GREEN STAR JAPAN

GREEN STAR JAPAN

Esperanto and the International Language Question, 1880–1945

Ian Rapley

University of Hawai'i Press
Honolulu

Paperback edition 2025
Printed in the United States of America

First printed, 2024

Library of Congress Cataloging-in-Publication Data

Names: Rapley, Ian, author.
Title: Green star Japan : Esperanto and the international language question, 1880-1945 / Ian Rapley.
Description: Honolulu : University of Hawaiʻi Press, [2024] | Includes bibliographical references and index.
Identifiers: LCCN 2024002841 (print) | LCCN 2024002842 (ebook) | ISBN 9780824897543 (hardback) | ISBN 9780824898809 (epub) | ISBN 9780824898816 (kindle edition) | ISBN 9780824898793 (pdf)
Subjects: LCSH: Esperanto—Japan—History. | Internationalism.
Classification: LCC PM8245.J3 R37 2024 (print) | LCC PM8245.J3 (ebook) | DDC 499.992—dc23/eng/20240214
LC record available at https://lccn.loc.gov/2024002841
LC ebook record available at https://lccn.loc.gov/2024002842

ISBN 9780824898861 (paperback)

Cover illustration: Banner from *La Revuo Orienta*, 1930, featuring the words to "La Espero," the unofficial anthem of the Esperanto movement. Republished with the permission of the Japana Esperanto Instituto.

Cover photograph: An Esperanto Class, 1920s. Image courtesy of the Japanese Esperanto Institute

Cover design: Melissa Olaivar Wong

University of Hawaiʻi Press books are printed on acid-free paper and meet the guidelines for permanence and durability of the Council on Library Resources

Contents

Acknowledgments

In researching and writing this book, I have worked on three continents at an ever-growing list of libraries, archives, and offices, as well as a second set of places that I have visited virtually or via email in pursuit of leads. I have sat stranded in Kiev airport drafting a chapter, in a high-viz jacket and hard hat reading League of Nations documents to the sound of drilling, and in cafes, sketching out plans, almost everywhere I have been over the lifetime of the project. I have read microfiche newspapers on a machine with a broken spool, tried and largely failed to decipher handwritten letters, and met the grandson of one of my historical actors while he was rewiring a library lighting system. I don't think that these experiences are exceptional for historical research. Nevertheless, the chance to do this work has been a privilege in an age of increasing pressure on academic budgets, and it is not one that I take lightly. Moreover, each of these steps has brought me into contact with a growing array of librarians, archivists, Esperantists, scholars, and others, who have helped me to better understand the material I was studying. Again, this is something for which I am deeply grateful.

The project was inspired by a conversation with my doctoral supervisor, Sho Konishi (although I suspect I misunderstood him when he suggested I work on *something like* Esperanto in Japan), and I also received formal support from John Darwin, Ann Waswo, Ian Neary, Linda Flores, Janet Hunter, and Rana Mitter while at Oxford. I was incredibly fortunate to be able to participate in the intellectual environment fostered by my fellow students and peers, especially Naomi Cross, Alice Freeman, Nadine Willems, Katya Hertog, and Judith Froelich.

I would like to express my gratitude to the librarians and archives in places I have visited in person—Tōno, Aomori, Akita, Tsuchizaki, Kyoto, Nagoya, and more—as well as those I dealt with electronically, in particular, Izumi Tytler, Yuki Kissick, Rie Williams, and Hitomi Hall at the Nissan Institute for Japanese Studies. Likewise, a series of workshops and conferences were pivotal in helping me to retain enthusiasm and refine my thinking. These included the EAJS doctoral workshop in Käsmu, run by Verena Blechinger-Talcott, Harald Fuess, Matthais Zachmann, and Reiko Abe Austedt; the stream "Sounds and Scripts in

Motion" at the Fourth Inter-Asian Connections conference in Istanbul, convened by Ronit Ricci and Jing Tsu; and "Beyond the Sinosphere," organized by Anna Belogurova and Nicolas Schillinger. My original research was funded by a studentship from the UK Arts & Humanities Research Council, as was a subsequent fellowship at Nichibunken in Kyoto, where I was hosted by Takii Kazuhiro.

I have benefited immensely from the support of a number of Esperantists, both in Japan and elsewhere: everyone involved with the Japana Esperanto-Instituto in Waseda, the Kansaja Ligo de Esperanto-Grupoj, Usui Hiroyuki, Gotoo Hitosi, Kobayashi Tsukasa, Hagiwara Yōko, and Ulrich Lins. Most of all, I owe thanks to Mine Yoshitaka and his wife, who hosted me in their house and sought to press more books and documents on me at every available opportunity. The generous welcome from all of these people has come to be a fundamental part of my understanding of what Esperantists mean by the *interna ideo*.

Finally, there is a less well-defined group of people who have helped and supported my work in different ways over the years: Josh Fogel, Joseph Essertier, Gotelind Müller, Hōjō Tsunehisa, colleagues past and present in the History Department at Cardiff University, and finally Masako Ikeda, the editors, and my anonymous reviewers at the University of Hawai'i Press. To them, and the others whom I have neglected to mention, I would like to offer my thanks. Most of all, I am grateful to Emma, Joseph, and Isobel, for giving me patience, inspiration, and distraction, in equal measure.

Some of the content of this book is derived from previous publications. Chapter 1 is expanded and derived in part from an article published in *Japan Forum* (32, no. 4 [2020]: 511–530) as "Sekaigo: Esperanto, International Language, and the Transnational Dimension to Japan's Linguistic Modernity," copyright the British Association of Japanese Studies, available at https://doi.org/10.1080/09555803.2019.1594342. An early version of the parts of chapter 4 considering Esperanto in Aomori was published in *Language Problems and Language Planning* under the title "When Global and Local Culture Meet: Esperanto in 1920s Rural Japan" (37, no. 2 [2013]: 179–196). John Benjamins Publishing should be contacted before republishing this material. Finally, the essay "A Language for Asia? Transnational Encounters in the Japanese Esperanto Movement," published in *Transnational Japan as History* (Palgrave MacMillan, 2013), while not directly connected to any specific part of the book, was an important staging post in the development of my ideas.

Introduction

As the four ships that comprised Matthew Perry's mission to Japan sailed northeast from the Ryukyu Islands in early July 1853, many of their passengers must have been deep in thought of what was to come: How would the Japanese respond to their arrival? Would they be successful in their attempts to establish formal relations between Japan and the United States of America? What would the wider consequences of the encounter be? One of those, Samuel Wells Williams, was certainly wracked by conflicting emotions: certainty that the Japanese policy of seclusion was wrong, wariness about the motives and likely conduct of Perry and the other military officers, and unease about the role he was personally due to play.[1]

Williams, aboard the *Saratoga*, was one of only a few members of the mission who was not part of the navy. He was a missionary, based in China, who had been picked up in Canton in order to act as an interpreter, at Commodore Perry's insistence. Williams's major concern was how effectively he would be able to serve in this position. What Japanese-language skills Williams possessed were the result of his participation, nearly twenty years earlier, in another American mission to Japan: an unsuccessful attempt to repatriate some Japanese castaways. He was both rusty and, having studied with sailors and fishermen, not experienced in the sort of language that would be required in an intense diplomatic encounter. In truth, Perry's options had been limited. He had rejected the German Philip von Siebold (who was of uncertain loyalty to the Americans, and liable to anger the Japanese, who had expelled him from the country some years earlier), deciding to take a team of linguists comprising Williams, a Japanese castaway named Sam Patch, a Dutchman named Anton Portman, and Williams's Chinese tutor.

In the end, Williams need not have worried. As the American ships entered Edo Bay, they were surrounded by a vast number of small Japanese boats. Eventually one drew near and some officials stood up. The second Japanese man to set foot on the American vessel said, "I speak Dutch," establishing that as the key language of communication.

While Williams's Japanese skills were therefore less critical to negotiations than he had feared they might be, he was nevertheless right at the heart of the encounter between the Americans and Japanese, called upon on a daily basis. He, often together with Portman on the American side as well as a range of Japanese interpreters and translators speaking Dutch or, later, English, was present at every major event and a host of other minor ones. Every undertaking, from the formal meetings to drafting the treaty Perry obtained through to the exchange of gifts, required interpretation and translation. And behind all the set pieces there was a seemingly endless number of smaller encounters: Japanese officials coming aboard the ships in order to deliver provisions, to haggle over the minutiae of the official meetings' locations and protocol, or to inspect the boats themselves and the Americans' equipment, for no discernable reason at all beyond mere curiosity and, eventually, seemingly out of friendship as well. The final result—the opening of Japan and the Treaty of Kanagawa that announced it—was thus the product of many hands, many voices, and, indeed, many languages: Dutch, Japanese, English, and Chinese were all used in one form or another. Without the presence of linguists on both sides, it would not have been possible.[2]

The underlying issue of identifying a suitable language for communication in international (or interlinguistic) encounters can be called the international language question. It forms the main subject of this book. That meetings between people from different communities require some language through which exchange can take place is sufficiently obvious that it is often ignored, but this book will demonstrate that the history of the international language question contains insights into the practicalities of international language, the consequences of international politics and power, the hidden histories of language study, and ideas about how the world is or even perhaps should be.

The majority of this book focuses on the twentieth century and on a language, Esperanto, that did not exist in 1854. However, the purpose of beginning with Matthew Perry's encounter in Edo Bay, a critical moment in modern Japanese history, is to stress that the international language question and the wider themes surrounding it have been central to Japan's modernity. For Japan, the onset of modernity was deeply and inextricably intertwined with its growing connections to the wider world (and in particular the network of Western powers); this book will demonstrate and explore the linguistic issues that resulted. Of course, there had been foreign contact before the Perry mission—most recently trade with the Dutch, the Koreans, the Chinese—to say nothing of informal and accidental interactions with whalers and castaways, each with their own questions of language.[3] Nevertheless, the events of 1853 and 1854 marked an inflection point from which those contacts grew faster and faster, featuring people, goods, and ideas flowing in increasing volumes both into Japan and out from it.

The reconfiguration of Japan as something recognizable as a modern nation-state, ushered in by the Perry expedition and Meiji Revolution, is usually studied as a set of internal processes—industrialization, social reform, governmental centralization, and so on. However, there was also an external dimension that reflects the reverse side of the nation as a fundamental watershed between domestic and international affairs. Just as Meiji Japanese leaders transformed internal relations between people and the state, they also reconfigured Japan's place in the world: they and others engaged in new forms of foreign relations from formal diplomatic relationships to new patterns of trade, exchanges of ideas, and a whole panoply of cross-border undertakings. In short, for Japan at least, the onset of modernity was profoundly international and global in nature.[4]

Critically, one of the practical problems thrown up by both the rapid growth of international contact in practice and the change in Japan's conceptual position in the world was the question of language. Every transnational moment, whether official or informal, required some medium of communication, some shared language. In some cases this might be simple—gestures, single words, facial expressions—but many contacts required much more sophisticated exchange, and some language in common had to be identified before real progress could be made.

While we often, for good reason, ignore the choice of language used in a transnational moment, preferring to focus on what was said rather than the language in which it was spoken or written, there is much to be learned by seeing which languages were used, and how and why. In 1853–1854, the onus fell upon the Americans, as the instigators of the encounter that led to the opening of Japan, to make the first steps in the identification of a language in common, but ultimately communication was made possible most readily by the extensive efforts the Japanese had made in learning Dutch. However, in subsequent years, as Japan regularized its position in the international order, Dutch would no longer serve to connect Japan to the world beyond its borders, and the Japanese themselves would have to address the international language question on a wider and more ongoing basis.

Taking Esperanto Seriously

This book uses one language in particular as a lens through which to think about more general questions of international language and transnational networking: Esperanto. Esperanto is the most famous of a class of what are known as planned languages.[5] These are languages that emerge not from the messy processes of usage and experiment that give birth to most languages used by humanity, but by a more deliberate process of design by one or more individuals. There is a rich tradition of language planning, dating back at least to the European Enlightenment, encompassing a range of motivations from philosophical experiments to personal projects to the design of languages spoken by fictional peoples of film and television.[6]

The language Esperanto specifically is a part of a subgenre of planned languages known by the somewhat cumbersome label of "international auxiliary languages": "international" because they are intended to be used in an international setting, and "auxiliary" because they are not and were not intended to replace existing native national languages, but to exist alongside them. Simply put, Esperanto and its like were proposals for a universal second language. Were one of these languages to achieve widespread adoption, people would still use their native languages in the home and national social settings; they would make use of the international auxiliary language when communicating in international or interlinguistic encounters.

Esperanto was neither the first nor the last international auxiliary language to be devised, but it has proven to be the longest lived and most widely used. It was developed by a Jewish resident of the Russian Empire, L. L. Zamenhof, in the 1880s.[7] Zamenhof was a resident of the town of Bialystok in an age of globalization and increasing interconnectedness, which proved to be a strong motivation for the development of an international language. It took until the early twentieth century for Esperanto to emerge as the dominant candidate for universal adoption, rising over rivals with names such as Nal Bino, Solresol, and Pasilingua, and subsequently surviving a challenge by those who wished to develop a revised, or improved, form of Esperanto named Ido.[8]

For the purposes of this book, rather than delve deeper into this history, it is enough to recognize a few basic characteristics of Esperanto as a language and movement. I would stress two key points: first, the structure of Esperanto, which is designed to be a language that is easy to learn and use, and second, the ideology underpinning and motivating the language: Esperantism, as I will term it.

Fundamental to Esperanto's intended purpose as a shared language for transnational communication is the idea that it is simple, so that many people can master it easily while retaining the capacity for the full range of expression. As a result, the grammar and pronunciation of the language were deliberately regular, shorn of all the oddities and irregularities that accumulate over history in most national and regional tongues. Word function (such as subject, object, verbal tense, adjective, and adverb) is indicated through a series of suffixes, while another series of prefixes and suffixes are used in word formation. For example, the Esperanto word *malgranda*, the adjective "small," can be decomposed into the stem *grand*, meaning large; the prefix *mal-*, indicating inversion; and the adjectival suffix *-a*, indicating the word's grammatical function. In principle, the grammar of Esperanto is contained in sixteen rules, laid out in an early text, *Fundamento de Esperanto*. In practice, there is a little more to learning the language than memorizing these rules; nevertheless, the basic ideal of reducing unnecessary complexity and irregularity in the interest of approachability holds true.

Most of the root words of Esperanto's vocabulary come from European, principally Romance, languages (*grand* being a good example). Some other planned languages had experimented with completely new vocabularies, but this proved a barrier to learning. However, that this made the language inherently and inescapably Western in nature unsurprisingly did not escape Japanese proponents and opponents alike. While Esperanto was easier for Japanese to learn than, say, French or English, it was also easier for a French speaker or an English speaker to learn Esperanto than it was for a Japanese speaker, chiefly because of the shared vocabulary.

The second point to stress here is the ideology of Esperanto. Esperantism, or in the language itself, Esperantismo, is the set of ideas about what Esperanto is and why it should be adopted. It is best seen as a debate rather than a single fixed position, as it has been the source of controversy over time; nevertheless, there are some central concepts or principles. Zamenhof's central idea (often called the *interna ideo*, or internal idea) was that a shared common language and the easier communication it would facilitate would foster mutual understanding between peoples and thereby work toward a world beyond war. That this language should be neutral—a planned language, rather than the selection of a particular national language—was seen to be important in the interest of equality. However, an extension of this idea of neutrality emerged that was somewhat opposed to Zamenhof's vision. This form of neutralism held that, to be truly universal, all views must be expressible within the language—even those antithetical to the cause of world peace—and so the link between Esperanto and Zamenhof's more idealistic ideas must necessarily be cut. At the first major congress of Esperantists in Boulogne-sur-Mer, the neutralists won out, resulting in the Boulogne Declaration—a statement that Esperantism should be seen as simply the advocacy of Esperanto as an international auxiliary language, with any other political or philosophical views simply those of the individuals themselves. Nevertheless, Zamenhof's *interna ideo*, as well as his broader philosophy, known as Homaranismo ("human being-ism"), have always been very influential and powerful in recruiting learners, not least in Japan.

Esperanto has long had at least a small presence in the English-language historiography of modern Japan and Asia, but it has been a marginal one: scattered across a wide range of topics and limited to passing references and footnotes. My interpretation of these marginal encounters with Esperanto is that they serve as a sort of marker of the exotic past. Whether it be an anarchist intellectual, diplomats at the League of Nations, or members of a religious community, the idea that these historical actors would devote their time and energy to something as esoteric-seeming as a planned language is a destabilizing experience, conveying an essential strangeness of the people and society of a time even as recent as the early twentieth century.

Happily, there is now a growing body of work on Esperanto in Japan, Asia, and more widely. Scholars such as Nancy Stalker, Sho Konishi, Nathan Shockey, and Edwin Michielsen have all produced work that includes engagement with Esperanto's history in Japan, while others such as Ulrich Lins, Gotelind Müller, Li Bichhin, and Brigid O'Keefe have worked on the language elsewhere in continental Eurasia.[9] In addition to this, there is a longer history of historical work on Esperanto in Japan and elsewhere written within the community of Esperantists themselves. Although this has not necessarily been read widely beyond this community, it has nevertheless proven an important source of information and insight in my research.

Framing the International Language Problem

The presence in Japan of a minority language of European origin might seem to be an unlikely subject of historical study. However, it is one that reveals greater insight into Japanese modernity than perhaps is immediately obvious. Esperanto never achieved the level of widespread adoption that its advocates imagined. However, the question of Esperanto's "failure" obscures a broader pattern of its use in the twentieth century (and into the twenty-first) and reflects a linguistic narrowing that has taken place in international exchange over a similar period.[10] In short, in Japan and elsewhere, people have been drawn to Esperanto over time, they have learned and used it, and they have created networks, forms of knowledge, institutions, and publications through and about it. This is not just a history of an imagined future in which Esperanto might have become a universal language ("what might have been"); it is also a history of what was: concrete achievements and actions, and the lessons which they have for us about the nature of language and transnational activity.[11] This is an example of a fundamental historical truth that history is not merely a story of how the present day came to look as it did (Esperanto's "failure") but also a quest to understand the past on its own terms.

The historiography of language in modern Japan has as its central focus the creation of a modern national Japanese language. Scholars such as Paul Clark, Nanette Gottlieb, Patrick Heinrich, and Lee Yeounsuk have explored how the processes of greater global connection discussed above led Japanese intellectuals to see the languages they spoke and wrote as flawed, and also the ways in which they consequently sought to rectify these deficiencies.[12] This led to a series of linguistic changes that had both a practical effect (the creation of a standardized and uniform form of spoken and written Japanese that could serve as a consistent language across the nation, and empire) and an ideological one (the identification of that standardized language with Japanese nationalism and identity). The developments also had knock-on effects for other aspects of Japan's linguistic world, including the relegation of regional variations to secondary status, and even more pressure on minority languages such as those of the Ainu and the people of Okinawa. These processes began in the mid to late nineteenth century, but language reform and change continued to take place well into the twentieth century.

These historical developments (and the scholarship tracing it) can be placed into a transnational context. At the same time as Japan, other countries were undergoing similar experiences and were engaged in similar projects of language reform as a result of their parallel experiences of globalization.[13] We might well think of a global moment in which ideas of language, nation, and modernity interacted in recognizable patterns across many different communities and states. Scholars such as Seth Jacobowitz and Nergis Ertürk stress that this was less a straightforward transfer of ideas from a modern West to a modernizing periphery than it was a pattern of similar and overlapping responses to technological and material changes that occurred broadly in parallel across the globe, early and late modernizers alike, with flows of cross pollination.[14]

That said, I think that where this book on the study of Esperanto and the broader international language question offers something new is in focusing on languages of transnational communication. Even where the existing scholarship on East Asian language reform and change is explicitly transnational in its focus—for example, the work of Lydia Liu and Douglas Howland—it generally focuses more on the impact of transnational influences upon domestic, or in-group, language.[15] This book documents, and seeks to understand and explain, a different (but contemporaneous and connected) phenomenon: the languages of use internationally, when communicating with people who spoke different native languages. In doing this, I hope to build upon the existing scholarship and open up a different dimension in the history of language in modern Japan and beyond.[16]

The book thus sits at the conjunction between two of the major "turns" that took place within the late twentieth-century study of history: the linguistic and global (or transnational) turns. At times I will frame the study of the international language question in Japan within one or the other of these, either arguing for the introduction of an international dimension to the historiography of modern Japanese language(s) or arguing for a greater awareness of the role of language in the study of inter- or transnational contact. Regardless of this choice, the broad structure of events remains the same: the increasing transnational contact that came with Japanese modernity revealed the international language question to be a pressing issue. Moreover, because the desire to engage with the world beyond Japan's borders was felt widely across the Japanese population, perception of this international language problem was, likewise, widespread—diplomats, officials, and intellectuals needed or sought to make transnational contacts, but so too did less-influential people spread across Japan and its colonies.

Esperanto was a radical potential solution to this problem, but it was also one with strong modern credentials: a rational, scientific approach to solving the issue of cross-cultural communication and a practical vision of simplicity and regularity. As a result, it appealed to many people who sought to exchange ideas with those beyond Japan's borders. This appeal was not limited to the political left or to the more liberal decades of Taishō democracy, but can be traced across the country and throughout the first half of the twentieth century.

The argument to follow has a broadly chronological structure, tracing Esperanto's history in Japan from the emergence of the international language question in its modern form in the late nineteenth century, through to the end of the Second World War. However, each chapter also examines different aspects of the language's presence in Japan, bringing different ideas to the fore. Throughout it, I follow not the institutional history of Esperanto organizations, but the broader (if less well-organized and documented) history of the language and its advocates within Japanese society.

Chapter 1 traces a series of languages through the late nineteenth century, culminating in the Esperanto boom of the early twentieth century. In doing so, it demonstrates that the international language question was present within the better-known Meiji-era debates about language change and reform that drove the creation and promotion of a standardized form (*hyōjungo*), the merger of spoken and written forms (*genbun itchi*), and the establishment of the ideological role of language within the process of nation making (*kokugo*). This goes beyond the focus of scholarship on translation and the injection of ideas and concepts into the Japanese language to instead consider other languages and their part in these debates, arguing for a wider conception of Japan's linguistic history.

Chapter 2 moves on to the Taishō period and transnational intellectual networks that were centered upon Tokyo. Here the twin roles of Esperanto as idea and language are highlighted. While the concept of a neutral international language as well as wider forms of Esperantism were important intellectual influences in Japan, we should not overlook the practical side of Esperanto as a language. This second wave of Esperanto activity saw its increasing use in real terms, permitting communication between individuals who otherwise did not share a common language.

Chapter 3 shifts the focus from Japan to Geneva and Paris, looking at the role of Japanese participants in language debates at the League of Nations. This reveals not only that Esperanto achieved a level of recognition at the heart of government, but also another key fact about the global nature of Japanese modernity. At the League, as with the linguistic reform proposals of the late nineteenth century, Japanese history was not merely being shaped by the global context—the recipient of waves of new ideas and the outcome of experiments taking place in the West. Rather, Japanese actors were participants in the generation of those insights and ideas, helping to shape the new world and being shaped by it. Moreover, I argue that Japan's position as a linguistic outsider forms a useful counter-perspective to that of Japan as a great power.

Chapter 4 goes to the opposite end of the spectrum, examining Esperanto's presence among groups in the far north of Tōhoku, showing that the desire to reach out beyond Japan's borders stretched far from the capital to touch every part of Japan. These groups, as well as the socialists considered in chapter 5, which focuses on proletarian Esperanto in Japan, put Esperanto to a diversity of uses and meanings, demonstrating that in "thinking and feeling beyond the nation," multiple identities both larger than and smaller than the national shaped the ways in which people saw themselves and their part in the world.[17]

The final chapter moves to the 1930s and early 1940s, revealing that Esperanto continued to have a role in the Japanese society of the "dark valley" of early Shōwa Japan. The history of "Patriotic Esperanto" is one part of an international language problem that arose in the Japanese Empire, demonstrating that transnational communication is more than just the concern of liberal internationalists.

Through this history, whether it was Meiji-era intellectuals debating the future of language, socialists teaching Esperanto in a factory, students singing the Esperanto anthem "La Espero" in rural villages, diplomats arguing for and against the language's expansion, or expatriates seeking to find a new lingua franca for Asia, advocates, users, and even opponents of Esperanto in Japan shared certain ideas: the importance of growing transnational interaction to Japan's modern future, the significance of language skills in facilitating those contacts, and the consequence of language choice in reflecting ideas of fairness, culture, tradition, and power. The history of Esperanto in Japan, therefore, is more than the history of failure; it is a history of Japan in the world.

CHAPTER 1

Sekaigo

The International Languages of Meiji Japan

In the spring of 1906, Japan was still in the afterglow of its unprecedented military victory over Russia the year before. Fêted abroad, Japan's domestic response was considerably more conflicted, with unrest originating from all parts of the political spectrum. Ōsugi Sakae, a leading Japanese anarchist, was arrested for his part in protests surrounding an increase in tram fares in Tokyo. He was sent to the jail in Ichigaya, where, far from idly waiting out his sentence, he got to work. Ōsugi was neither the first nor the last socialist to seek to make productive use of his time in jail. Like many, Ōsugi read various key texts, seeking to refine his theoretical understanding of Marxism and socialism, but (freshly graduated in French from the Tokyo School of Foreign Languages) he also chose to expand his language skills. He came to call this practice *ichihan ichigo* ("one crime, one language"): each time he was imprisoned he would choose another language to study. In later years, during other sentences, he would study Italian and German, but that first time in 1906 he chose a different tack: Esperanto. In a letter to a friend, he described his daily routine:

> First, in the morning, I read Feuerbach's "On Religion," and Albert's "On Free Love." In the afternoon I focus on Esperanto. Last month I just practiced reading but now I split my time half reading, half writing. Diligently running one-by-one through boring grammar exercises and the like is the sort of thing that, if one weren't in prison, would be totally impossible, I think. However, on my own, conversation is impossible. Then there are only a couple of hours between dinner and lights out. During that time, I am reading a collection of Tolstoy's short stories.[1]

While he fit in Esperanto amid a number of socialist thinkers and influential Western writers, prison, then, offered some opportunities for focus and concentration that ordinary life did not. And if prison denied Ōsugi conversational partners, in other respects he was far from alone in his newfound interest in the planned language: outside the prison walls, others were taking up Esperanto in Japan in increasing numbers.

They were doing more than just study: after the magazine *Chokugen* ran a profile of Esperanto in March 1906, May saw the creation of a national association, the Nippon Esperanto Societo (NES); a second one, the Nihon Esuperantisto Kyōkai (or JEA, after the Esperanto translation) was formed the following month, ultimately absorbing its forerunner. By the time Ōsugi was released in July, Esperanto in Japan was up and running and being covered by major newspapers such as the *Asahi Shinbun* and the *Yomiuri Shinbun*, clubs had begun to open in the major cities, and advocates were giving a series of promotional talks attended by hundreds, making for a full-fledged boom.[2] In the autumn, the *Asahi Shinbun* recognized Esperanto as one of the *ōzeki* (i.e., the highest rank) of the year's trends.[3]

Ōsugi's encounter with Esperanto was more than a passing fad. He attended the first national congress in September 1906, reading out an Esperanto translation of the Momotarō myth to a crowd that included other socialists, journalists, lecturers from various universities, and even Hayashi Tadasu, the foreign minister. From there, between other prison spells (and hence, of course, other languages), he continued to practice and promote Esperanto, teaching it to young Chinese anarchists and using it to disseminate information about the revolutionary struggle in Asia. But his was just one path to Esperanto—others came to the language not in prison, but in bookshops in Europe, while working in Manchuria or America, or via a wide range of friends and other intermediaries, and they would go on to make use of the language in a similar myriad of ways—writing letters, reading magazines, welcoming guests from overseas, and making trips themselves.

This rapid expansion of activity was unexpected and striking. However, while Esperanto emerged seemingly out of nowhere, an examination of the history of linguistic reforms and debates in the early Meiji period reveals a more complex story. Placing the explosion of Japanese Esperanto in 1906 into a wider history of Meiji linguistic reform demonstrates a strand of concern about international communication that coexisted alongside the better-studied efforts to reform internal national language. By tracing this chronology of thinking about international language, not only will I show how and why people felt the pressing concern with regard to the international language problem, but I will also reveal that they were willing to explore radical and surprising possibilities in order to solve it. Then, by expanding upon the network that both formed and was formed by the Esperanto boom of 1906, I will show that the transnational activities that revealed the international language problem and the proposed solutions to which they gave rise reflected Japan's growing modernity. This was a modern problem—if not born of new forms of contact, then certainly transformed by them—and thus one aspect of Esperanto's appeal was that it offered a modern solution.

The language debates of the early Meiji period have been well studied. Scholars have placed developments such as *genbun itchi* (the move toward a "unified style" of speech and writing) and the creation of *kokugo* (an ideologically charged, standardized language) into the broader process of late nineteenth-century nation-making.[4] This was a new form of the Japanese language that was perceived to meet the needs of a modern nation-state: uniform and standardized, reducing regional variations to the minority status of "dialects," and removing archaic elements deemed incompatible with a modern age.[5]

However, just as people were debating and experimenting with their native language for use within Japan, so too were they thinking about how best to communicate across borders. These debates reveal that the question of how to communicate with foreigners, whether they be inside or outside of Japan, was a pressing issue within the early Meiji discourse on language. The two strands, national and international language, were connected and intertwined: arguments about reforms to the domestic tongue included notions of facilitating access to foreign ideas, and questions of international communication held implications for the national debates as well.

From Mori Arinori's "English language proposal" of 1872–1873, to Japan's encounter with the planned language Volapük in the 1880s, and finally to the Esperanto boom of 1906, via the language of the treaty ports, and other suggestions, I will demonstrate that the international language problem was a fundamental element of Meiji Japan's linguistic modernity. In this context, Esperanto represented not a quirky and improbable pipe dream, but a modern, rational solution to a pressing problem of the globalizing world.

Languages, Foreign Contact, and Modernity

Of the early Meiji proposals regarding the modernization of Japan's language, the most famous is that of Mori Arinori. In a letter to American linguistic scholar William Whitney in 1872, and then again in 1873 in his book *Education in Japan*, Mori explored the possibility of adopting some modified form of English as the (or perhaps a) national language of Japan. Although his suggestion was met with polite skepticism by Whitney, and then by a range of criticism and ridicule by both Japanese and foreign commenters alike, it has had an afterlife as a key point of reference for other writers on the Japanese language.[6] While the conventional understanding is that Mori sought to replace the Japanese language with English, much of the postwar academic scholarship on Mori's proposal has focused on seeking to pin down exactly what Mori was suggesting. Indeed, there is considerable ambiguity in his writing, to say nothing of the possibility that his thoughts may have developed in light of his consultation with Whitney and elsewhere. While Mori advocated that the Japanese "adopt a language like that of English," the closest he came to pushing for abandoning Japanese was in the 1873 introduction to *Education in Japan*, in which he suggested that "all reasons suggest its disuse."[7] In other parts of the two documents he seems to suggest various overlapping ideas—the replacement of Chinese influence in the Japanese language by English, English and Japanese to be used in parallel, the Romanization of Japanese, and/or the creation of a written vernacular Japanese based upon the spoken form.

Exactly what Mori intended is unlikely to ever be settled; it seems entirely possible that he, an innovative thinker unafraid to test out new ideas, had not settled upon a single final proposal.[8] But however vague Mori's proposed solutions were, he was clear about the problems he sought to tackle. In his original letter he wrote:

> The spoken language of Japan being inadequate to the growing necessities of the people of that Empire, and too poor to be made, by a phonetic alphabet, sufficiently useful as a written language, the idea prevails among us that, if we would keep pace with the age, we must adopt a copious and expanding European language. The necessity for this arises mainly out of the fact that Japan is a commercial nation; and also that, if we do not adopt a language like that of the English, which is quite predominant in Asia, as well as elsewhere in the commercial world, the progress of Japanese civilization is evidently impossible. Indeed a new language is demanded by the whole Empire. It having been found that the Japanese language is insufficient even for the wants of the Japanese themselves, the demand for the new language is irresistibly imperative, in view of our rapidly increasing intercourse with the world at large . . . The only course to be taken, to secure the desired end, is to start anew, by first turning the spoken language into a properly written form, based on a pure phonetic principle. It is contemplated that Roman letters should be adopted. Under such circumstances, it is very important that the alphabets of the two languages under consideration—Japanese and English—be as nearly alike as possible, in sound and powers of the letters. It may be well to add, in this connection, that the written language now in use in Japan, has little or no relation to the spoken language, but is mainly hieroglyphic—a deranged Chinese, blended in Japanese, all the proportion of the letters of which are themselves of Chinese origin.[9]

A year later, in *Education in Japan* he suggested:

> In the style of expression, the spoken language of Japan differs considerably from the written, though in their structure they are both mainly the same . . .
>
> The words in common use are very few in number, and most of them are of Chinese origin. There are some efforts being made to do away with the use of Chinese characters by reducing them to simple phonetics, but the words familiar through the organ of the eye are so many, that to change them into those of the ear would cause too great an inconvenience, and be quite impracticable . . .
>
> The march of modern civilization in Japan has already reached the heart of the nation—the English language following it suppresses the use of both Japanese and Chinese. The commercial power of the English-speaking race which now rules the world drives our people into some knowledge of their commercial ways and habits. The absolute necessity of mastering the English language is thus forced upon us. It is a requisite of the maintenance of our independence in the community of nations. Under the circumstances, our meager language, which can never be of any use outside of our islands, is doomed to yield to the domination of the English tongue, especially when the power of steam and electricity shall have pervaded the land. Our intelligent race, eager in the pursuit of knowledge, cannot depend upon a weak and uncertain medium of communication in its endeavor to grasp the principal truths from the precious treasury of Western science and art and religion. The laws of state can never be preserved in the language of Japan. All reasons suggest its disuse.[10]

The problems that Mori identified in language in Japan can be enumerated as a general unspecified inadequacy for modern life, the role of Chinese influence on the language, the large number of homophones, the split (diglossia) between written and spoken Japanese, the difficulty in expressing law in written Japanese, and, notably, the need for a language with (international) commercial power and potential. This list stresses the weaknesses within Japan's domestic language system, but it also reveals that Mori was thinking internationally as well. English (in some role within Japan) was vital, Mori argued, for commerce, for the maintenance of Japan's independence, and for the gathering of knowledge. These three dimensions to foreign relations—trade, law/diplomacy, and intellectual exchange—were all of paramount importance to Japan's new situation, and thus he argued that it was vital that the restructuring of Japan's linguistic world facilitated progress in all three.

It would be possible to overemphasize the distinction within Mori's tripartite division into trade, diplomacy, and intellectual exchange: the actors and the activities involved in these different forms of international networking were often overlapping and interrelated, and it is indeed something of an arbitrary categorization. Nevertheless it does prompt recognition that different linguistic needs and different sets of problems arose from different types of foreign contact. The languages that emerged as potential solutions to these problems demonstrated different characteristics as a result.[11] So while, as outlined, the Perry mission negotiations involved the use of Dutch, Japanese, English, and Chinese in the search for a precise set of parallel translations,[12] elsewhere the spread of Western knowledge necessitated the creation of neologisms to convey new concepts as well as repurposed older phrases (highlighting the complexity of intellectual "translingual practice"),[13] and, as we shall see, in the treaty ports trade focused attention on the immediate need for pragmatic communication in order to get deals done.

Mori was by no means the only Japanese intellectual to think beyond the Japanese language, nor to focus on the question of trans- or international communication. In 1874, only a year after Mori's suggestions, the Confucian scholar Sakatani Shiroshi published an article in the *Meiroku Zasshi*, the forum for many of the debates over internal language reform. He turned his mind to the broader question of the nature of international contact and the strictures language placed upon those seeking to exchange knowledge. While growing numbers of Japanese were learning English, French, German, and more in their drive to pick up knowledge in fields from science to politics, Sakatani anticipated a different approach to international contact:

> Even after a hundred years, the various countries with whom we have relations will preserve their identity, and it will be necessary to use the English and French languages with the English and the French, the Russian and the German languages with the Russians and the Germans, and the Chinese and Korean languages with the Chinese and Koreans . . . We cannot avoid studying all these languages with utmost diligence since their use is already mandatory . . . How unfortunate it is that these differences consume so much time and seriously interfere with the spread of enlightenment to the five continents! If you ask me what should be done, the only solution is to make the languages of the world one.[14]

Sakatani imagined that his "common world language" (*tenchikan dōbun dōgo*, perhaps also translatable as "universal language") would be used primarily in public discourse, but that this might lead to a gradual decline in the private use of existing national languages. He linked it to European philosophers' hopes of putting an end to war, arguing that this was an unachievable goal until the nations of the world put aside their self-interest, and that a shared language for international communication was "an advantage for all countries alike without regard to their wealth or power."[15] These ideas—a diglossia of domestic and international communication, the connection to mutual understanding (and even world peace), and a common (neutral) language as a leveler, echoed some of Mori's arguments and at the same time prefigured many of the ideas that motivated the creation of, and support for, Esperanto, still some fourteen years from birth and thirty years from its explosion in Japan.

Sakatani's vision was one focused chiefly on the spread of "enlightenment" (*kaika*)—straightforwardly on what Mori had identified as intellectual exchange, but the "Ports lingos" that grew up in Yokohama and elsewhere were altogether more down-to-earth and immediate. Surviving evidence of the language, which has been variously known as Yokohama Kotoba or Yokohama Pidgin Japanese, and tagged using the exotic-sounding words *peke* and *sarampan*,[16] is very limited—almost all scholarship on it draws from two or three interconnected sources, the most significant being *Exercises in the Yokohama Dialect*, a pamphlet published anonymously in 1879.[17] As Basil Hall Chamberlain noted in *Things Japanese*, the pamphlet was something of a joke, making use of spoof quotes from fictional newspapers and increasingly ridiculous sample sentences, but nevertheless it documents a language being used to conduct everyday life in the early years of treaty port Japan.[18] Chamberlain speculated that while the Chinese treaty ports tended to use pidgin Englishes because the Chinese were adept at foreign language acquisition, Yokohama Kotoba was based on Japanese because the locals were less linguistically skilled. However, it was populated by words of Western origin and from other Asian languages, presumably imported alongside the growth of trade.[19]

The scantiness of the surviving detail of Yokohama Kotoba reveals something of the nontextual and informal nature of its practice (and also of how the historical archive is constructed and what it privileges). But what does survive serves as a reminder of the scale and imperatives of trade-driven contact in the treaty ports, and illustrates the pragmatism present in everyday encounters. That pragmatism might be most evident in daily life in the treaty ports, but it is no less important in other forms of transnational contact—especially when face-to-face. The simple need to get a message across, however it was done, was no less a part of diplomatic contact than it was of trade.[20] Yokohama Kotoba might have been a simple pidgin, and the conversations that took place in it might have been direct and uncomplicated, but it was nevertheless a medium of much trans-ethnic contact, and the facilitator of many encounters in a contact zone of considerable complexity.[21]

Sakatani's suggestion and Yokohama Kotoba not only represent two different of Mori's categories of transnational contact; they are substantially very different—the opposite ends of a spectrum between thought experiment and practical reality. But in 1888–1889, another language began to gain coverage in Japan, one that spanned the gap: born of serious philosophical and intellectual intent, but (at least in Europe) realized in patterns of actual use. This language was also the first in Japan to attract the name *sekaigo*.

Volapük: The First *Sekaigo*

Volapük was a forerunner of Esperanto, its immediate predecessor as heir presumptive to the status of international auxiliary language. A German priest, Johann Martin Schleyer, created and published it in 1880. During the subsequent decade, it gathered a community of speakers in Europe, spreading beyond Germany, most notably to France, to become the first really successful international language. There were numerous Volapük clubs and a range of publications, and three congresses were organized in 1884, 1887, and 1889, the last reportedly conducted solely in Volapük itself.[22] However, this last congress marked the effective peak of the language's spread, as it revealed the cracks forming in the community of Volapük speakers. Schleyer wanted to retain a veto on all proposed changes to the language; denied this, he boycotted the congress. Marred by internal fallings-out regarding potential changes to grammar and structure, the 1890s were a period of self-destructive argument around the language that caused a decline in its popularity. Although a small community of Volapük speakers continued into the twentieth century, by 1900 it had decisively been replaced by Esperanto as the leading candidate for widespread adoption.[23]

In 1888, as Volapük was reaching its peak in Europe, it attracted attention in Japan. This is no coincidence, of course, since a high level of activity in Europe was a strong selling point for Volapük (and later also for Esperanto), as well raising the likelihood of it coming to the attention of a Japanese audience. The first articles mentioning Volapük in Japan came as early as 1886—the first one written by the leading intellectual Katō Hiroyuki in the second issue of a new English language magazine, *The Student*, and the second the following year, this time in the *Japan Gazette*, a Yokohama-based English language journal. However, they led to little response.[24] It wasn't until a Dutch doctor, Willem van der Heyden, also based in Yokohama, began to make efforts to promote it that

Volapük began to attract a wider audience. The *Yomiuri Shinbun* was drawn to his suggestions, running an article introducing the language on December 30, 1887, and following it up with a series of pull-outs covering the basic grammar in the new year. Between January and April 1888, these inserts built up to form an introductory textbook. They were supported by a series of articles on debates both for and against Volapük.[25] (One of these suggested that Volapük might replace Yokohama Kotoba in the treaty ports, reiterating the point that while it might have faded from view in the archive, in early Meiji Japan the pidgin had a noted presence as a language of transnational use.) Finally, in 1889, van der Heyden, together with a colleague named Sasaki Hayashi, published a Volapük-Japanese dictionary, *Wayaku Sekaigo Jirin*, to help Japanese students learn the language.[26]

Despite this mainstream coverage and promotion, what is most notable about Volapük's introduction to Japan is the apparent total failure of the language to get off the ground. There were a few scattered individuals who began to study it, but despite calls in the *Yomiuri Shinbun* for the establishment of a Japanese Volapük association, this seems to never have come into being. After the flurry of activity in the pages of the *Yomiuri* over a span of about twelve months, Volapük seems to have died away in Japan.

This is not to say that there were no echoes of Volapük's brief time in Japan. Perhaps the most notable Japanese learner of Volapük was Oka Asajirō.[27] Later the most famous introducer and proponent of Darwinian evolution to Japan, in the late 1880s he was a student of biology and, perforce, also a student of several European languages. Learning about Volapük from the *Yomiuri Shinbun*, he ordered textbooks from overseas and began to study them.[28] However, after graduating, he put Volapük aside and instead began his own planned language project, Zilengo, before moving to Germany to study further. His encounter with Esperanto there (while in a bookshop searching for a textbook on Swedish) makes him perhaps the first Japanese person to study Esperanto, but he remained unconvinced that it was the best of the possible *sekaigo*, picking up alternatives such as Ido and Idiom Neutral, as they arose.[29]

Oka's own language, Zilengo—meaning "our language"—represents a variant of the style of Volapük and Esperanto; it uses the Roman alphabet, draws from a Latinate vocabulary, and makes use of suffixes for verb conjugation and grammatical structures in an effort to create a systematic, easy-to-learn language. However, Oka did draw from the Japanese language as well. Looking back at his project in 1940, he drew a parallel between suffixes in Zilengo and Esperanto and particles in the Japanese languages (*joshi*: short, postnominal words serving a range of grammatical functions). Whereas Esperanto uses the suffix *-o* to indicate subject and *-on* for object, Oka used *-a* and *-o*, respectively, echoing the Japanese particles *wa/ga* for subject and *wo* for object:

Language	Esperanto	Zilengo	Japanese
Subject	Patr-o	Patr-a	Chichi wa/ga
Object	Patr-on	Patr-o	Chichi wo

Some other minor characteristics were drawn from Japanese—the use of the suffix *-e* to indicate the dative case in rough parallel to the Japanese particle *he/e*, as well as the lack of a definite article and restricted indication of gender and number.

Oka never promoted Zilengo—it's unclear whether he intended it to be a serious proposal or a personal project-cum-thought experiment. Either way, when he discovered Esperanto in 1891 he put his own effort to one side.[30] Still, while it was never launched into the world, Zilengo places Oka into the tradition of auxiliary language at a time when it was still almost exclusively European. Where Sakatani in 1874 seems to have thought of his proposal essentially independently of the European language planners (largely before they had really got underway as a serious endeavor), Oka was very much engaged with their proposals.

Esperanto, 1906

If the precursors to the Esperanto boom of 1906 reveal an ongoing preoccupation with the role of language in foreign contact, then the event itself is also a snapshot of networks of popular transnational activity in late Meiji Japan. For those intellectuals and others seeking to get ahead in the new society, foreign sources of knowledge were vital, and while translations were increasingly available, going direct to the source was a more reliable route (or even expected within the upper branches of the education system). In the first instance, these intellectual connections and networks were paths through which knowledge of Esperanto could flow—in later years Esperanto itself became a vehicle for the transmission of other ideas and information: from knowledge *of* Esperanto to knowledge *through* Esperanto. These connections demonstrate the diversity of different forms of transnational contact, placing Japan in a web of people, objects, and ideas moving across borders, both to and from the West, but also circulating around Asia as well.

Typically, three distinct, complementary routes have been identified as the origins of Esperanto in Japan: The English language route (through the Welsh teacher Edward Gauntlett) provided a core population of Esperanto students. The French route through Nagasaki led Kuroita Katsumi to become the driving force behind the organization of the Esperanto movement. The Russian route, from Vladivostok, led Futabatei Shimei to publish one of the first Esperanto textbooks in the Japanese language, forming a key resource for new students. That these forces coincided in the years culminating in 1906 helped form the critical mass of activity that Volapük's advocates had conspicuously lacked. As the examples of Oka and others demonstrate, these three routes were not the only routes; rather, they have come to be seen as the most influential in the growth of the fledgling movement.

Route 1: The English Route

The Welshman George Edward Gauntlett, known as Edward, was one of a wave of Europeans and Americans who came to Japan as missionaries and to support the new Meiji education system. Born in Swansea in 1868, son of a canon of St. David's Cathedral, he traveled to North America before arriving in Japan in 1890. He worked as a teacher of English and Latin in a number of schools throughout Japan, in particular the Sixth Higher School in Okayama.[31]

Gauntlett was introduced to Esperanto by a Canadian friend, Daniel McKenzie, who was working as a missionary in Kanazawa. McKenzie suggested that the two might study Esperanto, "the new universal language," together during the summer of 1903, when Gauntlett was due to stay with him. Gauntlett recalled being skeptical: "That was the first time I had ever heard the word 'Esperanto,' and remembering that Volapük, another universal language had failed I wrote and told him that I thought Japanese was hard enough without going into a new language."[32]

However, when Gauntlett arrived in Kanazawa, McKenzie was temporarily engaged, so Gauntlett picked up his friend's Esperanto textbook, seeking to pass the time. He swiftly became hooked. Mindful of the failure of Volapük, Gauntlett was not an automatic believer in the power of a universal language and was wary of investing too much time into it. Comparing Esperanto's structure to an old Volapük textbook, however, reinforced his faith in Esperanto. Its simplicity stood in stark contrast to Volapük, whose inventor "was evidently no linguist." This simplicity, Esperanto's most powerful aspect, was deceptive: "At first, during the study of the language there is nothing specially interesting, but THE MORE YOU GO INTO IT THE MORE INTERESTING IT BECOMES AND THE MORE YOU ADMIRE IT."[33]

Gauntlett wrote his first letters in Esperanto within his first few days in Kanazawa; by 1905–1906 he estimated that he had received as many as seven hundred letters from perhaps seventy-five different nations. They covered commercial and academic matters in addition to the simple interest in corresponding with Esperantists based in Japan. Many of the letter writers mistook Gauntlett for a Japanese native.[34]

However, more significant than his correspondence was Gauntlett's work in spreading Esperanto within Japan. In 1905, he began a study group in Okayama including his wife, Tsuneko; brother-in-law, Yamada Kōsaku (who became a famous Taishō-era composer); and others. Then he began a correspondence course that was taken by over six hundred students across three intakes in 1905 and 1906.[35] It was a collaborative affair—Edward writing the lessons, Tsuneko running off mimeographed copies, and other members of the Okayama study group helping out where they could.[36]

The book from which Gauntlett learned Esperanto was a British one, *The Complete Student's Textbook*, by John Charles O'Connor. A number of other Japanese Esperantists also studied it as their first introduction to the language. For example, in 1903 Yoshino Sakuzō, the famous liberal academic, bought a copy. He had encountered Esperanto through a series of articles by the British Esperantist William Stead in the London *Review of Reviews*. Based upon these columns, Yoshino wrote an article of his own on Esperanto in the magazine *Shinjin*, published by the early Japanese Christian Ebina Danjō.[37]

Other, more active members of the early Esperanto scene, such as Fukuda Kunitarō and Abiko Teijirō, also encountered Esperanto for the first time through the *Review of Reviews* articles. Abiko Teijirō worked at a publishing company and book importer, Yūrakusha. In 1906 they began to import copies of O'Connor's textbook. Katō Misao, a young marine engineer in training, picked one up after he was introduced to Esperanto by a friend. Katō joined the British Esperanto Association after reading about it in the textbook and then went about creating his own Japanese Esperanto organization.[38] His Nippon Esperanto Societo (NES) held its first meeting on May 20, 1906, in a nursery school in Yokosuka.[39] About twenty people attended. They held a formal opening ceremony and then sang a translated version of the national anthem, with the wife of the school's owner playing the organ.[40]

Route 2: The French Route

However, the NES was eclipsed in June, a month after it was created, by the formation of the better connected Japana Esperantisto Asocio (the Association of Japanese Esperantists, JEA, or the Nihon Esuperanchisuto Kyōkai in Japanese), which was based in Tokyo. Displaying a notable lack of preciousness about his own group's primacy, Katō arranged for the NES to be folded into the JEA, first as a distinct wing of the organization, but by 1907 as no more than a Yokosuka branch. The key figure behind the JEA (and indeed the leading figure in Japanese Esperanto for its first decade) was Kuroita Katsumi, a young lecturer in classical Japanese literature at the Imperial University. Kuroita's interest in Esperanto was sparked by a similar yet different route from that of Katō Misao, Yoshino Sakuzō, or Edward Gauntlett: through the French teacher Alphonse Mistler, who was based in Nagasaki.

There are suggestions that French Catholic missionaries in Nagasaki studied Esperanto in the late nineteenth century, but Mistler was not involved with the language until 1902.[41] Mistler, a science teacher, had been in Nagasaki since 1893. His brother, Jean, was an active Esperantist; through him, Alphonse came in contact with L. L. Zamenhof and Esperanto. Once he had studied the language himself for a while, Mistler began to introduce Esperanto to some of the students at the Nagasaki middle school at which he taught. In total he had approximately sixty students; he also wrote a profile of the language for the English-language magazine *Nagasaki Press*, also in 1902.

It was this article that caught the attention of Kuroita Katsumi. The following year, Kuroita obtained a copy of Zamenhof's *Ekzercaro* (one of the first Esperanto textbooks) and began to study it. After a couple of years Kuroita felt confident enough to begin to seek to promote the language. In 1905, his first such effort took the form of an interview that the socialist Sakai Toshihiko turned into an article in *Chokugen*, the successor magazine to the newspaper *Heimin Shinbun*; the following year, the *Yomiuri Shinbun* ran a two-part article on Kuroita and Esperanto.[42]

Until these articles were published, Kuroita had been unaware that there were others in Japan who knew of and were beginning to study Esperanto. In the 1905 *Chokugen* article, Sakai wrote (based on what Kuroita had told him) that Kuroita and Mistler "and perhaps one or two others" were the only Esperantists active in Japan. Moreover, there were slight errors in the details of both Esperanto's history and grammar in these articles, which serve to highlight the extent to which Esperanto was still largely unknown territory. However, the articles helped to bring together some of those hitherto isolated individuals who had been studying the language—for example, Abiko Teijirō, who had been importing and selling O'Connor's Esperanto textbook on behalf of the publishing firm Yūrakusha, as mentioned above, and Muramoto Tatsuzō, a member of Gauntlett's study group in Okayama, who both got in touch with Kuroita.[43]

On June 12, 1906, three weeks after Katō Misao had founded the NES, Kuroita Katsumi, together with Abiko and the *Yomiuri Shinbun* journalist Usui Hidekazu, still unaware of the creation of the Yokosuka group, founded the JEA,

Figure 1.1. An Esperanto exhibition (date unknown). Image courtesy of the Japanese Esperanto Institute.

holding their first meeting in Kanda. There were ten people present for the first meeting, the others being mostly journalists and teachers. They set the membership dues at one yen per year and resolved to meet on a monthly basis. The creation was reported in the *Yomiuri Shinbun* (on June 10 and 27) and the *Asahi Shinbun* (June 26), which helped the distinct pockets of Esperanto activity to coalesce still further and attract new people to investigate the language. The second meeting, on July 12, was attended by Katō Misao from the NES; Ōsugi Sakae, newly released from prison; and others. The *Yomiuri Shinbun* continued to report on Esperanto events and activity throughout the subsequent months of 1906 and 1907. Organized Esperanto activity in Japan had begun in earnest.

Route 3: The Russian Route

The final major event of 1906 was the publication of Futabatei Shimei's textbook, *Sekaigo*. In seeking to recruit new members and new students of the language, the newly formed Japanese Esperanto groups had one key need: appropriate tools for Japanese students to learn the language. Gauntlett's course was based in English, and the other early adopters had learned the language through European-language textbooks, but there was as yet nothing available in Japanese. Consequently, the new Esperantists worked to fill the gap: the first

Japanese-language Esperanto textbooks were published in 1906 by Edward Gauntlett (in July, together with Maruyama Juntarō) and Katō Misao (in September);[44] two Japanese-Esperanto dictionaries were released in October 1906, one written by Kuroita Katsumi.[45]

However, although Futabatei came from outside of the new community, his textbook was to prove the most successful. It was published in July 1906, in parallel to the other books, but had a longer and more complex gestation. In 1902 Futabatei had resigned from a post at the Tokyo School of Foreign Languages in order to experience Russian society firsthand, visiting Vladivostok. There, he became friends with the then president of the Vladivostok Esperanto Society, Fjodor Postnikov. Postnikov, an early Russian Esperantist, had served as the third president of the earliest Russian Esperanto association, Espero, prior to moving east, and was keen to promote Esperanto in Asia.[46] L. L. Zamenhof personally pressed upon Postnikov the need to help spread Esperanto in Asia and make it truly a world language. As a result Postnikov had visited Japan as early as 1894, going to Nagasaki, where he left some European-language pamphlets about Esperanto with local residents (apparently without any lasting success).[47]

Postnikov and Futabatei hit it off. It is clear that they had much to gain from each other—Futabatei had found someone from whom to learn more about modern Russian society, and Postnikov had found an intellectual with an interest in language reform, the perfect candidate to help introduce Esperanto to Japan. Futabatei attended the Vladivostok Esperanto Society a number of times and went so far as to join it. Postnikov personally taught Futabatei the basics, and Futabatei agreed to work on a Japanese translation of the Russian Esperanto textbook.[48]

However, after less than a month in Vladivostok, Futabatei moved on to Harbin, where he stayed for three months, before returning to Japan via Beijing, apparently thinking no more about Esperanto. It was only when Futabatei received a letter from a French Esperantist while in Beijing and a second one once he was back in Tokyo, this time from Mexico, that his mind was drawn back to the language. Both letters inquired after the language's presence in Japan. Futabatei replied, composing his first—and apparently only—Esperanto letters.[49]

The cause of these letters was Postnikov. After parting company with Futabatei, he had contacted Zamenhof, confident that his goal of introducing Esperanto to an East Asian audience was going to be successful. Zamenhof in turn included the presumed-to-be-forthcoming Japanese textbook in a 1903 list of Esperantists and Esperanto publications, with Futabatei's name recorded next to it.[50] The textbook, however, was still more than three years from its eventual publication.

A year later, in late 1903, Postnikov visited Tokyo on his return from a trip to America. There he found Futabatei "sitting on a floor spread with tatami, translating the Russian-Esperanto textbook into Japanese."[51] The two worked together for a while before Postnikov left, leaving $50 toward the costs of publishing the completed book. Futabatei's work was once again interrupted, this time by the Russo-Japanese War, but this final delay led to the happy coincidence of the book's eventual publication with the launch of both the Yokosuka and Tokyo Esperanto associations. In addition to the translation, Futabatei wrote articles for *Jogaku Sekai*, *Gakusei Taimuzu*, and *Seikō* in September and October 1906, increasing yet further Esperanto's public profile and helping to ensure the book's success. Finally, he followed it up with a translation of Zamenhof's *Ekzercaro*, titled *Sekaigo Dokuhon*.

It's tempting to chart a connection between Futabatei's work in the reform of the Japanese language (the author of "Japan's first modern novel") and his contribution to the birth of the Japanese Esperanto movement.[52] However, despite going to the effort of writing these articles promoting the language, and indeed despite his self-description in the title pages of *Sekaigo* as a "member of the Vladivostok Esperanto Club," his engagement with Esperanto seems to have ended once his obligation to Postnikov was paid. Besides the letters he wrote in 1903, he seems to have spent little time studying the language. Once the books were published, he put Esperanto aside. So cleanly did he cut his contacts with the burgeoning movement that he even went so far as to pretend to be out when Esperantists (including Gauntlett) visited him.[53]

Other Routes

The three paths described above, and the individuals most fundamental to them—Edward Gauntlett, Katō Misao, Alphonse Mistler, Kuroita Katsumi, and Futabatei Shimei—played the most important roles in the emergence of the Japanese Esperanto movement in 1906, but there were other paths to Esperanto: Yoshino Sakuzō and others through the London-based *Review of Reviews*; Nakanome Akira, who discovered Esperanto while in Hungary; Sasaki Tadasu in Sacramento; Higuchi Kentarō in France; and others closer to home, including Akino Matsukichi in Vladivostok and Takahashi Kunitarō and Shimose Kentarō (separately) in Manchuria.[54] The diversity and number of these separate encounters reveals the ever-growing scope and range of Japanese society's networks of intercourse with the wider world, the growing profile that Esperanto had in the early twentieth century, and further examples of Japanese individuals who felt the potential of an easy-to-learn language of international communication.[55]

The Japanese Way Station

However, Japan was not merely an end point in this web of connections. As well as the recipient of the intellectual flows, Japan also passed on knowledge of Esperanto to other parts of Asia as well. In the early years, Ōsugi Sakae was the most notable figure to be involved in spreading Esperanto, specifically to China.

After his release from prison, Ōsugi was very active in seeking to recruit new learners. In September 1906, he founded an Esperanto night school, held in a primary school in the Hongō district of central Tokyo. Although some forty students of varying backgrounds enrolled in the course, the intensity of study (there were five ninety-minute classes per week) meant that only twelve students saw the course through to completion in December.[56] The school ran for a second term, this time in Kanda, starting the following January, but Ōsugi was back in prison later that year and a proposed third term saw far fewer sign-ups.[57] However, in 1908, in between two further spells in prison, Ōsugi was teaching Esperanto once more, this time together with socialism to a group of Chinese students in Tokyo. The group, based around husband and wife, Liu Shipei and He Zhen, and others, went on to be one of the sources of both Esperanto and anarchism in China.[58]

Sino-Japanese anarchist links ran throughout the late Meiji and Taishō period, with Esperanto as one thread of mutual interest and Ōsugi remaining at the heart of much of it. For example, in 1914, he sent a young member of his circle, the print worker Yamaga Taiji, to Shanghai in order to help out with a small anarchist magazine, *Voĉo de la Populo*.[59] Yamaga joined twenty or so members of a cell, working in secret in a residential suburb. The leader of the group, Liu Shifu (known by the pen name Sifo), was an intellectual heir of a Parisian group of Chinese Esperantist-anarchists operating parallel to Ōsugi's students in Tokyo. His personal vision of politics and ethics, influenced by Leo Tolstoy among others, included abstention from eating meat, drinking alcohol, using tobacco, riding in rickshaws, marriage, the use of family names, holding of government office, militarism, and religion.[60]

Yamaga stayed with this unorthodox group for less than a year before Ōsugi called him home, but he returned to China several times in the 1920s, including a trip in 1927 to teach Esperanto at the Shanghai Labor University (Shanhai Rōdō Daigaku) for four months, together with Ishikawa Sanshirō.[61]

Sifo and Ōsugi were examples of the small-scale but increasingly interconnected transnational networks of East Asian anarchists: Sifo writing for Ōsugi's magazine, *Kindai Shisō*, and an Esperanto magazine, *Orienta Azio*, and Ōsugi publishing a number of short essays in European Esperanto journals.[62] The relationship between socialism and Esperanto in Japan was, right from the outset, complex: overlapping but not synonymous, with left-wing Esperantists and nonpolitical or less radical Esperantists coexisting for the most part within a single community, at least until the end of the 1920s, as we will see in chapter 5. Yamaga Taiji is a good example of this. His work at the publishing house Yūrakusha brought him into contact with Esperanto and some of the anarchists involved with the language, but at the same time he lived and worked at the headquarters of the JEA as Kuroita Katsumi's secretary. Kuroita had broken any connections he had with the left in the wake of the Great Treason trial, but nevertheless he supported and acted as a mentor to Yamaga, even as the young printer built his contacts with the likes of Ōsugi Sakae and Ishikawa Sanshirō, drawn to an ideology that had "in a moment, changed the eyes through which he viewed the world."[63]

Theorizing *Sekaigo*

Separated by fifteen years, and with very different outcomes, the introductions of Volapük and Esperanto to Japan nevertheless had some distinct similarities. Both languages received the active support of a major newspaper in the form of the *Yomiuri Shinbun*, both involved a foreigner resident in Japan in a leading role, and both occurred in parallel to a booming European scene. There are also strong similarities in the ways in which the two languages were presented and conceptualized. For all that Japanese society and its relations with the wider world had changed between 1888 and 1906, the need to make contact overseas, and the linguistic issues that resulted remained tediously the same. As the following two quotes show, the primary appeal of a planned language was as a functional solution to a problem that was emerging in an era of expanding globalization:

> In recent times the association between all the nations grows by month and by year, and thus those who would engage in the least exchange between the members of other nations must learn one or two, or even four or five languages; for those who study, in politics or in trade, the inconvenience is not inconsiderable. (Van der Heyden writing in 1888)[64]

and:

> As world intercourse becomes more incessant with every day, so do the differences between the languages of all the nations make inconvenience

> and disagreeableness more and more keenly felt . . . It has been a yearning in the hearts of many how convenient, how agreeable it would be were peoples throughout the world to use the same language. In short, the idea of Sekaigo has come to pass. (Sakai Toshihiko/Kuroita Katsumi in 1905)[65]

Settling upon a single standard language of international communication would be of obvious advantage to the Japanese engaging with the wealth of European ideas and thus faced with a multitude of different languages of potential importance. But Tani Shintarō, who wrote the majority of the *Yomiuri Shinbun*'s articles on Volapük, argued that it would be of great advantage to all the peoples of the world. Though he had initially suggested merely that Volapük might provide a replacement for the Yokohama Pidgin and its ilk, it rapidly became clear to him that Volapük's bid to become an international language was not a challenge to minor trade slang, but rather to the major European languages, most particularly English.[66]

Faced with the suggestion that "English, which has emerged victorious from contact with other national languages" was the de facto international language and that no alternative was needed, Tani modified his claim regarding the advantages that would accrue to the nations of the world given the adoption of Volapük.[67] It would, he acknowledged, involve some short-term inconvenience—the necessity for everyone, even those who already spoke several languages, to study Volapük—however, he suggested that this was a small short-term concession in the name of longer-term progress. While the adoption of Volapük would require leading nations to put aside the self-interest of promoting their own mother tongues, the fact that progress in Volapük/*sekaigo* could be measured in months rather than years of studying English revealed how foregoing the benefits of Volapük/*sekaigo* because of the presence of English was akin to refusing to invest in the railways because of the existence of the roads.[68]

In 1905–1906, the early Esperantists, too, drew the parallel between their *sekaigo* and the developments of modern technology. Katō Misao called it a "new practical language of twentieth century reason,"[69] while Higuchi Kanjirō suggested that in a world with remarkable resonances to the contemporary process of globalization, language remained a key barrier:

> Now, the uncanny power of steam and the superhuman power of electricity have made the globe small and brought all the nations close; in the number of days it would have taken to travel from the north of Japan to the south thirty years ago, one can now go to any of the nations of the world, a ten Sen stamp is enough to communicate with all of the civilized

> nations and a few hours is enough to make contact by telegraph further than one thousand ri. Moreover, in recent years more telephone lines have been laid, and we are reaching an era in which radio communications will be of even more practical use. However, because the language of each country is different, there are many cases where new cultural conveniences cannot be made use of.[70]

While Esperantists also placed the language within a historical tradition of language creation dating back to the philosophical languages of Gottfried Leibniz and John Wilkins, presenting it as an incremental development rather than a disruptive discontinuity, nevertheless it was usually presented as a fundamentally modern phenomenon, to be compared to the railway and the telegraph in its power to enable communications.[71] Indeed, these comparisons to modern technology reveal something of the way in which Esperanto was perceived. Seth Jacobowitz's retelling of the development of modern Japanese and the unified style stresses the importance of technology in this history, showing how material technologies such as the telegraph and linguistic innovations including shorthand acted to catalyze the transformation of written Japanese, while Nathan Shockey charts the linguistic impacts of the rapid rise of print culture a generation later, also tying language change to material developments.[72] In effect, as presented in 1905–1906 and cast in the language of modern inventions, Esperanto was (as indeed Volapük had been before it) itself a form of intellectual technology. In later years the metric system, timekeeping, and longitude and latitude were also used to explain it through comparison, conceptualizing language as a phenomenon as amenable to rationalization as time and physical space.

In addition to revealing the ideas of rationality and modernity embedded within both this first wave of Esperanto and the wider ideas of language debates that presaged it, and connecting to the argument of other scholars on the link between language change and material or technological developments, the idea of Esperanto-as-technology also reveals an absence that is noteworthy in relation to the subsequent history of Esperanto both in Japan and internationally. By conceiving of Esperanto as a narrow solution to an emergent linguistic problem, a modern solution to a modern problem, it was chiefly positioned without any wider political, moral, or philosophical meaning.

Jacobowitz is keen to stress that Japanese linguistic reforms took place alongside a range of linguistic changes and experiments in the West, rather than in their wake, challenging a diffusionist narrative of Japanese modernity.[73] The same is largely true in the case of Esperanto in Japan. The first boom in Japan coincided with the first European Esperanto congress, in 1905 in Boulogne-sur-Mer (chapter 3 in particular will explore Japanese participation in broader global language debates). As mentioned in the introduction, the 1905 congress saw a fierce debate as to the appropriate understanding of Esperantism, the underlying philosophy of Esperanto, in which the idealistic forms of Esperanto of L. L. Zamenhof and others were rejected by the majority in favor of explicit neutrality.[74] Intense debates along similar lines to the European ones would be fought in Japan in subsequent years: many Japanese Esperantists argued for their language along moral and idealistic terms, arguing for linguistic fairness and equality, or with a vision of world peace. However, in 1905–1906, while European Esperanto was arguing this question for the first time, it appears to have been largely absent among the activities of the first Japanese Esperantists. In the first wave of Japanese Esperanto, arguments focused on the pragmatism of a simpler, more regular language as a tool for practical use.

This formulation of Esperanto as apolitical technology was what Fred Halliday referred to as the analytic side to internationalism: a "sober, non-utopian internationalism" that recognized the growing interdependence of modern world society.[75] I would describe these first articulations of the early Japanese Esperantists (as well as that of the Volapük advocates before them) as essentially descriptive forms of internationalism—that is, they were making a call to an international community or society that existed in the present and were seeking to ease the problems arising from its growth, rather than arguing for the use of a world language for the construction of some imagined future international community.

The major exception to this within the first generation of Japanese Esperanto were the socialists. While Ōsugi Sakae, Ishikawa Sanshirō, and their fellow socialists faced the same linguistic barriers as those keen to look to the West for knowledge, and so found in Esperanto a potential tool for the development of transnational networks, they also were developing a critique of the nation-state that looked to transnational solidarity. This, they thought, might offer the means to resist a repeating cycle of national wars that they saw as axiomatic to the Western international system. The Russo-Japanese War was critical in the development of this line of thought.

If the dominant line of thinking within the early Esperanto community in Japan conceptualized the language as an apolitical form of technology, then the socialists represented one locus where more ideologically charged conceptions of the language could be found, blended with the sort of socialist internationalism that they were developing. Radical thinkers such as Ōsugi, Fukuda Kunitarō (an Esperantist who helped to fund some of the early anarchists and who later appealed for Japanese Esperantists to "cast off their neutrality"),[76] and Kōtoku

Shūsui (who asserted to the Tokyo-based Chinese anarchists that an international language would come into being)[77] help to indicate the potential for a broader, more revolutionary imagination of Esperanto. These ideas, embryonic in the first flowering of Japanese Esperanto, became much more significant over time, most notably with the emergence of the proletarian Esperanto movement in the late 1920s, as explored in chapter 5.

If one *sekaigo* were to find long-term support in Japan, it is not surprising that it should be Esperanto and not Volapük. It would be odd indeed were the majority of Japan's international language movement to persist with Volapük in the face of the global preference for Esperanto, not least because the major criterion for the success of an international language is less some external measure of its perfection as a language than its realization in a network of actual usage. However, in addition to the longer-term persistence, one striking difference between the Volapük and Esperanto moments was that whereas Esperanto got started within the first year or two of its discussion in the mainstream national press—groups formed, and an organizational base was established from which further growth could develop—Volapük's introduction to a Japanese audience met with little to no enthusiasm and too few interested individuals to give rise to any broader movement. This perhaps represents the changing national context in which the two events took place. Between 1890 and 1906, the number of Japanese studying foreign languages and the degree to which Western learning had penetrated Japanese life had steadily grown. Moreover, in the wake of the victory over Russia, Japanese perhaps felt more able and willing to embrace and take a lead in efforts to mitigate the problems of international communication, rather than meekly accept the need to study European languages. In the words of Katō Misao, "Our people, who having received the laurel crown of victory [in the Russo-Japanese War] should launch out into the world, have a duty to take the lead among the great powers, and research and use this [Esperanto]."[78]

This chapter has demonstrated that the timing of the first Esperanto boom places it at the culmination of a series of experiments and proposals for an international language that ran in parallel to (and influenced) the better-known debates and reforms to the Japanese language in the early Meiji period. Katō's newfound confidence was correct in two ways. First, his exhortation that Japan look to take the lead in efforts to solve the international language question reflects Seth Jacobowitz's argument that Japan was increasingly a participant in rather than a recipient of global intellectual trends. But second, he spoke at the start of a Japanese Esperanto movement, which grew to become one of the largest in the world and, indeed, the largest outside of Europe. While the focus of activity for these first Japanese advocates of Esperanto was to spread knowledge of their language and to argue for it as a solution to the challenges of transnational communication, in subsequent years they and those who came after them built upon these foundations. From the Taishō period and into the early Shōwa period, they began not only to seek to drive greater awareness of Esperanto and hopefully its study, but also to find ways of using the language in more diverse practical ways. The next chapter and those that follow will demonstrate how Esperanto increasingly became not just an interesting (or to some even a compelling) idea, but rather a practical language that could be written and spoken to real purpose.

CHAPTER 2

A Portrait of the Blind Russian

In Shimo-Ochiai, central Tokyo, is a reconstruction of the home and workplace of the Taishō-era artist Nakamura Tsune. It is only two miles north of Shinjuku, perhaps the busiest railway station in the world, but it stands in a quiet residential block, an elegant wooden building ringed by a small lawn. The building has a couple of small rooms intended for daily life, but the main area is devoted to a single large studio. On clear days, as when I first visited, the high-ceilinged room is full of light streaming in through tall, translucent windows. It is clear that the space is ideal for an artist. Indeed, it was one of several similar studios and ateliers that was built during the early twentieth century in Tokyo.

In the center of the main room now stand two paintings of the same man: Vasilii Eroshenko, a blind Russian who lived in Tokyo on and off between 1914 and 1921. They were painted simultaneously, side by side. One, unsurprisingly, was painted by Nakamura Tsune himself; the other by his close friend and contemporary Tsuruta Gōrō.[1] Looking at them, one can recreate the positions of the three men: Eroshenko sat on a sofa pushed up against the wall, Tsuruta stood to his right, and Nakamura stood to his left. They were painted over the course of a week in September 1920; the following month, they were both exhibited at the second imperial exhibition (Teiten). Nakamura's portrait, in particular, attracted substantial attention and praise.

The story goes that Tsuruta noticed Eroshenko waiting at Mejiro station, cutting a striking figure, tall and with long blond hair, and asked him to sit for a portrait. Recently returned from Manchuria, Tsuruta lacked a workplace and so partnered with his friend Nakamura to combine subject and studio.[2] This serendipitous encounter may well have occurred, but all three men were also closely linked through a literary and artistic salon run by husband and wife business partners Sōma Aizō and Kokkō. The Sōmas owned a bakery called the Nakamuraya, which had its own atelier at the back; both Eroshenko and Nakamura had even lived there at different times.

A blind Russian might seem a strange choice to use in order to explore the intellectual networks of Taishō Japan. Nevertheless, his experiences and his

Figure 2.1. Nakamura Tsune's *Portrait of Eroshenko*. Image copyright the National Museum of Modern Art, Tokyo, licensed through DNP Art Communications.

relationships with the likes of the Sōmas, Nakamura, and Tsuruta; his connections to the bakery and elsewhere; and even the story of the two portraits of him together reveal the importance of transnational connections and influences in an era known for its vibrant urban culture and a rising middle class. The Taishō era was a fertile period for Japanese culture and intellectual life, and one facet of this was the flowering of rich patterns of exchange, flowing both into Japan from abroad and back out in the opposite direction.

Moreover, threading through this "Taishō transnationalism," the ideas of Esperanto and Esperantism (both the language itself and the philosophies embedded within its movement) were influential and important themes. The underlying international language problem remained a persistent issue in early twentieth-century Japan: ten to fifteen years after the first major wave of Esperanto activity had brought the language to the country, the Japanese Esperanto movement underwent a second, larger boom, setting volumes and patterns of activity that would persist well into the 1930s.

Alongside the language issue, the ideas of internationalism and cross-cultural understanding that had motivated L. L. Zamenhof to create Esperanto also found a receptive audience in Japan in the late 1910s and early 1920s. Esperantism was one of a number of different forms of internationalism or cosmopolitanism that flowered in the Taishō and early Shōwa periods, and the networks and practices of transnational exchange formed a concrete manifestation of these different (if related) ideas.[3]

Eroshenko became an important symbol of Esperanto's ideas and potential in this period. He was a European who came to Japan as much to learn as to teach, reflecting the complexity of the flows of people, ideas, and things. Despite being hampered by his lack of sight, he traveled the world, putting his faith in others to aid his passage and spreading his vision of an Esperanto future. This optimism and hope formed a powerful message for young Japanese, who were drawn to Eroshenko's charisma. However, his time in Japan ended in scandal and disappointment. In the spring of 1921, barely six months after the two portraits were exhibited to great acclaim, Eroshenko was served with deportation papers, citing his "dangerous thought" and secret meetings with revolutionary agitators. Despite outcry in the press and petitions by his supporters (by no means all drawn from the political left) he was bundled unceremoniously out of the country with little notice and no room for appeal.

The irony could hardly be more clear. On May 29, 1921, newspapers published the release of Eroshenko's deportation order, even going so far as to include photographs of him, letter in hand, being consoled by friends.[4] The very same day, a small item in the *Yomiuri Shinbun* announced an artistic exchange

between museums in France and Japan.[5] The following autumn, Nakamura Tsune's portrait was again the central attraction of an exhibition—this time in Paris. The image of Eroshenko stood as a marker of Japan's success in the artistic world, a high point of modern Japanese cultural achievement. And yet, the man himself was a threat to national security: so subversive that his very presence was intolerable. Nakamura Tsune succumbed to tuberculosis in 1925. Only the art remained, its subject deported and its creator dead.

To his friends, then, Eroshenko was a musician, a poet, and a storyteller, who wore his politics lightly and espoused views that were progressive and utopian without being saddled by theory or dogma. The state perceived him in a very different way from the students and intellectuals of Tokyo: as a dangerous radical spreading subversive thought and collaborating with socialists and those seeking to overthrow the state and its economic system. Eroshenko, Esperanto, and Esperantism were all examples of an increasingly globally connected and diverse Japanese society, with more voices clamoring to be heard, and influences drawn from across Japan, Asia, and the world.

Taishō Transnationalism and the Blind Russian

Vasilii Eroshenko, was born in 1890 in Belgorod, Russia, and lost his sight as the result of a childhood illness. He was educated in Moscow in a school for the blind.[6] After graduating, he worked for a while in an orchestra of blind musicians, but in 1912, aged twenty-two, he moved to London to study in the Royal Normal College and Academy for the Blind in Norwood. He lasted less than a year, returning to Moscow and the orchestra via Paris.[7] Japan, then, was not his first taste of a foreign country and society, but it was still a large jump: much farther than he had been previously and culturally more different from his previous European experience.

Eroshenko, however, did not choose Japan at random. His attention was sparked by the knowledge that the blind in Japan were taught massage as a profession. In order to learn firsthand about lives and livelihoods of the Japanese blind, he therefore began to prepare for a visit, studying Japanese through contacts he made through the Japanese consulate.[8] Once he had set the details of his voyage to Japan, he also arranged introductions through the Universal Esperanto Association (UEA). His first and most notable supporter was Nakamura Kiyō, a meteorologist of some standing in Japan and by the mid 1910s an elder statesman of the Japanese Esperanto movement. Nakamura welcomed Eroshenko to Japan, arranging his enrollment into the Tokyo School for the Blind and augmenting somewhat his Russian sources of income.[9]

These two points of contact, the blind school and the Esperanto community, formed the beginning of Eroshenko's network in Tokyo. His entry into the blind school was well timed: among his peers were a number of students who shared his desire to push at the edges of what society deemed them capable of. Fellow students such as Torii Tokujirō and Iwahashi Takeo would go on to be leading figures in a movement to expand the opportunities for the blind in Japan in the 1920s and beyond.[10] Their friendship with Eroshenko helped to both motivate them and steer their interests, not least into studying Esperanto. Blind Japanese Esperantists began holding a special subgroup meeting at the annual Esperanto congress in 1922, and in 1928 they formed a separate association the Japana Asocio de Blindaj Esperantistoj (JABE). They were supported by a series of textbooks and dictionaries specifically designed for them and printed in Braille.[11] Despite some efforts by the Tokyo School for the Blind to discourage its study in the wake of Eroshenko's expulsion from Japan, Esperanto was on the syllabus in schools for the blind in other cities, such as Osaka and Okayama, and studying it led students to make contact with other groups and individuals. As Kataoka Yoshiki, who entered school in 1923, later recalled: "The school authorities looked upon students who studied Esperanto with suspicion, but I wasn't too bothered. I visited Akita Ujaku, and became close to [Agnes] Alexander, Gauntlett, Abe Isō and so on."[12] Gauntlett here was, of course, George Edward Gauntlett, the pioneer of Japanese Esperanto discussed in chapter 1, and Abe Isō was a well-known lecturer at Waseda University and Christian socialist, but Akita Ujaku and (Agnes) Alexander are lesser-known figures. Both were leading participants in the Japanese Esperanto movement, both had close ties to both Vasilii Eroshenko and his activities, and both were involved in other branches of the Taishō-era intellectual networks.

Akita Ujaku was a playwright in the Waseda Bungaku school who was close to Shimamura Hōgetsu and deeply interested in the plays of Henrik Ibsen. He was originally from Aomori, in the far north of Japan; one possible source of connection between him and Eroshenko was that Akita's father was blind. The two men first met in 1915, becoming close friends and collaborators. As Akita wrote:

> [In 1914/1915] we lived for six months on almost no regular income. My two children waited for me like fledglings waiting for their parents to return carrying food in their mouths . . . Perhaps at that time had two or three friends not encouraged me . . . I might even have found occasion to commit suicide . . .
>
> At a time when I was absolutely despairing of life, becoming extremely nihilistic, I came to know Eroshenko who, while blind, was fervently

> working for the cure of world Esperanto . . . Thanks to it, I was able to look on life with new eyes.[13]

The two men met on February 21, 1915; on February 22 Akita took up Esperanto, an interest that was to last the rest of his life. Throughout Eroshenko's time in Japan, other examples abound of similar effects he had upon friends and acquaintances—inspiring and enthusing others through the example of his zest for life, his vision of a potential future, and his refusal to be hampered by his blindness.

At the same time that Akita became friends with Eroshenko and took up Esperanto, he was also introduced to Agnes Alexander. Alexander was the granddaughter of two famous Christian missionaries to Hawai'i; while also a missionary, she advocated not Christianity but Bahá'ísm. The religion Bahá'í was established in the middle of the nineteenth century in Persia; it teaches a syncretic series of beliefs respectful of other faiths and articulated a vision of a common humanity, overcoming national and sexual difference. It looked to Esperanto as a linguistic element of this perspective. The Bahá'í mission was established in 1914 by Alexander and another follower, George Augar: Alexander was a regular presence in Esperanto meetings in Tokyo, while Eroshenko's friend Torii Tokujirō was an early Japanese convert to the religion. Akita and Eroshenko worked with Alexander, and while they never seem to have become believers as such, they helped Alexander translate some Bahá'í texts into both Japanese and indeed Braille. Indeed, Eroshenko took to wearing a red fez, something often sported by Bahá'ís, and together with Akita formed a literary group they called the Red Hat Society.[14]

From these initial contacts among the blind students and Esperantists of Tokyo, Vasilii Eroshenko began to expand into other intellectual groups, making contacts across a spectrum of activities, chiefly focused on literary and what one might call progressive interests. However, as mentioned in the introduction to this chapter, the group he is most closely associated with, the one among whom he made the closest bonds, was the Nakamuraya Salon.

In opening their bakery, Sōma Aizō and Kokkō had originally wanted to run a coffee shop, eager to take advantage of Japanese students' interest in "*hai-kara*" (Western intellectual) cultural artifacts. However, they found that there was already one close to the Imperial University where they sought to operate (before later moving to Shinjuku), so they decided that baked goods met a similar demand.[15] Aizō was a graduate of Waseda University with ties to the Waseda Bungaku literary group, but the group that began to assemble around the bakery was at first mostly of sculptors and artists: Ogiwara Rokuzan, who had an atelier nearby the bakery; Kinoshita Naoe; Tsuruta Gorō; Nakahara Teijirō; and Nakamura Tsune. The Sōmas built their atelier on the grounds of the bakery in 1910, originally to house the artist Yamato Keisuke, but later home to a series of different residents.[16]

By the time Vasilii Eroshenko was settling in to life in Tokyo in 1914–1915, the salon was fully up and running, exploring literature and cultural issues in addition to the visual arts. It was Akita Ujaku who introduced Eroshenko to Sōma Aizō and Kokkō, together with a mutual friend, the journalist and socialist Kamichika Ichiko.[17]

There was, unsurprisingly, a good deal of mixing between the different groups: Agnes Alexander was a regular at Esperanto meetings in Tokyo, while Eroshenko's friend, the blind Bahá'í Torii Tokujirō, was an occasional visitor at the Nakamuraya. Eroshenko participated in many different circles, including the elite literary group Shirakaba-ha and the Shinjinkai student group born of the Imperial University's Law Faculty, both of which explored the language Esperanto as well.[18] Together with the likes of the Chinese students introduced to Esperanto by Ōsugi Sakai, discussed in chapter 1, Eroshenko represented a physical manifestation of the growing international dimension of this Japanese intellectual world.

Eroshenko signed letters to his friends "Ero."[19] While Taishō/interwar Japan has usually been described using a different *ero*—the "erotic grotesque nonsense" of a rapidly developing consumer culture—these networks of Taishō transnationalism reveal another dimension to the complex mix of domestic and international that characterize the period. The classic images of Taishō Japan reveal an urban culture that was influenced by overseas trends but was more than mere reproduction.[20] The Modern Girl, for example, was not merely the "Japanese flapper," but rather represented a response to modernity that drew on ideas coming from abroad blended and grounded in the specifics of the Japanese city. Similarly, the intellectual networks examined here were innately transnational in outlook and drew on European and American writers and thinkers, but they manifested in ways that were unique to Japan's position and context.

The intellectual networks also reveal that the flows of transnational encounter defied a simple West to East model: the Shinjinkai student group experimented with Esperanto not, as one might expect, to connect to Europe, but in order to allow Korean students to better participate in discussions, reflecting the growing importance of empire to Japanese life.[21] Similarly, the presence of the Bahá'í mission in Tokyo demonstrates the more complex directions in which connections were being made and knowledge was flowing: no longer a simple process of learning from the West, if that was ever truly the case, but now exchange with Persia, via Hawai'i. These were not just issues of networks or practice: the activities of these groups reflected differing conceptions of the world—differing forms of internationalism.

So, the Nakamuraya salon's participants were artists influenced by European art movements, as well as writers of the left, such as Akita Ujaku and Kamichika Ichiko, but Rash Behari Bose, perhaps the most famous resident at the bakery, reveals connections to Asia and Japan's political right. Bose was an Indian independence activist who, in 1915, was forced to flee India for his part in various revolutionary plots.[22] In Tokyo, he received support from the radical Asianist leader Tōyama Mitsuru, who arranged for him to evade extradition by hiding in the Nakamuraya. Eventually in 1918, Bose married Sōma Kokkō's daughter, Toshiko. We cannot, then, easily characterize the Nakamuraya as a left-wing group or one influenced purely by European thought.

This complexity is revealed by objects and places as much as ideas. Eroshenko's intellectual activities were embedded in the same urban environment as the erotic grotesque nonsense: Esperantists met in Ginza cafés and the graduate school of physics, the Nakamuraya salon participants studied in the bakery, and the spread of artists' studios in northern Tokyo led to the growth of an area that would come to be called "Ikebukuro Montparnasse."[23] While the Nakamuraya supplied students and artists with baked goods of a European style, they also introduced more world foods to Japan, including borscht from Russia and curry

Figure 2.2. The Nakamuraya Salon (1920s). Image courtesy of Nakamuraya Co. Ltd.

from India. In 1921, again inspired by Eroshenko, they introduced the Russian-style *rubashka* as uniform for the staff. Clad in a Russian shirt and a fez introduced by the Persian Bahá'í, eating Indian curry from a recipe provided by a member of the pan-Asian underground, and discussing (with Korean students, in Esperanto) French art or Russian literature, the participants of these circles reveal an emergent transnational modernity that was much more than narrow Westernization: it was a complex and unpredictable mix of influences from across the globe, each inflected and reinterpreted for a Japanese context.

The Asian Connection

The position of Asia in these intellectual networks and the concrete encounters that resulted form a vital part of the phenomenon of Taishō transnationalism. Perhaps the single most high-profile literary event during the mid 1910s was the visit to Japan of another Indian, the poet and writer Rabindranath Tagore. Tagore came to Japan in 1916, one of the first high-profile visitors in a growing pattern of tours that would later include the likes of John Dewey (1919), Bertrand Russell (1921), and Albert Einstein (1922).[24] His arrival was promoted for weeks in advance, promoting Pan-Asian sentiment through his position as the first non-Western winner of the Nobel Prize in Literature. This drum beating was wildly successful: it reached such a height that when Tagore finally arrived in Kobe he was met by a crowd of thousands, a scene that was repeated as he traveled across the country. When Tagore finally made it to Tokyo, arriving by train, Akita Ujaku, Eroshenko, and the Red Hat literary society were there (part of a crowd estimated at as many as thirty thousand) to shout a greeting in Esperanto across the platform.[25]

In Tokyo, Tagore spoke a number of times—his highest-profile speech at the Imperial University was attended by Akita, Eroshenko, and Agnes Alexander as well as dignitaries, including the British ambassador.[26] Elsewhere he met with the Bahá'í Mission and visited the Nakamuraya, surrounded by a varied mix of hangers-on and associates, such as the French poet Paul Richard.[27] The excitement around this visit drew Akita Ujaku and others to study Tagore's own work as well as Indian philosophy, such as the Upanishads.[28] However, the truth was that his reception was profoundly mixed, and his message was largely at odds with the prevailing sentiment in Japan. Tagore was struck by his experiences in Japan, at once perceiving a country uniquely in touch with its natural environment and yet troubled by its rapid modernization. He described Kobe as a "huge Chinese dragon with a twisted back . . . iron roofs so close together that they touch one another, glistening in the sun like scales."[29] Yet at the same time he drew comfort from Japanese gardens, Japanese flower arranging, and other aspects of daily life: "I met, at a wayside station, some Buddhist priests and devotees. They brought their basket of fruits to me and held their lighted incense before my face, wishing to pay homage to a man who had come from the land of Buddha. The dignified serenity of their bearing, the simplicity of their devoutness, seemed to fill the atmosphere of the busy railway station with a golden light of peace."[30] Tagore's central message to his audience was one of caution: to modernize was not simply to Westernize, nor to industrialize, and to miss the differences risked losing something of Japan's unique quality.

> One must bear in mind that those who have the true modern spirit need not modernize, just as those who are truly brave are not braggarts. Modernism is not in the dress of the Europeans; or in the hideous structures, where their children are interned when they take their lessons; or in the square houses with flat straight wall-surfaces, pierced with parallel lines of windows, where these people are caged in their lifetime; certainly modernism is not in their ladies' bonnets, carrying on them loads of incongruities. These are not modern, but merely European. True modernism is freedom of mind, not slavery of taste. It is independence of thought and action, not tutelage under European schoolmasters. It is science, but not its wrong application in life.[31]

This message was not well calibrated to a more sanguine Japanese audience: Stephen Hay calculates that of eighty-seven individual assessments of Tagore's speeches, only twenty-six were clearly positive.[32] Akita Ujaku confessed ambivalence, arguing that Tagore had Western culture right, but adding: "I must admit that I cannot say that I agree with most of his ideas, but I feel a strong sympathy with him as a poet, and the leitmotiv of his philosophy."[33]

Vasilii Eroshenko was reportedly much more critical still—in outright opposition with Tagore over the nature of human culture and society. Tagore articulated a clear division between the materialistic West and the more spiritual East, forming a clear split within humankind. By contrast, Eroshenko's Esperanto-inspired vision was more unified: identifying commonality, not difference, between the peoples of the world.[34]

In the middle of Tagore's lecture tour, Eroshenko departed Japan, heading out on a trip of his own. His intentions varied over time—sometimes talking of returning to Japan, at other times intending to return to Europe via South Asia and the Middle East—but the trip ultimately took him through Hong Kong and Singapore to extended stays in Siam, Burma, and India.[35] During the trip, he remained in close contact with a number of friends from Japan, discussing their activities at home; his experiences in Bangkok, Rangoon, and Calcutta; as well as his developing opinions on the varied international experiences of the blind.[36] Indeed, the trip was largely built upon introductions and contacts garnered through his network of contacts in Japan—chiefly blind teachers and Bahá'í. In addition, he stayed with Russian émigrés he encountered during his travels, ever ready to put his faith in people he had barely met.[37] Eroshenko supported himself financially using the massage skills he had learned while in Japan, often on Japanese clients, as well as sums he received from friends back in Japan and others he met on his travels. These connections once again demonstrate how Taishō-era Japanese intellectuals were increasingly tied into networks that spanned Asia.

The stated purpose of Eroshenko's travel was a survey of the lives of the blind (and in particular their education) in other Asian nations, including the possibility that he might contribute to the latter's development. In Bangkok he was frustrated in that objective and grew restless at a lifestyle that was purely centered on recreation and enjoyment. From there he moved on to Burma, where he was able to secure a job in a school for the blind. He was even led to believe that he might take on the position of headmaster there, but when push came to shove, he elected to move on. "Did I leave Russia in order to run a Burmese school? Did I leave Japan in order to live out my days in Burma?" he asked a friend, "Of course not—I have to move forward."[38]

When we think of transnational exchange in terms of translation, we have to be careful to recognize that the source and output are related, but different: the translation represents more than just a copy or approximation of the original, a function of the context in which it is produced. However, even when we are sensitive to this, translation is a model that suggests unidirectional flows: typically from the West into Japan. If, instead, we think in terms of circulations of knowledge, we can recognize flows moving in different directions—in and out of Japan, back to the West, to elsewhere in Asia, and so on. Eroshenko, seen as an avatar of Taishō transnationalism, reveals this more complex circulation in action: coming to Japan to learn, inspiring others in various ways, and making use of the contacts he'd made to travel elsewhere across Asia.

However, a lone Russian traveling with an unorthodox and unclear motivation inevitably attracted some official attention. In Hong Kong, Eroshenko struggled to obtain an onward visa to Singapore, his red fez raising suspicions he was a Muslim and questions about his sources of income provoking the provocative answer "I'm bourgeois!" Eventually his visa was secured in consultation with the Russian consulate.[39] Later, in Burma, he felt it necessary to keep his associations with the Bahá'í from authorities.[40]

This all came to a head in India. Eroshenko arrived in Calcutta in late 1917, in the wake of the October Revolution in Russia. Early the following year, a rumor spread that the British authorities were going to arrest all Russians in Calcutta, so the bulk of them fled on a homeward bound Russian ship. Eroshenko, however, resisted, eventually returning to Burma, hoping to take up the post of headmaster that he believed he had been offered the year before. However, he discovered that while the staff and students were supportive, the governors of the school refused, offering him only a regular teaching position. Frustrated, Eroshenko returned to Calcutta. However, this time he found an exit visa harder to come by, securing one only after the first Japan-bound ship had departed. When the second boat was impounded by authorities, Eroshenko changed his mind, deciding instead to seek to return to Europe. He hoped to attend the peace conferences about to convene in Paris. This, too, was resisted by the British authorities, who eventually put Eroshenko under house arrest in December 1918.[41] In June 1919, six months after his movements had been limited by the state and almost eighteen since the first rumors of a threat to Russians had caused him to change plans, the British eventually decided Eroshenko's case, putting him on a boat back to Japan. He arrived in July, three years after he had left.[42]

The Rise of Esperantismo

Eroshenko had left Japan in 1916, with Europe mired in a war that had quickly proven to be more deadly and more intractable than any before. He arrived in 1919 to a Japan that was, despite its distance from and only minor participation in the First World War, feeling the effects of a transformed international environment. While the emergence of the Soviet Union would ultimately make for a dramatic change in the perceived threat of socialism and communism, in the short term the sense of optimism that the peace conferences might enable the creation of a world beyond war proved a boost for progressive movements of all kinds, including the end of the "winter period" of Japanese socialism.

The place of Esperanto at the League of Nations and Japanese participation in those debates is considered in chapter 3, but the end of the war and this optimistic phase that resulted had a dramatic effect on Esperanto at home as well. During Eroshenko's first period in Japan, Esperanto activity had been at a fairly low ebb. The first wave of 1906–1910 failed to maintain its momentum, and the outbreak of war in Europe made for less support from abroad. While a lot of groundwork was done during the second half of the 1910s, with a new generation of leaders emerging in debates about the nature of Esperanto and its significance, this was eclipsed in the early 1920s in a new, more sustained period of growth.[43]

Here, it is useful to distinguish between two different facets of Esperanto as an intellectual movement. There are different ways of conceiving this: one might talk of Esperanto as a language and Esperanto as an idea or (as outlined in the introduction) talk of Esperanto (the language) and Esperantismo (the philosophy or ideology underpinning it). In short, Esperanto in this period was important, both seen as medium and seen as content. It was a language through which international communication could take place, but also a set of ideas about what such communication might achieve.

However, while ideas of Esperantismo appealed beyond the Esperanto community, within it, debates raged as to what the correct articulation of it should be. The *interna ideo*, the "intrinsic idea," of Esperanto, from its outset was that adoption of the language on a mass scale would promote mutual understanding and thereby prove to be a step toward peace. However, opinions on how to implement this in practice were more varied. For many, the idea went hand in hand with progressive political and social views, which led them to see Esperanto as similarly politically progressive. By contrast, others saw this view as problematic—if a language had embedded within it an inherent ideology, then how could it truly lay claim to universality? For Esperanto to be a world language, the latter group argued, it must be capable of being the medium for any phrase. Within this view, while the effect of Esperanto might be progressive, this outcome would only be possible if the language was explicitly politically neutral.

As outlined in the introduction, these debates were had across the Esperanto world, with the two key poles being Zamenhof's own views, typically called Homaranismo, and the position expressed in the 1905 Declaration of Boulogne: explicit neutrality ("All other ideals or hopes tied with Esperantism by any Esperantist is his or her purely private affair, for which Esperantism is not responsible").[44]

While the first generation of Esperantists in Japan had held rather unproblematically to this neutral standpoint, focusing on the language narrowly as a medium of communication, by the 1910s the debate was reopened and the new generation took a very different view. Vasilii Eroshenko, alongside other young Esperantists such as the anarchist acolyte of Ōsugi Sakae, Yamaga Taiji, and Fukuda Kunitarō (another anarchist) took the more overtly idealistic viewpoint, while they were opposed by some of the old-timers, for example Kuroita Katsumi and Takusari Kōki.[45] These tensions about Esperantism were evident as early as 1914, when Chifu Toshio, then editor of the official JEA magazine *La Japana Esperantisto*, caused uproar within the community with an editorial titled "Banzai," celebrating the Japanese capture of German-held Asian territory, including the Shantung Peninsula.[46] His overtly national perspective was contrasted by a much more emollient note struck by a German teacher at the First Higher School

named Junker, in a speech to the Tokyo Esperanto Club. Junker argued that, were Esperanto more widely adopted, the European war might have been avoided: essentially a direct application of the *interna ideo*.[47]

The end of the First World War was the spark of a more sustained argument over the true meaning of Esperanto. In 1923, Osaka Kenji, who would prove to be perhaps the single most influential figure in organized Japanese Esperanto over the next decade, published an Esperanto textbook together with Akita Ujaku, which started with Akita's explicit refutation of the Boulogne Declaration: "To be an Esperantist is not simply to practice Esperanto [the language]."[48] The year before this, advocates of this sort of explicit embrace of the *interna ideo* had sought to bring a motion in support of it at the annual Japanese congress, but withdrew it in response to appeals that the debate would prove divisive.[49]

Indeed, while it might not have happened in an official setting, that debate was bubbling up in Esperanto circles, and it was indeed provoking disagreements. A broadly left-wing Esperanto magazine, *Verda Utopio*, published by the anarcho-Esperantist Fukuda Kunitarō, ran an issue devoted to debates over Esperantismo and neutrality, giving space to both sides of the argument in what came to be known as the Esuperantisimo Ronsō. Chifu Toshio, by now the chief voice in support of the Boulogne position of explicit neutrality, argued there and in a separate pamphlet that Homaranismo was a shallow ideology that risked turning Esperanto into a cult of Zamenhof: "Remember that Esperantismo is not a religion, nor moral instruction: it is a pure linguistic movement which must be absolutely neutral for all religions, for all morals, and for all ideas; likewise [it must be] for all nations and peoples."[50]

Chifu was supported by another Esperantist of long standing, the engineer Takahashi Kunitarō, who argued that Homaranismo was an admirable but unachievable philosophy, and thus Esperantists should focus on more practical objectives. The two were fighting a losing battle, however. The congress motion might have been seen off in 1922, but by the 1924 congress, a group of young Esperantists had formed, calling themselves the Aĉuloj (roughly "the wastrels") and drunkenly celebrating the rise of the *interna ideo*.[51]

These young advocates of the Homaranismo interpretation of Esperantism were not only taking charge of the intellectual grounds of Esperanto; they were also becoming central to the institutional apparatus. The postwar environment was ripe for Esperanto to grow again, but the JEA under Kuroita Katsumi was not in a position to take advantage. Kuroita's (mis)management and personal absentmindedness meant that the finances were woefully confused and poorly handled. In 1919, their longtime publisher, Daidō-sha, broke with them over unpaid bills; finding a replacement printer for *La Japana Esperantista* proved hard given the level of disorganization.[52] The leading advocates of reform—Osaka Kenji, Fujisawa Chikao, and Asai Erin—ultimately concluded that they had to take the more radical step of creating a new body to promote Esperanto in Japan. They created the Japana Esperanto Instituto (Nihon Esuperanto Gakkai, JEI) on December 20, 1919.[53]

In the JEI, they created an organization that reflected some combination of the problems resulting from Kuroita's control of the JEA and the new, more egalitarian spirit of the times: it would have no single head, but rather a committee to guide it and regular limited terms of appointment.[54] It was also better able to support a new, growing interest in Esperanto among the Japanese public. Indeed, the expansion was dramatic and sustained: by 1919, there were only 280 paid-up members of the JEA; in 1922 the figure for the JEI was nearly 1,500, and it continued to grow from there.[55] The proportion of members surveyed who gave their occupation as "student" rose from 19 percent in 1919 to 43 percent in 1922, reflecting the influx of a new generation.[56]

The idea of an international language continued to appeal, as it had to the previous generation, but its more idealistic articulations, centered upon Homaranismo and the *interna ideo*, added another dimension to this appeal, bringing different constituencies into the broad Esperanto community. One example of the draw of a more idealistic articulation of Esperanto is the rise of the blind

Figure 2.3. An Esperanto Class, 1920s. Image courtesy of the Japanese Esperanto Institute.

language movement. As discussed, the late 1910s and early 1920s saw the emergence of an Esperanto movement within the system of schools for the blind. Vasilii Eroshenko's charismatic presence was one driver of this, as were the general conditions that helped boost Esperanto across society. Blind students were in this regard no different from students in other institutions, but they also put their own gloss on Zamenhof's ideas, reflecting their own unique situation. The idea of a language that broke down barriers between different peoples had a profound effect upon a generation of blind Japanese who were increasingly keen to escape the narrow confines that society had established for them. In the inaugural issue of *Orienta Blindularo*, Torii Tokujirō wrote:

> What is it that those oppressed by the darkness gasp for? What is the ultimate goal of the various movements of the blind world that will result from their struggle? It is a joint share in culture, equal opportunity with respect to society, and then to achieve the same happiness as sighted people . . .
>
> . . . what is it that we have invested our new light of hope in, in this deadlocked current oriental blind world of ours, in this acute need of ours? It is the international auxiliary language, Esperanto: we deeply believe in Esperantists . . . it is the sole key to achieving the realization of the principle of world brotherhood, further, it is the driving force to make the blind people of the world and the sighted one whole family, to realize a utopia drenched in the light of human love and humanism. There, the gap between sighted and unsighted might, even if not small, be smaller than it is in the present world. We truly feel that the light of the new age for which we struggle can only be seen in the flag of the green star.[57]

Religious groups, too, found Zamenhof's articulation of a world united by mutual understanding appealing: while the Bahá'í were Esperantists of long standing, others, such as a Buddhist group led by the abbot of Nanzenji, Shibayama Zenkei, emerged in the same period as the blind movement, crafting their own interpretation of Esperantismo.[58] By far the largest Japanese religious Esperanto movement, however, was that associated with Ōmoto-kyō, the largest of the prewar "new" religions. Ōmoto was introduced to Esperanto by a chance encounter between one of the leaders and a Bahá'í visiting Japan named Aida Finch. The early 1920s were a period of persecution at home for Ōmoto, following the first "Ōmoto incident," in which leaders were charged with lèse-majesté for perceived insurrectionary aspects of their teaching. Deguchi Onisaburō, head of the religion, responded to this domestic blow with efforts to find new sources of support and legitimation overseas. These included new ties to new religions in other parts of Asia, an ill-fated mission to Mongolia, and the engagement with Esperanto.[59]

Deguchi founded a separate organization to promote Esperanto, the Esuperanto Fukyū Kai (or EPA, from the Esperanto translation), and a magazine, *Verda Mondo* (Green world), as well as adding Esperanto columns in its regular publications. However, the most impactful article on Esperanto and Ōmoto was one written by a non-adherent, a student of the Third Higher School in Kyoto, Yagi Hideo. This, published in 1924 in a Swiss magazine, led to a wave of interest from Europe, as a result of which Ōmoto established an office in Paris, staffed by a follower, Nishimura Kōgetsu.[60]

Deguchi was interested in *kotodama*, an ancient Japanese idea about the mystic power of words and language; Esperanto seems to have represented to him some international form of this. He was personally involved in the effort to spread Esperanto through Ōmoto, and vice versa, writing poems to help learn vocabulary and often stressing his Esperanto engagement.[61] Between 1922 and the second, more comprehensive "Ōmoto incident" in 1935, Ōmoto was an engaged and distinct presence within Esperanto in Japan, hosting gatherings, publishing magazines, and participating in events organized by JEI, at the same time as developing their own networks of Esperanto clubs and overseas connections.

The loose set of values and aspirations that formed Zamenhof's idealistic motivation for Esperanto, then, was sufficiently flexible to admit religious interpretations of the language and its philosophy, interpretations that appealed to the blind and to others with varying different worldviews and objectives. The single most significant such link was that between socialism and Esperanto, attracting figures from all parts of the left—from sophisticated anarchist thinkers, such as Ōsugi Sakae, to the less theoretically engaged likes of Vasilii Eroshenko. This relationship is examined in more depth in chapter 5; here it suffices to stress that, contrary to the fears of the neutralists who pointed to the Boulogne Declaration, the rise of more aspirational visions of Esperantism proved to be well timed, connecting with the "Wilsonian moment" to expand the language's range of appeal.[62] However, the coincidence of the resurgence in Esperanto activity with the reawakening of the socialists in Japan, as well as the overlap in personnel between the two movements, made for greater scrutiny by the state.

Poet or Radical? Eroshenko's Expulsion

Vasilii Eroshenko had been the subject of observation since his arrival in the country, but the manner of his return to Japan (he was deported from the British

Empire) raised the stakes further—not only was Eroshenko more clearly labeled as a radical, but the actions of his associates were becoming a greater cause for concern.[63] This all came to a head in the spring of 1921, when a series of events probed the boundary between acceptable cultural/social subjects and subversive politics, and pitched police against activists. The start of this moment came when Eroshenko spoke alongside a number of socialists at a meeting of the Bungei Kōenkai in Kanda on April 18.[64] The meeting was large—attended by some 1,200 people, according to Akita Ujaku—and saw some of the speeches cut short by attendant police observers who noted that the list of speakers was drawn heavily from the members of the Shakaishugi Dōmei (the Socialist League), accusing it of being a political assembly, rather than a cultural one.[65] However, this was a small event in comparison with the May Day march the following month, the largest Japan had ever seen.

The weather on May 1, 1921, was good. Although leaders such as Ōsugi Sakae and Sakai Toshihiko were prevented from participating, having been rounded up by the police the night before, the audience turnout was impressive. Flags waved, and slogans and songs were chanted as the participants made their way from Shibaura in the south up to Ueno Park.[66] As the march progressed, there was a struggle between marchers and the police over banners such as that of the Socialist League, and a series of arrests took place along the route. These arrests caused shock in the press, not least because among those apprehended were a number of women and Vasilii Eroshenko.[67] Eroshenko was rapidly released amid the sense that perhaps some of the arrests might have been a bit of a publicity blunder.[68] He demonstrated little in the way of ill will toward the police: "I simply went along with four friends to see what was going on, but the police picked me up forcibly . . . The police chief was a good man—when it became clear that there were no grounds to hold me, he soon let me return home," the *Yomiuri Shinbun* quoted him as saying.[69]

The following week, however, Eroshenko was seized again, this time outside a meeting of the Socialist League, as a part of arrests of some forty would-be participants.[70] Unperturbed, Eroshenko continued to attend events: on the fifteenth of the month he was finally allowed to participate in a meeting, this time held by the Kensetsu Dōmei (which the police had cautioned should not become a rescheduling of the Socialist League meeting), despite others such as Ishikawa Sanshirō having their speeches interrupted by the attendant police.[71] Little did he know, however, that the Home Ministry had been working behind the scenes all this time. On May 5, four days after Eroshenko's initial arrest, officials had opened a file labeled "Regarding the expulsion of a Russian National."[72]

It took three weeks for Eroshenko's case to be fully considered and decided, but on May 28, police arrived at the Nakamuraya with an order expelling him from Japan and denying him the right to return.[73] Eroshenko was absent when the police arrived, out celebrating the completion of a new piece of work. By the time he returned, a couple of friends had heard the news and were there to console him, along with journalists and a photographer, who captured an image of the Russian together with Sōma Kokkō and Aizō.[74] The police returned later that night. Eroshenko was shaken and reluctant to stay alone in the atelier, so he remained in the main Nakamuraya building together with the Sōmas. After the restaurant had closed and the last of the trains stopped, as many as thirty officers forced their way into the bakery, breaking furniture, stomping across the tatami without removing their shoes, and seizing Eroshenko against his wishes, taking him away to be detained. Sōma Aizō was incensed by the act, accusing the police of illegal entry, while the press linked the invasion to the sanctuary he had offered Rash Behari Bose, four years earlier.[75]

However, there was little that the Sōmas or their friends could do. Akita Ujaku made the rounds of the major newspaper offices, seeking to raise popular support for Eroshenko; he and a number of others (including non-socialist figures such as Nakamura Kiyō and Kuroita Katsumi) petitioned the police and the Home Ministry for the chance to see Eroshenko, but they were consistently denied.[76] Inukai Ken, son of the leading politician Inukai Tsuyoshi, even offered to put up five hundred yen in bail for Eroshenko.[77] However, by June 4, it became clear that Eroshenko had been taken out of Tokyo already and was being put on a boat to Vladivostok ("from darkness into darkness" in the words of the *Asahi Shinbun*), rendering further petitions meaningless.[78]

Asking why the Russian was being expelled, Akita recalled being told "because he's having a bad effect [on Japanese society]." Akita responded, "But Eroshenko has no especial political views, he's a simple poet!" But the official was implacable: "That's so, but this poet is up to no good."[79] That exchange encapsulated a clash of two views over Eroshenko: to his friends and supporters he was an artist and writer with aspirational but largely apolitical views, but to the state, he was a dangerous influence on Japan, associating with undesirable figures from the radical left. The state was, unsurprisingly, able to force its view through, deporting Eroshenko without permitting any form of appeal or review, but in doing so they inspired a popular response. The overall tenor of this coverage was, even in the eyes of the government's internal documents, sympathetic, one respondent writing of her "endless tears as she bid farewell to [Eroshenko's] retreating figure," while others remarked about Eroshenko's "forlorn stance."[80]

For Fujii Shōzō, this popular sympathy for Eroshenko's treatment can be traced through the use of the appellation "the blind poet." Noting that Eroshenko really didn't write much in the way of poetry (preferring short stories, folk tales, and essays), Fujii traces the rise of this descriptor to the period between Nakamura Tsune's portrait in 1920 and the arrests and deportation of 1921.[81] Art journals described how Nakamura had painted Eroshenko "as a poet," and gradually newspaper accounts adopted the label "blind poet," until even the reliably conservative *Yamato Shinbun* was using it by the time of Eroshenko's deportation.[82]

Alongside the attempts by Akita Ujaku and the Sōmas to appeal Eroshenko's arrest or even just to visit him, there was a rich series of responses in the mainstream press. The first of these, in the days immediately following his arrest was an essay, "Eroshenko-kun wo okeru" (Farewell to Eroshenko) by Kisaki Hiroshi, an Esperantist, in the *Yomiuri Shinbun*.[83] This castigated the authorities' "blindness regarding universal language," as well as their claims about Eroshenko: "Eroshenko was a skilled musician, he had the disposition of a poet, and a naïve inspiration; he was neither very knowledgeable nor interested in politics and economics, and lacked any insurrectionary ideology or revolutionary spirit, so it's hard to imagine him spreading extreme, dangerous thought or the like."[84] Kisaki went on to argue that it was most likely Eroshenko's wanderlust, gregariousness, and curiosity that had led him into whatever problematic contact the state had identified.

Kisaki's main point was to argue that the Russian's deportation revealed that the police were fundamentally misunderstanding Esperanto's aims and social makeup, conceding that there were many socialists who advocated the language, but arguing there were also "cosmopolitans, nationalists, and Japanists; there were capitalists and workers; writers such as Akita Ujaku, journalists like Ōba Kakō, and scholars such as Kuroita Katsumi." He was not alone in eliding Eroshenko with Esperanto: in the wake of his arrest the *Yomiuri Shinbun* quoted Tokkō thought police suspicions that the Esperanto movement might be little more than socialism operating under the guise of a "cultural movement."[85]

Regarding the apparent incongruity of sending thirty officers to arrest a blind man, officials had the following to offer: "prior to his arrival in Japan, Eroshenko was deported from India by the British government, of late his activities have brought him close to groups involved with dangerous ideology and involved the promotion of socialism and anarchism . . . rather an a single incident, his presence in our country is having a bad effect on social conditions and endangering the maintenance of public security."[86] The state recognized the Russian as an intellectual threat and a dangerous radical; much of the press was not convinced. The *Niroku Shinpō* wrote of a "misguided approach to the control of socialism," while the *Asahi Shinbun*'s column "Tsunobue" went further: "How much propaganda could he, a blind man, really achieve? How great was the danger he would disrupt the system? Why punish this invalid? Anyone possessing emotion would find it unendurable: that most detestable action has been carried out in the name of the Home Minister."[87]

Leaving aside the air of condescension toward the capabilities of the blind (although Eroshenko himself had argued that "as a blind man, what could I do—I would be an impediment [to radical activity]"[88]) there was a clear gap between the argument of the state that Eroshenko was a clear threat to society and the impression of his friends and supporters, who saw him as an artistic figure with little interest in politics and no insurrectionary impulse.

The early 1920s was a period in which the police and state officials came to the view that the left represented a more complex threat than perhaps they had in the past. Ten years earlier, the Great Treason case of 1911 had centered around the possibility of an assassination plot, but a proposed bill in late 1921, shortly after Eroshenko's expulsion, sought to criminalize threats that were intellectual rather than directly violent. Although this bill was shelved the following year, it was a precursor to the 1925 Peace Preservation Law, which did pass, establishing the basic infrastructure for the "thought crime" arrests that dominated the late 1920s and early 1930s.[89] As a foreigner subjected to deportation rather than imprisonment, Eroshenko was an unusual example, but nevertheless his case came at a pivotal moment for the state's changing view of the left and was clearly tied up with issues of growing importance.

To a certain extent, the state was not wrong: Eroshenko's ties to the socialist movement went at least as far back as his time in London, where he had met the leading anarchist Piotr Kropotkin; he was close friends with Kamichika Ichiko; and he had other connections to the likes of Ōsugi Sakae and Ishikawa Sanshirō. And the British seem to have labeled him a radical in expelling him from the empire, even if the real root of that was unclear. In contrast, the bulk of his writing took the form of children's stories and fables: allegorical, of course, but only very lightly political in any direct sense. As Eguchi Kan put it: "Eroshenko was an anarchist. He was a cosmopolitan. He was a poet. He was a musician. But the world in which he lived was not at all the real world. It was a beautiful future country, a utopian freeland [*yūtopia furiirando*]. A world of poems close to a children's story. His anarchism and cosmopolitanism could only be the birthings of that world of beautiful poetry."[90]

What inspired people about Eroshenko was not his political views or his mastery of Marxist theory. It was the simple optimism with which he approached life. The faith in others with which he traveled—the willingness to trust in people he barely knew. In a way he embodied some of the ideals that drew students and others to Esperanto: proof that people could meet, befriend, and help one another, no matter their origin or nationality, and that an individual, even though blind, could travel the world and find support wherever they went. Individuals such as Kawai Hideo, a student at the Imperial University, saw Eroshenko speak, perhaps met him, read his short stories, and were inspired by his example (in Kawai's case using his stories to excite agricultural workers on a Shinjinkai effort at rural outreach).[91]

If his friends were to be believed, it was that wanderlust that attracted the attention of the state and ultimately brought its hostility down upon Eroshenko, but perhaps it was not just that his curiosity took him to places that officials found unacceptable. Eroshenko's cosmopolitan outlook—as articulated and as embodied—represented a repudiation of a narrower national state/subject relationship, and if he inspired young Japanese like Kawai, then perhaps this helps to explain why the state could no longer tolerate his presence in the country. It was that presence and what it represented, more than any intellectual argument or political views Eroshenko had, that provoked the state to act. In this sense, there is no contradiction to reconcile between Eroshenko's friends' view of him as a mere poet and the state's fear of his insurrectionary potential: as Eguchi said, he enacted a vision of another possible world, one that inspired and threatened in equal measure.

Vasilii Eroshenko left Japan in 1921, never to return, but he was neither forgotten by his friends nor at the end of his travels. The Japanese press documented his arrival in Vladivostok and his attempts to return to Europe. However, a combination of famine within the Soviet Union and ongoing struggles with White Russians in Siberia meant that he was refused entry and had to turn back.[92] Blocked once more, he found a new home in China, first in Shanghai and later in Beijing. He became close friends with the writer Lu Xun and his brother Zhou Zuoren; he taught Esperanto and lectured on various subjects, mixing with a variety of young Chinese. Eventually, in 1923, he was finally able to return to Moscow.

Eroshenko's time in Japan was only one part of a complex story of travel, of living out utopian ideals, and of the enactment of everyday anarchist and socialist politics of a form. But looked at through the frame of Japan, he was also a vivid manifestation of a transnational dimension to the vibrant urban culture that emerged during the Taishō period. Tying together religion, arts, literature, and, yes, politics, his activities provide one map of the interconnections of different groups active during Taishō democracy and the extent to which they were all profoundly transnational in outlook—touching not only the West for ideas and exchange, but also elsewhere in Asia. That these different groups were diverse and interconnected is perhaps a truism of our understanding of the intellectual and cultural world of the 1910s and 1920s, both in Japan and elsewhere. However, the appeal that Esperanto held for many of them tells us something more about the ongoing importance of language ability and language choice as well as, through the rise of Esperantism, the power of Zamenhof's idealistic vision of linguistic union—one of a number of different visions of internationalism that was manifested in the networks of Taishō transnationalism. The domestic arm of the state reacted to this, at least as represented by Eroshenko, with suspicion; however, as the next chapter will demonstrate, other parts of the government took a more complex view.

CAPTER 3

Language and Diplomacy

Japan and Esperanto at the League of Nations

The second boom in Esperanto in Japan, beginning in the late 1910s and accelerating during the early 1920s, and the developments within the Japanese Esperanto movement that took place as a result, were part of a wider set of trends within Japanese society during the period. But while chapter 2 explores a specifically Japanese context, there was also an international frame—a resurgence in Esperanto activity in Europe and elsewhere that arose as a part of the general sense of optimism and idealism resulting from the peace of 1918. The revival of Esperanto, whether in Japan or globally, was chiefly a popular phenomenon, driven not by state support but by bottom-up activism. However, such was its success that Esperanto became a topic of discussion within the sphere of international diplomacy. At the same time as they were developing small-scale transnational networks of popular participation, the Esperantists of Japan (and elsewhere) were also involved in attempts to gain a wider, official recognition for their language.

The main forum for these efforts was the League of Nations. The renewal in the popularity of Esperanto and the creation of the League of Nations were, broadly speaking, different manifestations of the same set of international trends after the end of the First World War. This "Wilsonian moment" was perhaps marred in various ways: the absence of three of the major powers from the League, the perpetuation of empire across much of Asia and Africa, and the uncertainty of what sort of diplomatic actor the world's first communist state, the Soviet Union, would turn out to be.[1] Nevertheless, for a period at least, it was possible to imagine that the world stood at the opening of a new, more peaceful age.[2]

The new, more open, and hence inclusive approach to foreign relations represented by the creation of League of Nations exposed an issue of language—what we might call a diplomatic language problem to distinguish it as a distinct subpart of the broader international language problem faced by anyone seeking to act transnationally. European diplomatic history had centered upon French as the standard language of negotiation since the eighteenth century.[3] However, the Paris Peace Conference revealed that the assumption that all negotiators could be expected to speak French no longer held—significantly neither British prime minister David Lloyd George (whose first language was Welsh) nor American president Woodrow Wilson spoke it.[4]

This placed English alongside French as the main languages of the negotiations, something that persisted at the League of Nations even once it became clear that the United States would not be a participant. However, participation of so many more and smaller nations at the League made for more diplomats with more varied linguistic abilities. Alongside the problems this raised, there emerged a sense of the importance of some form of linguistic equality—roughly, an effort to reduce the linguistic barriers to full participation in the League's activities.

Japanese actors were to play a significant role within the debates that resulted, and in particular in the encounter between Esperanto and the League. Three figures are especially noteworthy: Nitobe Inazō, as under-secretary-general, perhaps the Japanese figure most closely associated with the League; Fujisawa Chikao, a young Esperantist who worked with Nitobe in the League's Secretariat (the League's civil service); and Yanagita Kunio, an ethnographer and folklorist, who spent two years on the League's Permanent Mandates Commission.

Their activities reveal how the linguistic internationalism of domestic Japanese Esperanto was manifested within a diplomatic setting. While at home the police were turning a suspicious eye to Esperanto in the wake of Vasilii Eroshenko's deportation, actors within the diplomatic service overseas were considering the language in a much more positive light. The events in and around the League reveal that international language problems were ongoing, even within the elite of Japanese society and the highest circles of diplomacy; that Japan was not a passive recipient of developments within wider international Esperanto, but a participant in its ongoing evolution; and that the links formed through Esperanto could have concrete diplomatic outcomes. However, the events also reveal that different conceptions of internationalism could clash. For while the presence of Esperanto at the League of Nations was striking proof of its sudden rise, in the end Esperanto did not find the sort of support in the League that many thought or hoped that it might.

The idea of linguistic equality, perhaps unsurprisingly, appealed more to smaller nations, marginal linguistic identities, and unconventional actors in the sphere of international relations than to nations for whom French or English were national languages or career members of the diplomatic corps, who were steeped in the use of French. Thus, Japan's cautious embrace of Esperanto at the League casts the nation in a different light: rather than a conservative member of the great powers, unwilling to stray too far out of line, it reveals a Japan willing to side with smaller, less powerful allies, and to at least consider potentially radical proposals.

Before exploring the experiences of the three major Japanese participants, it is useful to lay out the main course of the League of Nation's language debates over its first three years. Language in general and Esperanto in particular were raised as topics in the first sessions of the League.[5] In one of the early sessions, several nations raised the possibility of Spanish being adopted as an official language of the League, reflecting the bloc of countries for whom this was the national language. They ultimately withdrew their motion, a decision involving "a spirit of self-sacrifice and devotion to the common welfare."[6] This formalized the basic principle that English and French were to be to main functional languages within the League.

The subject of Esperanto was raised at the same time as Spanish, but by contrast, the proposal put to the first Assembly made no immediate claims to official usage. Instead, the motion, proposed by a broad range of nations including Persia, South Africa, Belgium, and Brazil, sought to recognize the existence of the international language problem and give credit to the efforts of some member nations in the field of education:

> The League of Nations, well aware of the language difficulties that prevent a direct intercourse between the peoples and of the urgent need of finding some practical means to remove this obstacle and help the good understanding of nations, follows with interest the experiments of official teaching of the international language Esperanto in the public schools of some members of the League, hopes to see that teaching made more general in the whole world so that the children of all countries may know at least two languages, their mother tongue and an easy means of international communication, asks the Secretary General to prepare, for the next Assembly, a report on the results reached in this respect.[7]

Despite being accompanied by a broadly favorable report from one of the Assembly subcommittees,[8] when the motion reached the full chamber it was deferred without significant debate at the instigation of the French delegate.[9]

The second Assembly, in 1921, saw the Esperanto motion resubmitted, substantially unchanged from the previous year.[10] Edmond Privat, the head of the Universala Esperanto-Asocio (UEA) and later the Persian delegate to the League, had led efforts in the intervening twelve months to promote Esperanto among the diplomatic community in Geneva. Chief among these was an invitation extended to the secretary-general to send a representative to the UEA congress, held in Prague in the summer of 1921. Nitobe Inazō, as under-secretary-general the second highest ranking member of the League's permanent staff, attended along with Fujisawa Chikao, a fellow Japanese and the only active Esperantist working for the Secretariat. Nitobe submitted a report on his return, the bulk of which was later distributed to the member delegations.[11]

Faced with the second Esperanto motion in 1921, the committee considering the agenda for the full Assembly recommended that serious consideration of Esperanto be postponed, but that a survey be conducted of Esperanto education in member countries, as suggested by Nitobe in his report. This was agreed to by the Assembly, so the Secretariat prepared a report on Esperanto teaching, which was then submitted to the third Assembly, in the autumn of 1922.

However, in 1922 Esperanto met with more serious opposition. The French delegation was more hostile than ever, while other nations came out in support of English, or merely against Esperanto.[12] Eventually the question of Esperanto was referred to the Committee for Intellectual Cooperation (Committee VI) for further consideration. French influence on this committee was great, so the referral essentially represented a victory for those hostile to the language. The end result was that in 1923 the committee rejected Esperanto in favor of finding a natural language best suited for international communication.[13] There, the major consideration Esperanto at the League of Nations came to a close, after four years in which it was passed between different organs of the League, of which only in the final committee was Esperanto debated in any detail, and then with a negative outcome. There was one final twist in 1924, with the passing of a proposal by the Persian delegation that Esperanto be accepted as a "clear" language for use in telegrams, reducing the cost of its use.[14]

It has been suggested of Esperanto's experience with the League of Nations that "her apologists refer to [it] as a 'success' and her opponents call [it] a 'failure.'"[15] The end result was little in the way of official acceptance by the League as a whole but generally positive reception in unofficial capacities—for example, Nitobe's report. However dissatisfying the outcome, that Esperanto was considered at all at the League was itself a mark of the degree to which it merited recognition as a popular movement. To characterize it as a failure, then, is in part fair but misses the significance of the events as a symbol of Esperanto's wider success. Indeed, perhaps it was the Esperanto activity among the peoples of different nations around the League of Nations that was the most noteworthy endorsement of Esperanto's success, rather than the events within the League's chambers and committees themselves.

Bringing Japanese Esperanto to the League of Nations

As one of the diplomatic great powers and a permanent member of the Council of the League of Nations, Japan was the most significant non-European member.

What is more, as a non-European nation and a relative newcomer to conventional Western diplomatic circles, Japan felt the presence of the diplomatic language problem more closely than did perhaps other nations of a similar status. Thus, it is perhaps of no great surprise that Japan was closely involved with the debates over language at the League, but also that Japan occupied a position that was both that of an insider and that of a more marginal player.

Japan's permanent seat on the Council of the League of Nations marked it out as a member of the elite circle of international politics—only France, the United Kingdom, and Italy shared the honor (the United States of America, Germany, and the Soviet Union all being absent). It was the culmination of the rise to great power status that had begun with victory in the Russo-Japanese War. From a position of endangered sovereignty in the mid nineteenth century, Japan had not only secured its independence and emerged into contact with the wider world, but it had done so with unprecedented success.

However, Japan's rise in the world was not absolute. During the First World War, Japan's opportunistic twenty-one demands on China led to a backlash from the United States and Great Britain, revealing that Japan could not act without regard for the European and American powers, even in Asia. Moreover, there was a perception that not all great powers were equal. Japan's efforts to achieve a racial equality clause in the Versailles treaty negotiations proved unsuccessful.[16] This along with laws perceived as anti-Japanese in California and elsewhere in the United States of America were received poorly by the Japanese public and media. For all that Japan might be called a great power, there was a sense that Euro-American racism still stood as a barrier between Japan and real equality on the international stage.

The creation of the League of Nations was regarded, even by leading liberal intellectuals, as at least partially hypocritical—as a tool for the maintenance of Franco-Anglo-American hegemony, rather than the search for true internationalism.[17] Within the Foreign Ministry, there was a struggle between two traits when the idea of the League first began to circulate. Institutional conservatism resisted the idea of a new alternative to conventional forms of bilateral diplomacy. However, contrasting this was a long-running desire within the ministry to remain in step with "prevailing currents of world affairs" (*taisei junnō*)—that is, to avoid conflict with any perceived emerging international consensus.[18]

Thus, when it became clear that the League was to be a reality, the Japanese state committed wholeheartedly to it. The government established an office under the auspices of the Parisian embassy and sent Baron Megata Tanetarō from the House of Peers to attend the first session as the honorary head of the delegation. As will be seen, this pattern of initial conservativism followed by a move into line with the perceived trend of international affairs has a parallel in

Japanese diplomatic policy toward Esperanto. In the years that followed, Japan would prove to be a diligent, albeit perhaps not particularly inspiring, member. Within the Foreign Ministry, a term at the League often led to further high-profile positions and career success, suggesting that the League was considered an important part of the diplomatic firmament, and one to which talented members of the diplomatic corps should be sent.[19]

The general public and government attitude toward the League of Nations, then, was one of cautious optimism: not uncritical, but committed to trying to make it work, nonetheless. However, the Japanese Esperanto community was more positive on the whole. Just like the global Esperanto organization, the UEA, the JEI in Japan saw the League of Nations as an opportunity to advance the cause of Esperanto. Prior to the first sessions of the League, Osaka Kenji, the newly appointed president of the JEI, and Ga Morizō, another influential Esperantist, went on a round of meetings to promote the international cause of Esperanto among those with influence on the forthcoming delegation to the League. They met with several leading members of the Japan Association for the League of Nations, such as Shibusawa Eiichi, Prince Tokugawa Iesato, and Tagawa Daikichirō, as well as Baron Megata, first head of the Japanese delegation.

The Japan Association for the League of Nations was a quasi-governmental organization, set up and funded by the Foreign Ministry in advance of the official launch of the League, modeled upon similar organizations in the United Kingdom and the United States. Its goals were initially to raise consciousness of the role and aims of the League; later, it played an important role in disseminating information around Japan regarding the League's activities—for example, sponsoring domestic lecture tours by Nitobe Inazō.[20] It attracted widespread support from politicians, statesmen, and businessmen.

Although official Japanese interest in international Esperanto activity can be traced back to the 1907 World Esperanto Congress, held in Dresden, when Shinmura Izuru, a linguist then studying in Germany, attended as an observer on behalf of the state (making Japan one of the earliest nation-states to engage with the international Esperanto organizations),[21] after that there had been little or no official Esperanto activity by the government.[22] Nevertheless, the outlook for the JEI representatives seemed very positive—their efforts were well received, and several of the League of Nations Association members had prior knowledge of and positive opinions regarding Esperanto: Prince Tokugawa knew of Esperanto well, Soeda Juichi had studied it himself, and Megata "listened attentively . . . and promised that he would consider the problem of international language at the League."[23]

In addition to these efforts at lobbying the Japanese League of Nations delegation, there was another, more direct voice of Japanese Esperanto at the League:

Fujisawa Chikao. Fujisawa was the son of Fujisawa Rikitarō, one of the first to study Western mathematics in Meiji Japan. He was something of a linguistic prodigy—learning French, German, English, Russian, Italian, and Dutch while still a student, going on to join the Ministry of Agriculture and Commerce after graduating from the Imperial University's Law Faculty, where he often acted as an interpreter.[24]

The exact details of Fujisawa's introduction to Esperanto are somewhat unclear, but he was one of a younger generation who began to take on leadership of the Japanese Esperanto movement at the close of the First World War, closely involved with Osaka Kenji in the creation of JEI in 1919.[25] Around the same time he visited Vladivostok, writing a series of articles on his experiences in *La Revuo Orienta*.[26] He left the Ministry of Agriculture and Commerce in 1919, but later traveled to Europe as a member of a government delegation to a conference in Genoa. Although the delegation then continued on to the United States, Fujisawa remained behind, traveling around Europe and eventually obtaining employment within the information section of the League of Nations Secretariat.[27]

Fujisawa brought with him an optimistic and idealistic attitude toward both the League and Esperanto—the former would "open up a new epoch . . . in a world still full of injustice," and he took pride in the opportunity to play a central role in that task and to advocate Esperanto and Esperantism while there.[28] This rather more wholehearted embrace of the ideals of the League of Nations than the sort of cautious, qualified optimism common among even liberal Japanese intellectuals was perhaps typical of those who were drawn to Esperanto, especially those for whom Homaranismo was a compelling message, but it also reflects Fujisawa's own enthusiastic personality.

Fujisawa brought a unique personal opinion to his advocacy of Esperanto, derived from his experiences of working for the state. Fujisawa's direct experience of Japanese efforts to use foreign languages in government business tempered his enthusiasm about the potential impact that Japan could play at the League of Nations, while flagging the potential advantages to Japan of the use of Esperanto: "I fear that the delegation recently sent from Japan will repeat the same failure [as that of the Genoa conference]—due to inability at French and English. Thus the adoption of Esperanto as the sole language of international communication would be a very opportune proposal for the interests of Japan."[29]

Despite, or perhaps because of, his own linguistic prowess, Fujisawa's opinion of the overall abilities in foreign languages of even those Japanese within the diplomatic service was dismal, and he thought that this was a real and concrete barrier to wider international success. But Esperanto might present a possible solution. Not only was Esperanto a great project that sought equality for all mankind, but it was a tool of real and practical advantage to a nation such as Japan, revealing a coincidence of internationalist ideals with (Japanese) national interest.

Fujisawa sent letters back to his colleagues at the JEI, revealing details of the Esperanto-related activity at the League. Given the positive impressions given by the senior members of the Association for the League of Nations, it seemed likely that, should the language receive consideration by the League, the Japanese delegation at least would be in support of the language. And Fujisawa was not the only JEI member at the League—another, Usami Uzuhiko, was a junior member of the Japanese delegation. So expectations were running high.

However, when news began to be received in Japan of Esperanto's failure to gain recognition at the first Assembly of the League, what they learned was as puzzling as it was disappointing. Not only was the 1920 motion rebuffed by the League, but the Japanese delegation was reported to have played a key role in the rejection. It took some time for the full picture to become clear, but it turned out that the Japanese delegation had supported the French in their desire to reject the Esperanto motion.[30] Unsurprisingly, the response from the Japanese Esperantists was angry and confused. In a set of open questions posed to the Japanese delegation, published in *La Revuo Orienta*, veteran Esperantist Takahashi Kunitarō pointedly highlighted the issue of diplomacy and language: "Which national language did you use when you expressed your opinions against Esperanto . . . Whose is the blame, that Japan cannot free its diplomacy from some or other foreign language?"[31]

Matters were further confused when the offices of the JEI began to receive telegrams from Esperantists around the world, congratulating them on their success in recruiting the Japanese delegation to the League in support of the language. The Japanese delegation in Paris, too, was the recipient of these congratulations. Eventually this was revealed to have been a misunderstanding whereby an article written by Fujisawa Chikao for the *Yomiuri Shinbun* titled "Urgent Need for the Introduction of Esperanto" was translated and included within a League-published collection of international articles related to League activities, incorrectly indicated as coming from within the Japanese delegation.[32]

Rather than fall into despondency when faced with this setback, Fujisawa joined the major Esperantist in Geneva, Edmond Privat, in reinvigorating their efforts at promoting Esperanto to League participants, seeking to set the stage for a resubmission of an Esperanto motion at the second Assembly, to be held in the autumn of 1921. Fujisawa organized study groups and an internal magazine for the Secretariat, as well as lobbying delegations to support the Esperanto motions and writing articles on the League's Esperanto activities for newspapers at home.[33] In addition, he joined Nitobe Inazō as an official League representative at the 1921 UEA Esperanto congress in Prague.

Nitobe Inazō is perhaps the single Japanese statesman most associated with the League of Nations. His time at the League was spent as under-secretary-general of the Secretariat—that is, as the assistant head of the League's administrative staff, an employee of the League itself, rather than as a member of the Japanese delegation. This placed him in a somewhat ambiguous position, one perhaps reflective of both Nitobe's entire career and the very nature of the League's attempt to reform international relations. On the one hand, Nitobe was nominated by the Japanese state, his position was both a symbol of Japanese status and a useful position for the furthering of Japanese aims, and Nitobe himself had a keen sense of Japanese national interest and achievement. On the other, in the words of the Balfour report of 1920: "The members of the Secretariat, once appointed, are no longer in the service of their own country, but become for the time being exclusively officials of the League. Their duties are not national but international."[34]

Nitobe encountered Esperanto, then, not in a private capacity or as a representative of the Japanese state, but on behalf of the League of Nations itself. His general response, despite no evidence that he studied the language himself, was quite positive: not only was his official report generally supportive, but others, such as Fujisawa Chikao, Yanagita Kunio, and Nagata Hidejirō, mayor of Tokyo during the 1920s, all recalled him as supporting the language in their private interactions.[35]

Nitobe and Fujisawa attended the 1921 congress as a result of an invitation from the UEA. Nitobe was very keen to avoid making a firm statement in favor of Esperanto and indeed also to prevent his mere presence being seen as somehow a statement of official support. He stressed that he was at the congress "*not* because it was Esperantist, but because it was international,"[36] and suggested that any effort on behalf of the League of Nations to find and adopt a common international language would be slow work.[37] Nevertheless, he noted that the Esperanto community looked to the League of Nations as a body that shared many of their goals. He described them as "victims of derision and indifference from principalities and powers . . . in search of an authority to endorse their cause," who, "feeling a common bond . . . look to the League as their most probable patron and protagonist."[38] He was not wrong.

Returning from the congress, Nitobe wrote a report on his experience. He expressed great regret that somehow the press had reported him suggesting that the League would be adopting Esperanto shortly.[39] Such an enthusiastic statement sounds much more like Fujisawa Chikao, the idealistic young Secretariat employee and Esperantist, than the more circumspect diplomat Nitobe. It seems likely, then, that this misunderstanding arose from another case of misattribution involving Fujisawa Chikao—the ebullience of the junior Secretariat employee attributed to the senior.

While he was unwilling to make an outright endorsement of Esperanto, what Nitobe did recognize and admit was the presence of a real and pressing international language problem. This was not insignificant. Indeed, his analysis of the problem was in many respects fairly radical. It has been suggested that Nitobe used his report to further the Japanese government's interest in the issue of racial inequality.[40] To what extent this is true, and to what extent his Asian origins gave him a perspective in which the racial elements of the language problem were more readily apparent than they might be to a European, I think that the bulk of his report carries a fairly clear sense of genuine internationalist spirit, rather than an instrumentalist attempt to use the issue for national advantage (notwithstanding the coincidence of the two identified by Fujisawa Chikao).

Within Nitobe Inazō's life, there is much that can be seen as examples of what might be termed a benevolent paternalism—an elitism that "included a sense of responsibility for those in less fortunate circumstances."[41] Thus we see Nitobe the progressive colonial administrator, improving agricultural techniques of the native subjects; Nitobe the moralizing headmaster, leading his students; or Nitobe the League under-secretary-general, giving a consideration to those nations outside of the great powers. The idea of less-civilized nations helped along the path of development by more advanced ones has a long (and problematic) presence within the history of imperialism, but in considering solutions to the international language problem, Nitobe was not merely arguing for the support of minor nations by the great powers; he was arguing that there was a principle of equality by which the major (linguistic) nations owed an obligation to those nations on the periphery.

Nitobe's analysis was to seek a solution to a practical problem that nevertheless gave a consideration to this question of fairness and justice. Not only in the fields of commerce, science, and labor was there a need for a language of international communication, he argued; the field of diplomacy also was faced with problems of language. The new era of multilateral relations pressed upon the League of Nations an unprecedented requirement for translation into and out of a rapidly growing number of different languages.

Nitobe argued that the answer to these problems must include an element of "justice."[42] While acknowledging that English and French had their own respective advantages, not least of all being the languages of the Covenant of the League, he argued that they should not be considered as acceptable answers to the problem—he claimed that Norwegian was the only national language to have been proposed convincingly, based on its simplicity and uncontentious position. He suggested, however, that "a neutral language claiming no nationality" represented the best option.[43] While he strenuously sought to avoid presuming the wider League's support for Esperanto, this analysis certainly accepted quite positively Esperanto's broad analysis of the diplomatic and international language problems.

While Nitobe's support for the idea of at least opening the question of the appropriate language of international diplomacy was at odds with the stance taken by the Japanese delegation to the League in the first Assembly, 1921 saw a complete about-face in the official Japanese position. After playing an active role in the rejection of the first year's motion, the Japanese were among the list of nations proposing the motion to the second Assembly. Fujisawa Chikao was in no doubt as to the cause of the reversal: the personnel involved. Japan was represented in the League chambers by various ambassadors to European nations, chief among them Ishii Kikujirō, ambassador to France, and thus the head of the embassy in Paris, where the delegation's offices were located. However, it was Adachi Mineichirō, ambassador to Great Britain, who was the Japanese signatory on the Esperanto motion of 1921.

Fujisawa described Adachi as "that strange thing in the Japanese diplomatic world: a competent French speaker," who as a result fully understood the difficulties involved in Japanese efforts to learn European languages. By contrast, the ongoing rejection of Esperanto by Ishii Kikujirō and Hayashi Gonsuke (the third major ambassador to represent Japan at the League) was made all the more inexplicable given their inability to master French, English, or German.[44]

From 1921 onward, the general stance from Japanese diplomatic officials toward Esperanto remained more positive. The Japanese Association for the League of Nations expressed the view that "*Esperantismo* wholly accords with the purpose of the League of Nations,"[45] Japan was an advocate of Esperanto in its further contacts with the League,[46] and the Foreign Ministry was involved in extensive back-and-forth with the Ministry of Education regarding the League's survey of Esperanto teaching, while the Ministry of Agriculture and Commerce explored various efforts toward developing the use of Esperanto in trade.[47] Elsewhere, the Japanese representative to the International Labor Organization was a cosponsor of a motion to have the ILO increase its internal and external use of Esperanto.[48]

If Adachi Mineichirō was the prime mover in the Japanese switch on the Esperanto question at the League, nevertheless it seems unlikely that he had a free hand to determine official policy on the issue, so there remains the question of how he was able to persuade the other major figures in the delegation and Foreign Ministry hierarchy to accept the change in policy. The events during the period 1920–1921 may have helped sway others with a say in the issue: Nitobe's report, Fujisawa's own work in promoting Esperanto around the League (for example, a petition by a number of Japanese individuals in and around the League in favor of Esperanto, which was eventually presented by Yanagita Kunio to the Diet),[49] and perhaps even the confused telegrams received by the delegation in the wake of the first assembly. One way of explaining the shift then would be in terms of the conservatism / "prevailing currents" dualism within Meiji and Taishō-era Japanese diplomatic institutions. The initial position resisted a potential threat of change within conventional diplomatic norms and supported the position of France, a fellow great power, but in the face of what seemed like a wave of international enthusiasm for Esperanto, Japan's position changed to one that embraced the new ideas of linguistic equality.

That said, in making the shift, the Japanese were not following the lead of fellow great powers but rather siding with another group of countries entirely. As a vision of equality between all nations, Esperanto as articulated at the League of Nations appealed more to smaller, more marginal linguistic groups than to the diplomatic powerhouses. In his report to the secretary-general, Nitobe identified a postwar trend toward the growing proliferation of smaller, niche national languages—such as Gaelic, Czech, and Flemish—and remarked that it was among these "smaller nationalities, eager to develop their own national tongue," that a core base of Esperanto support was found.[50]

Seen this way, when Japan moved to embrace Esperanto, it was adopting a position not of a great power, but of a diplomatic outsider. The proposers of the motion at the first Assembly in 1920 were a mix of smaller European, South American, and Asian nations: Brazil, Belgium, China, Chile, Colombia, Czechoslovakia, India, Haiti, Italy, Persia, and South Africa. (South Africa's presence on the list was the result of the British citizen Lord Robert Cecil, the head of their delegation, a "staunch liberal internationalist," and something of a thorn in the side of the British government.)[51] The following year, Japan was joined by Romania, Finland, Albania, Venezuela, and Poland in adding their names to the list of proposing nations.

There were other nations with minority national languages that opposed Esperanto—for example, Norway and Sweden—but, as suggested, chief in opposition to the group was France.[52] While the position of French as the language of diplomacy had been dealt a blow at the Versailles peace conference, the dual use of English and French in the text of the Versailles Treaty and the Covenant to the League of Nations, as well as their use as the de facto operating languages of the League, at least meant French retained a shared status as a diplomatic language. Likewise, the British had no great incentive to embrace an alternative international language, seeing it as holding the potential for undermining national interests.[53]

Yanagita Kunio and Esperanto

For all that the question of Esperanto at the League was a meeting of national interest with internationalist spirit, and of various different institutional bodies with their own motivations and goals, it was also an encounter that involved individuals who brought their own personal perspectives and experiences to bear on it. While Nitobe Inazō and Fujisawa Chikao were both noted for their ability with foreign languages, the final Japanese participant at the League considered here, Yanagita Kunio, was not. Yanagita's struggles at the League will be familiar to many of us with rather less facility at language learning; what is more, they were fundamental to his interest in Esperanto. He was not a direct actor in the League's Esperanto debates to any significant degree, but his experiences reveal the practical reality of the diplomatic language problem. For Yanagita, Esperanto represented a possible solution to communication problems he experienced in the most direct way; for him, it was a means of ensuring a greater involvement in the new international society for individuals and nations who would otherwise find full participation impossible.

Yanagita Kunio is famous as the father of a Japanese school of folklore studies that sought to record and preserve the different patterns of rural life in Japan's regions. While he is usually seen in a domestic frame, he spent two years at the League. He came to the League at the suggestion of Nitobe Inazō. The two had met through their shared interest in rural affairs in 1910, forming a study group called the Kyōdo-kai (usually translated as the Native Place Association). This coincided with the publication of the first edition of his seminal work, *Tōno Monogatari*, although he continued his career within the Japanese bureaucracy until 1920, when he left to join the *Asahi Shinbun*.[54]

Yanagita came to the League to serve on the Permanent Mandates Commission (PMC). The PMC was set up to monitor the workings of the League's new mandate system: formed from colonies seized from the losing powers of the First World War, the mandates were a compromise between new ideals of self-determination and the colonial ambitions of the winning powers. Major member nations took over the administration of the new mandates, but they did so in the name of the League. The mandates themselves were classified into three categories—A, B, and C—according to the degree of development of the resident population and potential for becoming independent nations. Japan received control of the southern Pacific mandate—a set of islands seized from German control and classified in band C, the lowest level of development.

While it was suggested that the mandates represented an innovation in colonial rule whereby for the first time territories were administrated from abroad in the principal interests of their own people, rather than in the interests of the colonizers, the formation and administration of the mandates retained similarities of an older imperial colonialism (which, of course, had their own discourse of development, in the form of the "white man's burden").[55]

The PMC on which Yanagita sat was established to monitor the administration of the mandates by the member nations such as Great Britain and Japan. Yanagita represented a perfect choice for Japan. The members of the PMC nominally represented the interests of the mandates' peoples, not of the administrating nations, so government employees were expressly excluded from serving as members on the commission. From the perspective of the Japanese government, Yanagita, only recently removed from the bureaucracy, was one of their own, who, while known for being outspoken, still understood the systems of priorities and compromises involved in running the Japanese state.

The PMC was a small, intimate body; Yanagita immediately found that his language skills were not sufficient to allow him to play a full role. Despite an elite education and being a voracious reader of European authors throughout his life, Geneva proved to Yanagita that there was a great deal of difference between reading a foreign language and using it in a live setting. The inability to contribute significantly to the sessions of the PMC was intensely frustrating to him; although his contributions increased over time, the result of significant efforts to improve his language skills, he ultimately resigned from the post as a direct result of the issue.[56]

However, right from his arrival in Europe, Yanagita Kunio saw Esperanto as a potential solution to his, and others', language problems. In a postcard written shortly after his arrival in Geneva, Yanagita mentioned the language to his collaborator, Sasaki Kizen, suggesting that Sasaki, too, should take it up. He expanded in a later letter:

> [For Esperanto], it is not simply the grammar, but as regards the language, simplicity, clarity, even a good sound, are particularly important; perhaps more than important, they are fundamental. The text which I admire most is a biography of Zamenhof, written by a young scholar here in Geneva called Privat. If it is hard to obtain in Japan, perhaps I should send you a copy now. I even think that through Esperanto, the Japanese language might also improve its style.[57]

Yanagita recommended Esperanto to Sasaki, advising him to make a contact with the mutual acquaintance, Akita Ujaku. (Sasaki's own experiences of Esperanto are explored in chapter 4.) That Yanagita already knew Akita was an Esperantist reveals that he was acquainted with the language already, but he had not previously been involved with it: Yanagita's direct experience of Europe convinced him almost immediately of the need for and value of an international language. Yanagita engaged with the Esperanto community enthusiastically:

> At just that time there was a movement for the recognition of Esperanto under-way in the League, and the reason for the greater than usual interest I had in it was straightforward. If adopted, I too could express what I thought. Further, it valued the smaller nations: because those [League] representatives who were not diplomats were all suffering, even if it were not to reach the level of [usage of] English, or French, I thought it might be more freely used [in international circles].[58]

In addition to offering smaller, non-European nations the chance to participate more fully in diplomatic circles, Yanagita Kunio also saw Esperanto as a way of allowing the voices to be heard of those from beyond the diplomatic profession. Although as graduates of Tokyo Imperial University, and one-time bureaucrats, neither Fujisawa nor Yanagita (nor Nitobe) can really be considered as outsiders, it is noteworthy that neither were they career members of the Foreign Ministry. An unconventional idea, Esperanto appealed more to these unconventional diplomats.

This is supported by the views of some of the career diplomats. Where Fujisawa and Yanagita looked to a neutral language for the solution, others were less radical. Ishii Kikujirō, ambassador to France, as described above, was one of the chief figures that Fujisawa identified as driving the Japanese delegation to reject Esperanto in the first Assembly. He was, however, no less aware of the problem of language in Japan's diplomacy than Esperanto's supporters. In his memoirs, he cited the language barrier as one of the causes in Japanese diplomatic failure (the other being a lack of experience).[59] Yanagita recorded that when he went to Ishii to resign his position on the PMC, citing his struggles with language and communication, Ishii replied that everyone suffered from the problem.[60] However, Ishii identified the only way forward as improvements to the Japanese foreign language education system—a system described by Nitobe Inazō as prioritizing the written word to the almost total exclusion of the spoken.[61]

It has been suggested that Yanagita's experience in Geneva helped to form an image of Japan as an isolated "island nation," and that he "longed for a space where he could communicate in his native tongue," writing entries in his diary such as "I did not see a single Japanese face the whole day,"[62] but in his letters he also wrote of his adventures in Esperanto—of the vast numbers of nations represented at a meeting to celebrate Zamenhof's birthday, of his teacher, a Russian woman named Umansky, or of his trip to the Esperanto club in Venice—reflecting a more outgoing internationalist perspective.[63]

Like Fujisawa Chikao, Yanagita's overseas experiences shaped his perspective on Esperanto in ways that differed from the typical ones shared by many of the new Esperantists taking up the language in Japan at the same time as he was in Geneva. Although he shared the sort of ideas of fairness and equality expressed by Nitobe, which undoubtedly shared something with the idealistic views of the new generation of Japanese Esperantists, his expression of it was expressly built upon his experiences at the League; he spoke of the language in practical terms as a tool for the exchange of views and opinions and for the inclusion of a wider range of participants in discussion, and did not seem especially drawn to ideas such as the *interna ideo*.

Yanagita's Esperanto-related activities were extensive in Japan, as well as in Geneva. After his first session at the PMC, in the autumn of 1921, he returned to Japan briefly and there he met with many leading domestic Esperantists. Back in Europe for the next set of meetings, he was very active within Esperanto circles there, holding meetings at his own house and engaging a private tutor.[64] His letters to Sasaki include accounts of the larger meetings he went to in Geneva and Venice, and he was instrumental in the submission of a petition to the House of Peers from Japanese in Geneva, advocating serious consideration of Esperanto.[65] He went on to be an active member of the Japanese Esperanto community upon his return to Japan in 1923.

However, despite the rapid growth of his interest in Esperanto, Yanagita made no mention of it in the context of his work on the mandates and their inhabitants. Indeed, he even addressed the question of language in the mandates without bringing Esperanto into the frame. In his most extensive contribution to the PMC, a report titled "The Welfare and Development of the Natives in the Mandated Territories," submitted to the 1923 sessions of the commission, Yanagita explored which languages were most suitable within the context of the educational system of the mandates.[66] Yanagita compared two cases in colonial Africa: one where the French had imposed French upon the territory, and another where the German administration had sought to make use of a local language, Ewe. Although he regarded both as failures, Yanagita argued that the latter was the preferable choice because, while it potentially involved a difficult choice of one local language among many, this was less divisive than the split that resulted within a local population from the use of a European language—the creation of "two mutually incompatible classes of natives—the class which is in contact with civilized people and the class which is not."[67]

It is perhaps possible to make too much of an absence, but there is something intriguing in the coincidence of Yanagita's embrace of Esperanto as a tool of great potential for cross-cultural communication at the League with his failure to make even a passing reference to it in the context of his consideration of languages in the mandates. Perhaps Esperanto would be just another foreign language, the imposition of which would be as divisive as in the French case.

But equally I would suggest that it represents an example of the internal ambiguity in a League of Nations seeking to embrace Wilsonian ideas of self-determination for nations, yet still featuring colonies, mandates, and empires. Linguistic equality was one potential aspect of a new, idealistic international relations system that was centered upon a League of Nations in which all members could have their voice heard. However, a necessary condition of membership of this club was statehood—only those people who could form a nation-state capable of retaining their own sovereignty could participate; those who could not do so were not able to speak and thus had no need of Esperanto. Just as the principle of national self-determination seems to have been applied in Europe but not in other parts of the world, for all the popular appeal that Woodrow Wilson's speeches may have inspired,[68] so too is it possible that Yanagita's silence on Esperanto in the context of the mandates reveals an implicit assumption about the necessary conditions of development for joining the international community: the mandates were as yet not developed sufficiently for full statehood and membership of the League, and thus they as yet had no need of an international language.

The difficulties of internationalism within a setting more complex than that of an autonomous sovereign nation-state can also be seen in the ambiguous presence of Esperanto in Japan's colonies. Although Esperanto clubs formed in both Taiwan and Korea with mixed-nationality memberships, they had something of a troubled existence. The first clubs in Taiwan faced opposition from governing officials until the meteorologist and leading Esperantist Nakamura Kiyō intervened while on a lecture tour in 1915.[69] Even in 1922, *Verda Ombro* (Green shadow), the magazine of the Taiwanese Esperanto association, reported the opinion of a Japanese official in Taiwan, revealing the potential power of language as a political issue:

> Despite studying the same Esperanto, whereas for the Japanese the choice is undoubtedly simply as an international language of world exchange, a symbolic language of the inevitable rise of racial harmony, or perhaps a

> result of the love of the Japanese language; in the case of a Taiwanese the conditions are different. For them it is not the case of doing a world language as one of the peoples of the world; quite the opposite, it is fully imbued with the meaning of opposition to the Japanese language. Since language and thought have a relationship of connection, rejecting the Japanese language must be seen as rejecting Japan itself. The Japanese colonial policy must not tacitly allow such rebels.[70]

That is, Esperanto in a colonial setting was explicitly an act of resistance to colonial rule: reaching out to a wider community of mankind potentially represented a direct challenge to the authority of Japan's imperial presence.[71]

Esperanto Diplomacy: Gustav Ramstedt and the Åland Islands

For the Japanese delegation at the League, then, Esperanto represented a variation on the binary between great power conservatism on the one hand and the embrace of the "tide of world affairs" on the other. In the case of Esperanto, the division was between Japan as a great power and Japan as a linguistic minority or relative diplomatic neophyte. The first Assembly saw Japan joining its great power partner France in preventing even a modest motion in support of Esperanto from being raised, but the experiences of Nitobe, Fujisawa, and Yanagita and the support of Ambassador Adachi Mineichirō led to the more experimental stance of support for the language. While this stance, which allied Japan alongside some of the lesser powers at the League, might be an unusual way of seeing Japanese diplomacy, here I want to suggest that it was not without consequence. Esperanto diplomacy, and the connections that the Japanese made through it, offer one potential explanation for one episode at the League: the case of the Åland Islands.

The Åland Islands are a chain of islands in the Gulf of Bothnia in the Baltic Sea. In the wake of the Russian Revolution of 1917, the culturally Swedish population of the islands found themselves a part of the newly independent state of Finland. This led to a dispute over the right of the islanders to self-determination (i.e., to join Sweden) as well as the military strategic significance of the islands.[72]

The League considered the matter, issuing a resolution in 1921 that allowed Finland to retain control of the islands, subject to guarantees about the cultural autonomy of the people of the islands and their demilitarization.[73] What is significant here is that the Japanese were noted to have paid particular interest to the matter—both the delegation (which had relevant papers translated into

Japanese) and Nitobe Inazō himself, who oversaw the case (to the extent that it has been called "the Nitobe settlement").[74]

There are a few reasons why the Japanese should have been interested in a dispute over some small distant islands with few residents: an earnest commitment to their role on the Council in its first years of operation and a sense of solidarity with Finland and Sweden regarding their common neighbor the USSR, but also the input of the Finnish chargé d'affaires, Gustav John Ramstedt.

Ramstedt was appointed the first chargé d'affaires to Japan and East Asia for the newly independent Finland, arriving in 1920. His background was as a linguist specializing in the Altaic family: he was pressed into diplomatic service because of his experience in Asia, specifically through field trips to study the languages of Mongolia. These linguistic skills rapidly gave him a proficiency in Japanese that stood out from the diplomatic norm; he was also charismatic and outgoing. As a result, both Finland and Ramstedt became rapidly popular in Japan.[75] His connections reached the Japanese at the League: teaching Finnish to Toyama Kiichi, secretary (and nephew) of the delegation's head, Megata Tanetarō, and meeting Yanagita Kunio when the latter was back in Tokyo in 1922, after the Åland Islands case had been resolved.[76]

Ramstedt was also an Esperantist—something that came to light before he even arrived in Japan. He was visited by Fujisawa Chikao and others almost immediately upon making landfall,[77] and throughout his time in Japan he spoke to Esperanto groups nationwide, often on the subject of his home nation and its literature and culture.[78] Both Ramstedt and other Finnish observers were in no doubt that the combination of Nitobe, presiding on the council sessions as under-secretary-general, and the interest of the Japanese delegation—permanent members of the Council who came out in support of the Finnish position—played key roles in determining the outcome.[79]

The line connecting Esperanto at the League to Japan's intervention, such that it was, in the case of the Åland Islands is not a direct one. Nevertheless, Gustav Ramstedt's influence, and Esperanto's part in that, do help to explain in part why it was that Japan was drawn in to the affair to the degree that it was. And in doing so, it helps to show that the position of Japan as linguistic minority, as it was in the Esperanto debates at the League, had some concrete impact, rather than serving simply as a slightly unusual sideline in the League's early years.

For all that they found easy sympathies between Esperantism's wider ambitions and the goals of the League of Nations, the advocates of Esperanto at the League of Nations struggled to gain wider acceptance of the language's potential. Although the motions in favor of Esperanto proposed at the League of Nations were fairly modest in their explicit goals—articulation of the potential of Esperanto within the sphere of education, and recognition of the existence of an international language problem—nevertheless many of the participants on both sides of the debate clearly saw in them the potential to open a door to a wider issue—that of the potential of Esperanto to fulfill some role within mainstream international relations. Whether for questions of national prestige and advantage, a threat to their own position, innate conservatism, or skepticism regarding the more aspirational, utopian visions of Esperanto's potential, the majority of the diplomatic mainstream at the League seem to have remained reluctant to engage with the language.

The reasons given for this failure include the result, chiefly within France, of the resistance to the League's more lofty goals (as embodied within the language);[80] the failure of the Esperantists at the League to anticipate major power hostility;[81] and the result of a clash in the underlying conceptions of internationalism that were represented by Esperanto and the League.[82] All three of these have some power in explaining the events: while the ideas of justice that were used to motivate Esperanto at the League found a clear degree of harmony with the ideals of the League and many of the actors involved, nevertheless it was exactly the more powerful nations and the better-established diplomats who stood to lose the most with the adoption of a new, fairer language for diplomacy, and thus, with this intransigent force at the center of international relations, the adoption of Esperanto was ultimately improbable.

The Japanese participants in these debates, as well as Gustav Ramstedt in Tokyo, reveal that it was not only nations from outside the linguistic and diplomatic mainstream who most readily embraced Esperanto; it was also unorthodox diplomats. Adachi Mineichirō was the only Japanese career diplomat to come out explicitly in favor of the language; Fujisawa Chikao, Nitobe Inazō, and Yanagita Kunio all came to the League by unusual paths, and none of them were strictly there to represent the Japanese government. Likewise, Ramstedt's diplomatic career was the result of his linguistic specialty, and he appears to have remained an unusual, if effective, diplomat.

That said, the Esperanto debates at the League, and the Japanese participation in them, are revealed as more than just a symbolic representation of the language's wider unofficial growth: they reveal a Japan that still found linguistic barriers to its effective diplomacy (something that would be raised again in the 1930s when the country was seeking to defend its aggression in Manchuria) and a range of individuals open to the possibility of more radical experimentation. Moreover, the events reveal the Japanese Esperanto movement as more than just a distant offshoot of a European endeavor: the Japanese actors at the League were key participants in one of the most noteworthy moments in Esperanto history. Japanese Esperanto was a fundamental part of the wider global language movement.

If this series of events marks the highpoint of Esperanto's official recognition, it is worth recalling that the bulk of the language's movement remained popular and decentralized, both in Japan and worldwide. Diplomacy, as important as it is, is only one form of transnational communication and contact among many. The next chapter shifts perspective dramatically from center to periphery, and from elite actors to ordinary people, to look at Esperanto and the international language question as experienced in rural Tōhoku.

CHAPTER 4

Tōhoku Modern

In early August 1925, Akita Ujaku returned to his birthplace in Aomori Prefecture. He departed from Ueno station on the evening of August 5, eventually arriving in Hirosaki at three p.m. the following day. Discovering that it was hotter up north than it had been in Tokyo, he took a short break in the park before boarding another train to Kuroishi, a small town best known for its apple orchards. There, he was met by twenty to thirty schoolchildren—students of Esperanto—who had been assembled by two of Akita's friends in order to welcome him home. Akita discovered that they had developed a large and active group of Esperantists in the town—over the following days they held a congress, perhaps as many as one hundred people marching through the streets singing "La Espero," playing music, and holding a series of meetings and dinners in venues dotted around the town.[1]

Through the course of the 1920s, Akita spent several summers back in Aomori and Kuroishi. Akita's ties to and influence in Kuroishi clearly played some part in the development of Esperanto there, but he was not the only one: Narumi Yōkichi, a childhood friend, had picked up the language nearly a decade before Akita in the first wave of Japanese activity. What is more, the international language group that emerged in Kuroishi in the 1920s was only one part of the broader "Local Arts movement" that sought to advance the culture of the region and shake off a perception of northern Honshū as a laggard in Japan's modernization.

Tōhoku, the northern part of Japan's main island, Honshū, is known for its cold winters and seemingly impenetrable dialects. In the early twentieth century, a discourse developed surrounding the region that portrayed it as backward and falling behind other, more advanced parts of the country.[2] In addition, postwar scholarship has also seen Japan's rural areas as less progressive than the major cities: reservoirs of conservative values, which the armed forces found healthy recruiting grounds, and retaining patterns of landownership and wage labor that sustained regressive class relations.[3]

All the more surprising, then, to find a hotbed of Esperanto in this inhospitable, apparently backward part of the country. However, the purpose of this chapter is to chart a series of international, transnational, and cosmopolitan activities across Tōhoku, demonstrating that in fact international language and transnational engagement were by no means limited to the major cities. Indeed, I will demonstrate that the cosmopolitan movements of Aomori, Akita, and Iwate Prefectures brought their own local sensibilities and situation to their movement, blending local perspectives alongside national and global ones. If the previous chapter sought to show that international language problems reached the center of Japanese government and even impacted diplomatic relations, this chapter moves in the opposite direction, demonstrating that they also touched some of the smallest communities in Japan, ones that have not typically been seen to possess a transnational or global dimension. In short, the urge to act transnationally was felt nationwide.

In a 1992 essay, Mitchell Cohen defined "rooted cosmopolitanism"—a form of cosmopolitanism that found a union between a sense of common humanity and a recognition of cultural difference. This "cloth of many threads," he argued, might see the human community as a single tree, made up of "many roots and branches," and demonstrated "the legitimacy of plural loyalties, of standing in many circles but with common ground."[4]

Rather than see cosmopolitanism as implacably contrasted against nationalism, a binary of deracinated universal and parochial particular, Cohen's argument seeks to provide a means of viewing the two as more compatible, but the reference to "many circles" represents the possibility of further forms of identity, also overlaid on one another. Thus we might think of regional identities that lie between the global and the national—"macro nationalisms" such as Pan-Asianism, for example—and also crucially local communities on a level below that of the nation.

The movements in Tōhoku examined in this chapter did exactly this: they made imaginative and concrete contact with the world beyond Japan's borders, but at the same time they retained a deliberate sense of their own immediate place. In Cohen's language, they stood simultaneously in the circles of the world, the nation, and their own villages or towns. They did not see contradiction or tension in reaching out to the wider world while maintaining their own sense of identity and specificity. "Thinking and feeling beyond the nation" did not, in interwar Akita or Aomori or Iwate, require the abandonment of one's local allegiances.[5] Just as Vasilii Eroshenko, the Bahá'i, and the other participants in the Taishō transnationalism of chapter 2 represented a variety of different forms of internationalism or cosmopolitism (contrastable with the more conventional internationalism of chapter 3), so too do the actors considered in this chapter present ideas of their own.

However, before considering the rooted cosmopolitanism of Tōhoku's Esperantists, it is important to briefly consider the early twentieth-century ideas about the region and its position. In 1913, a group calling itself the Tōhoku Shinkō Kai (Society for the Advancement of Tōhoku) was established in order to challenge the growing perception of Tōhoku as a laggard by promoting and seeking to enhance the economic viability of Tōhoku's produce. The founders, notably, were a group of "Seiyūkai bureaucrats and Kantō-area industrialists"—that is to say, figures drawn largely from the national center.[6] Although Hara Kei, a native of Morioka, was involved, his perspective seemed to owe more to his position as a national politician (serving variously as home minister and later prime minister) than his northern roots. He had some harsh words for the region, arguing that its workers were lazy and its entrepreneurs merely in pursuit of easy profit. "In such a situation," he wrote, "it is hard to see the development of Tōhoku's society accelerating."[7]

Hoyt Long argues that a sense of specific place with its own identity must be articulated through broader frameworks—that is, in order to know where *here* is, we must have ways of seeing how it is different from *elsewhere*.[8] In the context of this early twentieth-century discourse of Tōhoku's lack of development, the first frame was clearly national—Tōhoku was seen to have fallen behind other parts of the country. While Satō notes that eventually Tōhoku residents did come to join the Tōhoku Shinkō Kai, the very fact that this is a noteworthy finding reflects a strong sense of the whole endeavor as a part of a discourse of peripheral backwardness projected upon the region from the center.[9] By contrast, this chapter demonstrates not only that Tōhoku residents themselves were invested in the advancement of their own locales, but also that in attempting to achieve this they sought to articulate themselves in more ways than just as a subpart of the nation. Esperanto and transnational engagement offered the people of Tōhoku alternative ways of imagining themselves and strategies to combat or bypass a national discourse that positioned them as a backward periphery.

In order to demonstrate that Esperanto's appeal reached beyond the major cities of Japan to small rural communities, and that in doing so it manifested in different ways according to specific, local context, this chapter explores three cases from the three northernmost prefectures of Tōhoku. First I examine the emergence in Akita prefecture of the *Tane Maku Hito* magazine in the early 1920s. Next I return to the local Esperantists of Aomori and Kuroishi in particular. And finally I look at the relationship between Sasaki Kizen and Miyazawa Kenji, two of Iwate's sons, in the early 1930s. Each case demonstrates that members of the rural backwaters of Japan might be as eager participants in Japan's growing encounter with the wider world as residents of metropolitan cities. In each case, Esperanto played a role in facilitating a vision of how these communities might relate to the wider world, revealing again the importance both of language in transnational activity and the strength of Esperantism as a vision of how the world might be. Finally, crucially, each movement or activity represented its own articulation of both cosmopolitan vision and local identity, demonstrating their own forms of rooted cosmopolitanism.

Esperanto in Tōhoku

The first Japanese Esperantists came from across the country, but the clubs that formed as they came together tended unsurprisingly to be in the major cities—Tokyo, Osaka, Kyoto—and to spread out from there as the movement grew. It was only with the second great wave of Japanese Esperanto in the wake of the First World War that the organized movement really became nationwide. Tōhoku reflects this trend: while continuously active clubs seem to have emerged most consistently in Tōhoku during the 1920s, there were nevertheless individual Esperantists practicing from the Russo-Japanese War onward.

Aomori prefecture demonstrates this well. One of the early Esperanto leaders, Takahashi Kunitarō, an engineer, was an Aomori native. However, he encountered the language first while working in Manchuria, and while he was active in the national movement, he seems to have retained little connection to his birthplace.[10] By contrast, another of the early adopters, Narumi Yōkichi, retained much stronger links to the region but worked more on an individual basis rather than within an institutional framework. Narumi was, by chance, a school friend of Akita Ujaku's, but he took up Esperanto almost a decade before the latter's encounter with Vasilii Eroshenko: in 1906, the year before he graduated from teaching college. Narumi worked as a teacher in Aomori and Hokkaido, all the while seeking to promote Esperanto, painting the windows of his classroom green at one school and, in his spare time, traveling around the region seeking new learners. A poet, he wrote of his early years as an Esperantist: "For mankind and for the world, I preached Esperanto, in the towns of the peninsula," and "Failing to notice I was missing meals, crying as I advocated Esperanto: that was me."[11]

As suggested, while individuals such as Narumi represented the first presence of Esperanto in Tōhoku, the early 1920s saw the growth of a fuller, continuous presence. The first club in northern Honshū was formed in the regional center, Sendai, in 1920–1921 when an experienced organizer, Mutō Oto, moved to work in the local electricity offices.[12] By 1923, Sendai could boast three clubs—one city based, one at the Imperial University, and one at the Second Higher School.[13] Other Esperanto clubs formed in Akita city and Funakawa in Akita Prefecture (1921–1922), and in Aomori city, Hirosaki, and Kuroishi in Aomori

Prefecture (1923–1924).[14] 1924 saw the national congress come to Sendai, marking the completion of organized Esperanto's arrival in Tōhoku.

This process was facilitated by the relative proximity of Tōhoku to Tokyo. Although it was considered a cultural periphery, it was not particularly hard to reach the region. Various Esperantists visited Tōhoku and Hokkaido to promote the language: in 1921, students from Tokyo universities; in 1922, Gustav Ramstedt the Finnish diplomat and Osaka Kenji, the JEI president; and then in 1923, another group of students and authors.[15]

The 1923 trip was well coordinated: five speakers funded by a pair of publishing houses stayed in lodges and hotels in towns up the east coast on the journey north and the west coast on the return trip. In May and June 1923, they undertook a series of public speeches and events to promote the language, typically speaking to schools during the day and local associations at night. On top of that they held impromptu sessions in public squares, hung banners out of their hotel windows, and gave short lessons to people sharing their train carriages. The five men were all young—only one over thirty—and strongly in favor of the aspirational forms of Esperantism.[16]

Esperanto, then, was an increasingly established presence in Tōhoku from the early 1920s. It is worth stressing that it stretched beyond the formal national organizations' reach. In Aomori in 1922 there were only eight members of the JEI and there were no officially documented JEI-affiliated clubs; across Tōhoku in total there were perhaps 150 members.[17] However, the 1923 tour spoke to audiences totaling nineteen thousand individuals (counting both Tōhoku and Hokkaido), and they met with a series of town mayors and dignitaries as they went.[18] Of course, not all of these listeners were present or future Esperantists in the making; indeed, many of the school attendees may not even have been willing participants. Nevertheless, while organized Esperanto in Tōhoku was still in its infancy in the early 1920s, the time and conditions were proving ripe for its spread.

As will be seen, the three case studies that follow represent transnational activities with Esperanto connections or dimensions; they are all only indirectly connected to the JEI and what we might call official Japanese Esperanto. As such, they can be seen to reflect well the general trend demonstrated here of a growing presence of the national movement, with a larger range of smaller local initiatives around it.

Akita: *Tane Maku Hito*

The magazine *Tane Maku Hito* is generally regarded as the origin of Japanese proletarian literature, the literary and artistic wing of Japanese Marxism in the

1920s and 1930s. The creation of Komaki Ōmi (1894–1978), a child born from a marriage between two wealthy merchant families from Akita, the magazine can be thought of in three distinct frames: as the Japanese manifestation of the global Clarté campaign, as the origins of the national proletarian literature movement, and as one of any number of local artistic magazines, in this case hailing from the northern port town of Tochizaki. By thinking of it as all three, we can see how its authors—Komaki, together with two old school friends—expressed a desire to participate in national and international debates and discourses, without sacrificing their local identity. In short, it represents an example of Cohen's rooted cosmopolitanism in action.

First, the global perspective. The magazine was ultimately the product of Komaki's experience in France during the years surrounding the First World War. Komaki had accompanied his father, a member of the national Diet, to an international conference in Belgium in 1910. When his father returned to Japan, Komaki remained, enrolling in the Lycée Henri-IV in Paris.[19] His father's political career and hence finances hit a rocky patch in the following years, so Komaki bounced from the lycée to a free school for laborers, before managing to enter the Sorbonne.[20] One way or another, he remained in France throughout the First World War, returning to Japan only at the end of 1919.[21]

The Great War, of course, was a pivotal moment in the thinking of many if not all of the European leftists who would go on to be influential in the interwar period: Komaki's intellectual development followed a similar trajectory. He not only read European writers of the time but also was drawn to the emergence of a humanist strain of Japanese thought led by Mushanokōji Saneatsu and the Shirakaba-ha group.[22]

By the end of the war, Komaki was not only intellectually influenced by progressive European thinkers; he had begun to be active in their literary networks and the negotiations that ultimately led to the formation of the Third International, the international organization later known as the Communist International, or Comintern.[23] Komaki himself was unable to attend the inaugural meeting of the International as he had been drafted (on account of his linguistic ability) into Japan's mission to the Versailles peace conference.[24] However, Komaki was able to meet Henri Barbusse later that year, recording the Frenchman "looking him straight in the eye and, gripping his hand, saying 'when you return home, don't forget Clarté.'"[25]

Clarté was the name of a new pan-European antiwar movement, named after one of Barbusse's novels. Together with figures such as Anatole France, H. G. Wells, and Stefan Zweig, Barbusse sought to be a "light amid the darkness," advocating social reform and international peace.[26] Komaki indeed did not forget Clarté: *Tane Maku Hito* magazine was his attempt to bring the movement to Japan.

Komaki saw himself very much as a conduit of ideas between Europe and Japan—not only seeking to bring what he had learned in France back home, but also working to show to Europeans that Japanese intellectuals had a contribution to make to their debates. Back in Japan at the start of 1920, he consulted with Mushanokōji Saneatsu (whose work he had translated into French during the war) about the prospects for developing a Japanese wing of the Clarté movement. Mushanokōji was lukewarm, however, so in the end Komaki looked not to the leading Tokyo intellectuals to help him, but to some old school friends.[27]

The three men who came together to found *Tane Maki Hito*, Komaki Ōmi, Kaneko Yōbun, and Imano Kenzō, all grew up in Tsuchizaki, a port town now subsumed into Akita city. While Kaneko had been drawn to Tokyo through his work as a journalist, Imano remained in Akita, bouncing between a number of jobs—tofu salesman, apprentice artisan, and kimono shop assistant, for example—before settling on work as a *benshi*, a live narrator of silent films.[28] As luck would have it, Kaneko was close to Mushanokōji Saneatsu, while Imano had exchanged letters with Arishima Takeo, another intellectual whom Komaki had approached regarding his ideas.[29]

While all three had some degree of connection to the literary establishment in Tokyo, they nevertheless were also tied to their hometown, and it was there that they sought to publish and print their new magazine.[30] Komaki got the wheels rolling on the project at new year in 1921 in a notably cold winter; the first three issues of their new magazine were published between February and April. They chose to call it *Tane Maku Hito* (The sower), a name derived from a Millet painting, which was also adapted to form the magazine's cover.[31] The magazine took a French subtitle, *Cahiers Idéalistes des Jeunes* (Idealist notebook of youths) together with a quote (also from Millet), "I am the peasant's peasant; my focus is [my] work."[32]

Small-scale, local literary magazines (*dōjinshi*) were a common phenomenon in the regions of Taishō-era Japan. *Tane Maku Hito* was, on one level at least, one of any number of literary coterie magazines published by a small circle of local young writers. In addition to the three founders, there were also essays contributed under pseudonyms by other friends and relations from Akita.[33] Although the impetus for the magazine's creation had come from Komaki's experience in Paris, and although its genesis had begun in conversations between Komaki and Kaneko in Tokyo, they not only recruited writers from their hometown, but they went back there to turn it into reality.[34]

According to Ōwada Shigeru, the decision was one part pragmatism (cheaper printing costs) and one part recognition of agricultural workers as an important part of Japan's labor class.[35] The magazine's title and cover image were another element of this—while the sower can be seen as a metaphorical representation of the authors as a vanguard of the socialist movement, it can also be seen as a direct representation of one tranche of society whose hardships they sought to highlight and relieve.

These first issues were slight—barely more than pamphlets in comparison with some of the general-interest journals, such as *Kaizō* and *Taiyō*. These first issues of the magazine were printed in Akita and sold through Akita bookstores, promoted through the local press and read in Akita.[36] Nevertheless, the magazine had an expansive perspective from the outset: Komaki wrote early essays on the Third International (issues 2 and 3), Kaneko wrote on Chekhov's "Peasants" (issues 1, 2, and 3), and Imano wrote on his feelings reading Romain Rolland (issue 3).

From the outset, then, the magazine melded a specifically local presence with a global awareness. This proved to be something of a problem. As its subject matter increasingly broached political subjects, it was required under the newspaper regulations to post an insurance bond of five hundred yen, a sum far in excess of what the small-scale organization could reasonably fund.[37] As a result, after the first three issues, the magazine went into hibernation.

It returned in the autumn, in a new form, this time published and printed in Tokyo (albeit not without ongoing issues of finance and government intervention).[38] From the outset, this second manifestation of *Tane Maku Hito* had distinct differences: it was larger (starting at roughly sixty pages but growing to a hundred or more versus the original twenty), it carried advertisements in the back, and its authors were a range of leading left-wing figures, including Akita Ujaku, Ishikawa Sanshirō, Yamakawa Kikue, Arishima Takeo, and others.[39] Still, Komaki was the central figure in ensuring that the magazine had a second life, recruiting a set of supporters and writers to ensure that his vision of a Japanese outpost of the Clarté movement continued, and that his two old schoolmates continued to be centrally involved. In its new format, it would continue to publish for two years, until the 1923 Kanto earthquake forced the magazine to take what was initially supposed to be a temporary break but turned out to be permanent.[40]

Another change that took place in the transition from Akita to Tokyo was the introduction of Esperanto to the magazine. In the three Akita issues of *Tane Maku Hito*, Esperanto isn't mentioned, French being the primary foreign language used (no doubt reflecting Komaki's background). However, when the magazine was relaunched in October, Esperanto made regular appearances. The French subtitle was replaced with an Esperanto one, *La Semanto*; there were regular international language items; and there was later an irregular Esperanto column. The magazine's (much censored) mission statement was printed in Esperanto translation in some months (and French in others). This introduction owed much to the new wave of contributors. The likes of Akita Ujaku (who had been in correspondence with Komaki on the subject of Barbusse and Clarté for some time), Sasaki Takamaru, and Ishikawa Sanshirō were all long-standing Esperantists.[41]

Esperanto and Clarté were only two of a number of ways in which the magazine continued to demonstrate its international perspective—for example, for the majority of its run, the most pressing issue was the Russian famine relief effort, seeking to provide support to the new Soviet Union. Nevertheless, and importantly for my argument here, in the shift to a national stage the magazine retained its subnational perspective alongside its international concerns. Among the regular items were the world column and the local column, each tracking socialist events and activities within and beyond Japan's borders.

Aomori: The Local Arts Movement

While the Esperanto dimension to *Tane Maku Hito* magazine came from its rebirth on a national stage—that is, from the center—the next movement I examine was one that engaged with Esperanto on a distinctly local level, using the language as one means of articulating the relationship between sub- and supernational. The young Esperantists who met Akita Ujaku's train in Kuroishi in 1925 were a small part of a local arts scene that sought to meld transnational engagement with an effort to promote local development.

In 1919, writing in opposition to a widespread perception that Aomori was "inherently both materially and spiritually behind other prefectures," the native author and translator Yanagita Izumi outlined his "stance regarding the local arts."[42] Yanagita's answer, in particular to the problem of the (perceived?) backwardness of the people, was to promote artistic cultivation and the Local Arts movement.[43] What emerged, growing out of the local tradition of haiku and tanka magazines in a way not dissimilar to the emergence of *Tane Maku Hito* only a little way down the coast, was a movement of artistic, philosophical, and social exploration, expressed through a series of magazines and activities. The operative imagery of the movement was one of birth, growth, and spreading influence—magazines taking titles such as *Reimei* (Daybreak), *Taiban* (Placenta), and *Kōkyō* (Reverberations)—again, not so different to Komaki Ōmi's metaphor of the sower.

Alongside the publications, a practice emerged of holding "summer universities"—short festivals of lectures and classes on the same sort of literary, social, and political topics, which the Local Arts movement had been established to consider. Every year from 1920 until at least 1924, starting in Kuroishi, Aomori Prefecture hosted the events, which centered on local residents but also saw speakers come from Tokyo. As a regular summer visitor to his hometown, Akita Ujaku was a key participant in these efforts, speaking on familiar topics including Esperanto, *Tane Maku Hito*, and the Russian famine relief movement.[44] Others who made the trip up from the capital included Abe Isō, a Christian socialist and "the father of Japanese baseball," and Ishiguro Yoshimi, whose encounter with the movement began with the 1923 Esperanto lecture tour.[45]

As with the origins of *Tane Maku Hito* magazine, the Local Arts movement and the summer universities retained a strong sense of their local origins, at the same time as engaging with international topics. They represented a new way for the residents of Tōhoku to educate themselves and keep up with current affairs and preoccupations, and while they did this with assistance from people from Tokyo, they did it at home: in Kuroishi in the first instance, not even in the prefectural capital. Photos of the events reveal a mix of attendees—mostly young men, but a number of women (including some carrying infants) and older people, too.[46] In contrast with the Society for the Advancement of Tōhoku mentioned in the introduction, there is a strong sense of a movement that was grounded in Tōhoku itself (in this case, Aomori), rather than one originating from the center.

Esperantists formed a significant part of this Local Arts movement. Even prior to the expansion of the summer universities, the early magazine *Taiban* had taken the Esperanto subtitle *La Placento*.[47] This expanded once the full movement was underway. The 1922 summer university included a short course in the language, the first of a number of courses in the town. In August 1923, Akita Ujaku was involved in a ten-day course, which was reportedly taken by a hundred students (eighty finishing all ten days).[48] The following year, the Kuroishi Esperanto Club was founded, running the following on a poster as a form of promotion: "For a long time before Esperanto's birth, it lay hidden in humanity's heart. We must remain aware that we are both national subjects and at the same time members of humankind. Esperanto is the Latin of Democracy. Esperanto is the standard language [*hyōjungo*]; national language [*kokugo*] is the dialect."[49]

This short set of ideals reveals the extent to which the young activists of Kuroishi and the Local Arts movement were keen to reach out to a wider sense of common humanity, provincializing the idea of the nation as (just) one form of identity among many. The year 1924 also saw the creation of the Aomori Prefectural Esperanto Association, which hosted an annual Esperanto congress for the rest of the 1920s.

However, neither the Local Arts movement nor local Esperanto activity grew without challenge. In particular, the key voice of opposition to the grounded cosmopolitanism of the Local Arts movement came from another local son, Fukushi Kōtarō. Fukushi was a poet and critic who, like his senior, Akita Ujaku, had relocated to Tokyo to pursue a literary career. He returned to his home region in the wake of the 1923 Kanto earthquake, in which large stretches of Tokyo were laid waste. Returning to Aomori, he became concerned about the vibrant Local Arts movement, with its left-wing politics and explicitly cosmopolitan calls. In response, he articulated his own vision of Tōhoku's renaissance, one he called *chihō-shugi* ("regionalism").

Fukushi's regionalism and the Local Arts movement originated by Yanagita Izumi have some distinct similarities: both sought to promote local literary and cultural endeavors in the pursuit of local rejuvenation; both were grounded in a distinct sense of their place. Fukushi sought to advocate "each of the ethnicities [*minzoku*] of the world's ethnic characteristics [*minzoku seishitsu*], and within the nation, each of the local people's [*chihō jin*] local characteristics."[50] Indeed, Fukushi's own starting point was not dramatically different from those of participants in the movement he sought to overturn: he was a translator of Tolstoy and shared many literary influences with Akita Ujaku.

However, where Fukushi's vision differed dramatically from those of his rivals was in the nature of the local culture both sought to promote, and the relationship that both imagined between the local, the national, and the global. The Local Arts movement built a reputation as progressive, seeking to find a happy merger of local arts and new trends, but Fukushi saw the two as more directly opposed. Trends emerging from the center, he argued, were overriding local context and tradition: "By neglecting ethnic realities and with them local realities, the ubiquitous adoption of 'culturalism' has become a slave to the cosmopolitan (universal, worldist) socialism."[51]

Fukushi's critics charged him seeking to celebrate local culture as a fixed tradition—perpetuating "the vice of uncritical kowtowing to . . . power."[52] Embracing an essentialized notion of fixed local traditions, they suggested, was a form of antiquarianism born of the center, in comparison with the Local Arts movement, which grew out of their experiences living in the villages, talking with and working alongside the rural poor.[53] Seeking to rectify his views of cosmopolitanism and socialism, one writer suggested that Fukushi look to Homaranismo as an alternative concept.[54]

Perhaps unsurprisingly, Fukushi was also a stern critic of Esperanto. In 1925, he wrote an essay for the *Hirosaki Shinbun* challenging an article in another local newspaper written by Taniyama Sōzō.[55] Fukushi argued that "A language can only preserve its complete authenticity through its connections to historical things, old forms, rules of use, customary spellings. Truly, lacking all of these things, Esperanto cannot be said to have authenticity."[56] Needless to say, this sparked a response from the Esperanto community, marking an extension of the previous clash that had taken place in the local press surrounding the Local Arts movement.

While Fukushi's movement was joined by some local Aomori residents, for the most part he failed to win his struggle with the Local Arts movement, while Esperanto remained a key part of the local cultural scene throughout the 1920s. Nevertheless, his proposal and the disagreements it provoked help to stress the role of Esperanto and wider engagement with the wider world within the Local Arts movement. Central to the clash between Fukushi and the Local Arts proponents was a disagreement over the relationship between universal or cosmopolitan ideas and those of the local region: Fukushi saw the global as a deracinating force that would erase tradition, while the Local Arts movement saw it as a means to separate local identity from older patterns of "ignorance, superstition, hunger and oppression."[57]

Given the left-wing inclinations of the Local Arts movement and the tenor of Kuroishi's Esperanto group, Kuroishi retained something of a reputation for progressive and socialist inclination. As a result, when national suppression of the proletarian movement began to ramp up, Aomori was included: one Kuroishi resident was arrested in the nationwide sweep of the Communist Party in April 1929, while the high point of raids in the prefecture took place in November 1933, with fifty-nine arrests, nearly half of which (twenty-five) were from Kuroishi.[58]

This was a significant blow to the Local Arts movement, essentially bringing it to an end. The various participants went in different directions, acting variously on a local and/or national scale. Akita Ujaku's relationship to the broader proletarian literature and socialist Esperanto movements is explored in the next chapter. Another Kuroishi Esperanto / Aomori Local Arts participant who continued to be active in progressive politics was Aizawa Ryō. Aizawa was one of the youngest members of the movement, learning Esperanto in Kuroishi in 1927 when only seventeen. By 1929 she was a teacher herself, running a course for younger learners and organizing students studying alongside her at the Imperial Women's Medical College. At the same time she was active in the Communist Youth League; as a result, she dropped out of college and was arrested the following year. This proved to be the first of a series of arrests (during which time she continued to promote Esperanto among her fellow arrestees) culminating in a five-year sentence, handed down in 1935. The following year, she developed a sudden illness and died shortly afterward.[59]

Back in Kuroishi, progressive politics took more of a back seat in the wake of the crackdown. Takagi Iwatarō, an Esperantist introduced to the language in the early years of the Local Arts movement, attempted to revive the summer universities in the early 1930s but was halted by the local police.[60] Esperanto continued to be practiced in Aomori during this period, but it took an explicitly neutral stance, disavowing ties to the previous incarnation and any link to "thought activities" (i.e., socialism) in general.[61]

Iwate: Rasu Chijin-Kai

The two examples considered so far—*Tane Maku Hito* magazine in Akita and the Local Arts movement of Aomori—were broadly group initiatives. The last case, from the third of the northern three prefectures of Honshū, Iwate, is a paired study that focuses more on individuals. Nevertheless, as will be seen, both Sasaki Kizen and Miyazawa Kenji, the two individuals involved, explored similar themes of local identity and global connection to those of their neighbors to the north and west. The two men lived only a few miles apart, a short train ride away from one another. They were brought together by their shared interest in Esperanto, one dimension of their parallel engagements with the global and the local, a few months before they both died, only a week apart and both in middle age.

Both Sasaki Kizen and Miyazawa Kenji are closely associated with and celebrated in their hometowns: Sasaki for his role in the creation of the *Tales of Tōno*, perhaps Japan's most famous collection of folktales, and Miyazawa more broadly for his reimagination of Iwate across a range of his children's stories. However, both figures also connected this strong sense of local place and identity to an interest in the global, in many ways bypassing the national frame in a similar fashion to the Local Arts movement in Aomori. Once more, this serves to challenge a naïve conception of the nation as a necessary stepping-stone between local and cosmopolitan, but it also stresses the individual nature of these articulations. Most obviously, neither Sasaki nor Miyazawa's rooted cosmopolitanisms were explicitly left-wing in the way that *Tane Maku Hito* magazine and the Aomori Local Arts movement had been.

Sasaki Kizen was born in Iwate in 1886 and is best known for his close working relationship with Yanagita Kunio. The two met in Tokyo while Sasaki, who came from a wealthy farming line, was studying at Waseda University. Sasaki had initially sought to study medicine in Iwate but dropped out and enrolled in a literature program.[62] His encounter with Yanagita, facilitated by their mutual friend Mizuno Yōshū, was the origin of *Tales of Tōno*, a collection of folktales and ghost stories from Iwate and the north. Sasaki, drawing on a childhood spent at the knee of his grandfather (a famous oral storyteller), provided the stories, and Yanagita transcribed and edited them. Exploring a range of fantastical stories and stressing Tōno's remoteness and the strangeness of its local dialect, the book (with Yanagita, the narrator and avatar for an urban audience) played into Tōhoku's reputation as a periphery.[63] After the book's publication in 1910, it would form the foundation of Yanagita's school of folklore/ethnology, *minzokugaku*, and of a lifelong mentor/mentee relationship. However, Sasaki fell ill shortly after the work was done and left Tokyo to rehabilitate back in Tōno, where he would spend the rest of his life, collecting local stories and researching local customs and religious traditions.[64]

Ten years after *Tales of Tonō* was published, Yanagita was also Sasaki's introduction to Esperanto. As discussed in chapter 3, Yanagita was drawn to Esperanto by his experience of foreign language use at the League of Nations; one of the first things he did on arrival in Geneva was recommend the language to his friend back in Japan: "Europeans know nothing about Japan—I feel the need to establish the Esperanto movement. Get in touch with Akita [Ujaku?] or someone and see if he'll help you."[65]

There was a fundamental difference in the way that Yanagita and Sasaki experienced the international language: Yanagita as a potential solution to problems of spoken communication, and Sasaki as a more conceptual phenomenon and chiefly as a written language. One of the obvious differences that this provoked was in the urgency that each man felt. While Yanagita threw himself into study, Sasaki had a more uneven introduction, one no doubt familiar to many of us who have tried to teach ourselves languages:

> Two or three years ago I had a go, but in the countryside there is little interest in this sort of thing, so I eventually left it at that . . . Because Sensei [Yanagita] recommended it, yesterday I picked it up again. When I contacted Akita [Ujaku] for help he too was very happy. If there was just some folklore it would be good—is there any? I stopped reading *La Revuo Orienta* too, but I'll pick it back up again.[66]

This second attempt in 1924 appears to have stuck, and Sasaki to have remained an interested student of Esperanto ever after. Although he did join the JEI, for the most part he doesn't seem to have participated in much centrally organized Esperanto activity.[67] The closest JEI-affiliated club was down the valley in Morioka, but it was many years after he had taken up study that he appears to have visited it.

Esperanto formed one part of Sasaki's work and home life. He taught local children the language, but for the most part he engaged with it through reading, writing, and thinking. He was a prodigious reader and writer, both privately (letters and diaries) and publicly (local and national journals). Esperanto appears in each of these different modes of imaginative transnational engagement: discussing the language in his correspondence with Esperantists and non-Esperantists alike, dropping Esperanto words into his diary entries, reading *La Revuo Orienta* and other Esperanto literature, and discussing it in some of his newspaper essays.[68] He even made use of it in his work and bought Esperanto translations of tales from Switzerland, Bulgaria, and Russia.

While Sasaki was also a semi-regular writer for the magazine *Rōmaji*, printing articles in Romanized Japanese, he doesn't seem to have written about the rōmaji movement in the same way he did Esperanto, indicative of a more sustained, intellectual engagement with the latter.[69] Tucked away up a mountain valley, deep in a region known for its backwardness, in a town that was a byword for Japanese folk tradition, Sasaki conceptualized Esperanto in a way that was very different from that of his mentor, Yanagita. Like the Aomori Esperantists, and many of those who took up the language in the early 1920s, Sasaki was strongly drawn to L. L. Zamenhof's ideal of Homaranismo, but he put his own spin upon it, calling it an instance of "whole-worldism" (*zen-sekaishugi*). He placed this at the heart of Esperanto—a moral or ideological vision, rather than a narrow solution to the international language problem, stressing the name *sekaigo* over the more technical *kokusai hojogo* (international auxiliary language). He called the latter an artless and vulgar term, noting that it was absent from Zamenhof's own work and suggesting that it labeled "a profound and subtle, precious language" with the resonance of a "factory owner's language."[70]

This reverence has an almost religious quality to it; indeed, elsewhere Sasaki called Zamenhof's principles of world peace and pure world love (*sekai heiwa shugi* and *sekai jun'ai shugi*) "a religion that does not rely upon a god."[71] Sasaki's own religious beliefs were complex: at different times he was baptized as a Christian in Tokyo; embraced a local form of esoteric Buddhism, *kakushi-nenbutsu* (hidden *nenbutsu*), with elements of secret practice; and finally, around the same time that he was introduced to Esperanto, was drawn to Ōmoto-kyō, the most successful of the pre–Second World War Japanese new religions.[72] Ōmoto's interest in Esperanto, through loose connections to Bahá'ism, no doubt shaped Sasaki's vision of the language—its magazine *Verda Mondo* (Green world) was another part of his regular reading.

In seeking to articulate Esperanto's significance, Sasaki compared it to other world-changing inventions: wireless communications, the steam train, Buddhism, and Einstein's theory of relativity. This list echoes the technological perspective stressed by other advocates, but it also captures the specific cultural and historic moment—the time and place—of Sasaki's own encounter, blending his interests in his own community's religious traditions and in an encroaching modernity. Tōno was seen from Tokyo as a rural backwater, but it too was changing: the train line reached the town in 1914, and the early 1920s saw an extended project to establish electric lighting across the town.[73]

Sasaki discussed Esperanto within this setting in a miscellaneous essay published in the regional journal *Tōhoku Hyōron* in 1923. The essay addressed four topics: Esperanto, Einstein's theories, Shinran Buddhism, and his penchant for European-style tea, putting universal language alongside modern science, a specifically local form of religion, and European culture. The universal sat alongside the local, the modern alongside the ancient, and all of it was parsed through and united within Sasaki's personal experience. Sasaki articulated less a rigorous framework for understanding the place of the local within broader national and global settings, and more an "everyday cosmopolitanism," describing his daily cup of milk tea and the memories of Tokyo it evoked, as well as his struggles to understand Einstein's work (a popular activity in the wake of the physicist's visit to Japan in late 1922) and his own research into local religious practices. And within this, Esperanto had its place as one of his regular activities.

Sasaki Kizen never went overseas, and he spent only a few years in Tokyo before returning to Iwate. But nevertheless, he remained integrally connected to the wider world through his correspondence and his reading, as well as through his daily practices and studying Esperanto with his friends and local children. In doing so, he brought the global and local together, not in a political/cultural movement like the Esperantists of Aomori or the writers for *Tane Maku Hito*, but in the small activities of his everyday life.

This was a very personal, individual articulation. However, in blending Buddhism, Esperanto, science, and Iwate, Sasaki was not alone. Thirty miles or so down the valley, in a town called Hanamaki, another figure was exploring these different ideas in his own way: Miyazawa Kenji. Miyazawa was a writer of children's stories who struggled to find an audience during his lifetime but has since become famous in Japan and beyond. Like Sasaki, he is closely associated with his hometown and the surrounding region.

The two men seem to have had brief contact with one another at the end of the 1920s, but they met in person only in 1932, when Sasaki came to Hanamaki to teach a short introduction to Esperanto. While there, he visited Miyazawa, who was ill in bed at the time. A subsequent account suggested that "Whenever Sasaki came to Hanamaki, he would without fail visit Miyazawa. When Miyazawa criticised Sasaki's religion, Ōmoto-kyō, Sasaki didn't object . . . 'He's a genius that man, he's a genius, absolutely a genius,' Sasaki would say."[74] Only a year after they first met, both men died: Sasaki aged forty-six and Miyazawa aged thirty-seven.

At the point of their meeting, Sasaki had been an Esperantist for about a decade; Miyazawa had been practicing for about half that, having taken up the language in 1926. Like Sasaki, Miyazawa practiced outside of the JEI-organized mainstream but still within a framework that melded local, national, and global. For Miyazawa, this took the form of the Rasu Chijin Kyōkai (Rasu Farmers' Association), his agricultural collective/school, aimed at relieving rural poverty and cultivating local arts and culture.[75]

Late in 1926, Miyazawa took a break from his work on the association to visit Tokyo. His immediate goals were to study the cello and the typewriter, but during these studies he accompanied an Indian friend to a talk at the Tokyo International Club (Tōkyō Kokusai Kurabu), where he met Gustav Ramstedt, the Finnish diplomat and leading Esperantist. It was Ramstedt who introduced Miyazawa to Esperanto as a means to access a more international readership for his children's stories.[76] Miyazawa took a short course in Esperanto while still in Tokyo, before returning to Iwate, where he added the language to the syllabus of his farming collective.

The creation of the Rasu Chjin Kyōkai in 1926 was roughly contemporaneous with a number of experimental villages formed in Japan during the interwar period—other leading examples being Mushanokōji Saneatsu's Atarashiki Mura and Arishima Takeo's Hokkaido farm (formed in 1918 and 1922, respectively). By the 1930s, the Japanese village came to hold a totemic position for many ultranationalists, but these experimental communities had their own visions and objectives.[77] Where the Atarashiki Mura sought the aesthetic fulfillment of its volunteers through artistic cultivation and agricultural labor, and Arishima's donation of his farm to its tenants was articulated in anarcho-socialist terms, Miyazawa's vision was an idiosyncratic blend of his own artistic vision and his prior work with local farmers.

Miyazawa's scientific agricultural work was straightforwardly a blend of universal and local knowledge: bringing scientific principles to bear on local conditions in an attempt to improve his clients' productivity.[78] His stories, too, demonstrate an attachment to his homeland—many are set in a land called Ihatov, a fantasy reflection of Iwate—as well as cosmological themes such as that of his most famous work, *Night of the Milky Way Railway*.[79]

The Rasu Chijin Kyōkai's manifesto, *A General Introduction to the Farmers' Arts*, written by Miyazawa, summarizes the vision like this:

> We all are farmers, our busy work is also hard;
> We seek the path to a brighter, more vibrant life;
> Among our aged teachers there were such people;

> We aim to debate a blend of the scientists' proofs, the seekers' experiments, and our own intuition;
> So long as the world is not wholly happy, we cannot achieve our own happiness;
> We will steadily develop the consciousness of our selves, from individuals to groups-social-cosmos.[80]

This explicitly ties the farmers' own fulfillment to a wider global frame, as well as placing scientific knowledge, religious(?) visions, and farmers' own perspectives on a level with one another.

Part of the appeal of Miyazawa's stories that has ensured their posthumous popularity is the uniqueness of his imagination. Indeed, his life and ideas reveal an individual unafraid to explore his own intellectual path along many very different subjects and, what is more, unafraid to attempt to put it into reality. Thus, his conception of Esperanto as one means by which the farmers of Iwate might seek to connect their work to the wider world cannot be seen as representative of a wider movement. Nevertheless, the conjunction of Miyazawa with his colleague Sasaki Kizen, the *Tane Maku Hito* writers, and the Local Arts movement of Aomori reveals a cluster of different movements and activities that shared some common features in the ways in which they imagined their connection to a common humanity.

Of the cases examined, only the first—the *Tane Maku Hito* movement—would be likely to be identified within a conventional history of Japanese internationalism. By contrast, while Miyazawa is a relatively well-known figure, his idiosyncrasies mark him as far from a conventional example of internationalism in action, while the Local Arts movement in Aomori and Sasaki Kizen remain little known. Thus, they would likely pass by a conventional study that focused on internationalism as a movement linked to the state and/or nongovernmental organizations.

Nevertheless, the cases document groups and individuals who were internationally engaged despite their apparent peripheral locations. While their articulations of internationalism or cosmopolitanism may have been nonstandard and less influential than those of more central bodies, I would argue that they represent a striking proof of the central claim of this book of the widespread desire to engage internationally in prewar Japan, and the role of Esperanto as a language and idea in mobilizing and facilitating this.

Moreover, there is no reason to suspect that these examples were isolated phenomena. While the ties between the different groups explored in this chapter and singled out as significant elsewhere in this book undoubtedly shaped their engagement with the language, a brief survey of the regional reports in the JEI magazine *La Revuo Orienta* indicates that Tōhoku was no more or less active than the rest of the country. The "Enlanda Kroniko" (Domestic chronicle) column detailed activities of the various different local clubs and associations across the Japanese movement; clubs from the three Tōhoku prefectures are mentioned fairly regularly, but not obviously out of proportion with other regions.

Central to the argument of this chapter is the idea that different locales found expressions of Esperanto that matched their own specific contexts and priorities—forming their own "rooted cosmopolitanisms." Thus other parts of the country (and other local Esperanto groups worldwide) will have found their own expressions of the relationship between their setting and their vision of global community. Other regional and local Esperanto initiatives within the Japanese movement paralleled those examined here. For example, the Kyūshu Esperanto League emerged on the southernmost of Japan's four main islands in the early 1920s, while in the Ryūkyū Islands, a location with a distinct linguistic identity and a history of controversy regarding national language policies,[81] the Esperanto movement also involved at least two pioneers of the movement to protect local culture and arts, Iha Fuyū and Higa Shunchō, suggesting again a complex interplay between the local, the national, and the cosmopolitan. The Esperanto groups in the Ryūkyū were closely involved in local struggles between anarchists and Marxists over the direction of the socialist movement, and it is this—the relationship between Esperanto and socialism—to which the next chapter turns.

CHAPTER 5

Green on the Outside and Red Within

Socialism and Esperanto

One of the central arguments of this book is that the international language problem has been experienced widely in modern Japan and, as a result, the appeal of a rational, relatively easy solution to it was also widely felt. Thus, while those on the left—from Ōsugi Sakae, to Yamaga Taiji, to Vasilii Eroshenko, to many of the young participants of Aomori's Local Arts movement—formed a vital constituency within Japanese Esperanto as a whole, it was only a subpart of the wider whole. This is noteworthy: while Japan's Esperanto movement was fairly politically diverse, other national movements, such as the Chinese, were more closely tied to socialism and/or anarchism.[1]

Not only was Esperanto never subsumed completely within the left in Japan, even among those who saw the language as necessitating a left-wing perspective, the relationship between progressive politics and planned language was neither uncontested nor fixed: people debated and disagreed over how Esperanto might contribute to the pursuit of global revolution, and the conclusions they came to changed over time, reflecting the development of theory, local context, and the wider international setting. Moreover, how they organized and practiced the language changed too to reflect these intellectual developments.

For the development of the Japanese left, the most important among the developments that took place over the first half of the twentieth century was the rise of the Soviet Union to dominate international socialism. This represented a key ideological development and a further dimension to the Japanese state's prior suspicion of socialism.[2] Thus, the particular period of focus of this chapter, which focuses on the relationship between Esperanto and socialism between the mid-1920s and the late 1930s, was one in which the Japanese left increasingly looked to Moscow and the Comintern for guidance at the same time as the Japanese state was particularly keen to suppress it. The activities of individuals and organizations that sought to advance Esperanto in the context of the left reflected these two trends.

While I argue that left-wing Esperanto was heterodox and variable over time, nevertheless there were some structural elements of harmony between the language and the politics that, in Peter Forster's words, meant that "socialist ideology has been highly compatible with the democratizing spirit of Esperanto."[3] First, when seen from Japan, there were superficial similarities between socialism and Esperanto: both were new ideas, imported from Europe at a similar time, and both had a progressive and rational, if radical, vision of global social change.

Moreover, socialists had an innately international outlook: sharing experiences and strategies as well as keeping in touch with the latest theoretical developments through networks of movement and communication. While these activities all butted up against the sort of transnational language issue that prompted scientists, politicians, scholars, and more to turn to Esperanto, for the socialists there was also an important international sense of common cause—solidarity—that was deeply embedded within their ideology and practice. Thus the sort of transnational connections enabled by Esperanto had both practical and emotional value for those on the left.

Finally, inherent within both the Marxist movement and Esperanto was a complex balance between the realities of the present day and the utopian possibilities of the future. Both were what I would term partially realized utopias: movements with a utopian vision of the future but also concrete achievements in the present day. For the socialists, the realities of everyday politics and the Soviet Union's example could be balanced against the communist state of Japan that might result from a proletarian revolution; for the Esperantists, the realities of the networks they were building and the ways in which they were using their language today sat alongside the anticipation of the *fina venko* (final victory) of universal adoption with all its concomitant benefits. Over the course of the first half of the twentieth century, while the nature of socialism and Esperanto's relations ebbed and changed, these different factors—the sense of international solidarity, the practical value of networks of communication, and the vision of a perfected future—represented three pillars of connection between the two.

As suggested, socialists formed an important part of the first generations of Japanese Esperanto. They had their own interpretations and meanings for the language, but they were for the most part content to operate beneath a single umbrella that combined almost all Japanese Esperantists. While there were the occasional spats, such as the arguments over Esperantism in the Taishō period, Japanese Esperanto was a diverse and fairly integrated network, bringing together a variety of different perspectives in a mostly well-functioning organization.

However, toward the end of the 1920s, this ceased to be the case: socialist Esperantists broke away from the mainstream, formed their own organizations, published their own magazines and textbooks, and generally operated a parallel movement distinct from the existing JEI-centered activities. I use the term "proletarian Esperanto" to signify these groups and this period in order to recognize them as a distinct subpart or subphase of a broader, less concretely defined sphere of left-wing Esperanto in Japan. The split—effectively the end of the broad church of prewar Japanese Esperanto—was the result of two processes: the development of Marxist thinking on the question of international language, and the pressure put upon the movement by the Japanese state. In short, the socialists began to drift away from their less radical colleagues, and the state's response to the Japanese communist movement was a powerful incentive for the mainstream Esperantists to make clear their difference from the progressives.

The emergence of a new body of theory, derived from the Soviet Union, led to new ideas about the nature of language and the significance of Esperanto in particular. This proved increasingly hard to reconcile with existing apolitical or liberal Esperanto activities, driving socialist Esperantists to rethink their position within the "bourgeois" movement. While there was a specific linguistic dimension to this, it was a part of a broader phenomenon of Soviet influence. The Comintern guidance at times sought to make national communist movements distance themselves from center-left liberal politics, which were deemed inherently antirevolutionary; the proletarian Esperantists followed this lead.

From the perspective of the Japanese state, the role of the Comintern in guiding international Marxism marked domestic communism and communists out as more than just an unwelcome and alien political ideology: the ideology of class loyalties superseding national ones threatened the very existence of the very state itself, and ties to the Soviet Union and the Comintern identified communists as a fifth column through which a malign and foreign influence was being introduced to Japan. Throughout the 1920s and into the 1930s, the Tokkō police sought to pursue and suppress a political movement that was flagged as inherently threatening to the *kokutai*, the fundamental foundations of Japanese state and society.[4]

For the Esperantists who were not allied with the communist movement, this was an alarming development. The expulsion of Eroshenko in 1921 had seen suggestions that their language movement might be synonymous with or a cover for the communists. They had worked hard to prove that this was not the case, but as the proletarian Esperantists became more outspoken in their radicalism, the suspicion reemerged. Thus, as the proletarian Esperanto movement was beginning to pull away from the conventional liberal movement, so too were the liberals keen to stress the ideological difference between them and the socialists in order to avoid being caught up in any police activity. In short, the socialist Esperantists opened a gap between themselves and the mainstream, and the scrutiny by the state helped to place a wedge between the two halves, separating them more clearly.

The threat of government suppression was very real. Proletarian Esperanto was an identifiable separate movement from the JEI and its orbit from about 1928, with distinct organizations, publications, theories, and practices. However, along with the rest of the proletarian arts movement of which it formed a part, the Esperantists struggled to operate legally and individuals found themselves arrested, often repeatedly. In the end, the central proletarian movement collapsed under the weight of arrests, disruption, and surveillance in 1934. From that point onward, left-wing Esperantists went one of two ways: back to the JEI and less directly political activities, or on to much smaller local or individual endeavors.

There were roughly three phases of socialist Esperanto in pre-1945 Japan: up to the mid-1920s, when it was integrated well with the liberal/bourgeois mainstream movement; from the mid-1920s, when a distinct proletarian movement emerged until 1934 when it fell apart; and the less-coordinated smaller-scale activities that survived the collapse of the organized proletarian phase. The second phase, of organized proletarian Esperanto, is a case study of the relationship between left-wing politics and the planned language. It reveals different people (both from within the left and from without) wrestling with the idea of Esperanto's relationship with socialism. Moreover, it shows that while the left approached Esperanto with its own theory and ideas and developed its own practices, nevertheless the core themes of an interest in international engagement, a sensitivity to language problems, and the appeal of Esperanto as a solution to them were common to those on the left and those who were not.

Debating the Relationship between Language and Socialism

Debates over the relationship between Esperanto and socialism were a specific case of a wider question of the relationship between language and culture. Was a given language a transparent medium for communication, or was it perhaps imbued with certain inherent cultural and intellectual qualities? On the one hand, unlike most national languages, Esperanto lacked the underpinning presence of a nation, state, and culture, which argued that perhaps it was uniquely free from cultural baggage.[5] On the other hand, the presence and weight within the international movement of ideas of *interna ideo* put the lie to the suggestion that, at least as a movement, Esperanto lacked some ideological ties.

Within the Esperanto movement itself, this question of Esperanto's innate character played out in the sort of arguments over Esperantismo discussed in chapter 2: those who wished to embed Zamenhof's hope that language could unify inherently within the language and its movement against those who believed that to be truly international, a language had to retain the potential to write or say anything. In the wake of the Eroshenko affair, a different debate arose in general Japanese society: the question of whether the language was inherently "dangerous"—that is, socialist. When the Home Ministry suggested that the Esperanto movement might be a cover for radical leftists, advocates of the language took issue with them. Nitobe Inazō wrote, "[Esperanto] has been indicted as being a channel of radical thought, but it is well known that more propaganda literature of 'dangerous ideas' exists in other languages,"[6] while a Japanese Esperanto magazine argued,

> What is a dangerous language? When we speak of "trifling with dangerous language," what do we mean—the language, the people, the ideas? It goes without saying that it is the ideas. There are among the Japanese, and the English and the Germans, those who hold so-called "dangerous thought." It is clear we cannot therefore regard these national languages as dangerous. So too, is the case for Esperanto. This is different from saying that English is for trade, German is for medicine, and Italian is for music. While we might use this logic to say Russian is dangerous (i.e., because of the Soviet Union), this does not hold for Esperanto.[7]

The view that a language is no more than the sum of its grammar and vocabulary did not convince many: Esperanto's appeal to those with generally progressive viewpoints seemed self-evident. The passing comment by *Esperanto en Nipponlando* that other languages have their own domains—international commerce, science, or diplomacy, for instance—seemed to be a commonplace. Socialist theorists came to call the stance that one could look at a language in a vacuum "linguistic fetishism," arguing instead that true understanding of a language has to include its social, ideological, and political dimensions: "that which we call a language is not knowledge written upon paper, but a living craft used by living beings."[8] In short, while a language might not have an innate character, and while its grammar might permit the expression of any viewpoint, it nevertheless had a social and cultural embeddedness in the world that were real and required understanding.

The specific question of Esperanto and the left continued to be debated over the early 1920s. As described, socialists had been participants in the Japanese Esperanto movement from its outset, but so too had nonsocialists, and even among the socialists there remained ambiguity about what the nature of the relationship was or what it should be. In their Esperanto textbook of 1921, Akita Ujaku and Osaka Kenji suggested that simply learning the language was not enough to make one an Esperantist, but they left it up to the individual what further progressive beliefs were required. Vasilii Eroshenko is reported to have said "All Esperantists must be socialists, and all socialists, Esperantists," but others took a different view.[9] The young socialist Esperantists who emerged in the mid-1920s called themselves "watermelons" (*akvo-melonoj*): green (Esperantist) on the outside but red (socialist) within, conceding at least the perception of a semantic gap between the two visions: politics and language, red and green.[10]

In 1926, the *Asahi Shinbun* ran a six-part article exploring the relationship between socialism and Esperantism. Its author, the Esperantist and medical doctor Asada Hajime, had first encountered Esperanto through the anarchist Ōsugi Sakae's work, but he was not a socialist; he described the political left as a social disease. His article made an extended analogy, comparing socialism within society to the rise of cancer in the body. Socialism, he argued, arose in parts of society subjected to unnatural stimuli—unemployment, poverty, and the like—just as cancer was found in habitual pipe smokers and big drinkers.[11] In his view, Esperantism and socialism were two political visions that were best thought of as alternatives to one another rather than complements or compatibles.

Asada expressed the view that Esperantism might provide a potential antidote to the spread of socialism—one that might prove more sympathetic than arrests and punishment. This view of Esperantism as a route away from socialism has some fore-echoes of the ideas of redemption and reintegration embedded within the rehabilitative apparatus for *tenkōsha*—those socialists who renounced their beliefs in the face of police pressure.[12] Indeed, in 1938 and 1939, Hirata Isao, one of the architects of the *tenkō* system, wrote articles in support of Esperanto, its role in Japan's international affairs, and the sympathies between Esperantism and Japan's nationalism.[13]

Unsurprisingly, the socialist-Esperantists took a very different view to Asada's opposition between the two movements. From the outset, the likes of Ōsugi Sakae had argued for a practical and ideological affinity between the language and left-wing politics, but in the middle of the 1920s a new generation of socialist-Esperantists began to articulate a more theoretically informed, complex vision. It was one that originated from the Soviet Union and the Comintern, drawing on developments in Marxist-Leninist thought.

From the early 1920s, what emerged was a theory of "worldism" (*sekai-shugi*) defined in opposition to internationalism (*kokusai-shugi*): worldism was proletarian and superseded the nation, where internationalism remained bourgeois, merely building upon, rather than challenging, the nation-state and its supporting ideology, nationalism. Within this perspective, the predominant trend of Japanese Esperanto up to the early 1920s was clearly an internationalist linguistic phenomenon. Although socialists participated, the general tenor was not revolutionary. An early articulator of this distinction, Sasaki Takamaru, argued that conventional internationalism (and the world peace movement) was "no more than a specter of militarism," whereas "the true meaning [of world literature (*sekai-bungaku*)] is the literature of the proletariat."[14] On the one hand stood internationalism, the nation-state-based international order, bourgeois capitalism, and the existing Esperanto movement; on the other hand was worldism, a socialist fraternity beyond borders, the proletariat, and the need for a more explicitly working-class Esperanto movement.

Sasaki distinguished between the existing movement in support of Esperanto, which could straightforwardly be categorized as bourgeois internationalism, and the language itself, which he saw as more "a manifestation of the highest ideals." He preferred terms such as *sennacia lingvo* (non-national language) for Esperanto over technical descriptions, such as "international auxiliary language."[15] However, the fuller development of this theory went further, arguing that Esperanto was at best a transitional step. This model, based upon the works of the linguist V. Y. Marr and articulated by the Esperantist and Soviet official Ernest Drezen, was a Marxist model of language evolution tied to the materialist path of economic and political transitions. National languages were directly tied to the modern development of the nation-state and hence were inherently bourgeois; Esperanto, as a language operating between national languages and built upon the framework of nation-states, was similarly bourgeois in nature. In the Japanese proletarian movement's terms, it was an international language, a *kokusai-go*, not a world language, a *sekaigo*. What was needed—or what was to come—was a true *world* language built (as Sasaki Takamaru had articulated in relation to literature) by and for the working classes.

Sasaki's name for Esperanto, *sennacia lingvo*, drew upon the most significant European socialist Esperanto organization of the 1920s—the Sennacia Asocio Tutmonda (SAT; Global Non-National Association), which was founded in 1921 by an idiosyncratic French Esperantist, Eugène Lanti.[16] The SAT embodied some of the complexities of Esperanto's relationship to socialism: for a time the organization precluded parallel membership in the SAT and any politically neutral, bourgeois Esperanto group, but it simultaneously had a fractious relationship to the Soviet Union and the Comintern. This eventually led to the creation of a separate, Comintern-controlled group, the International of Proletarian Esperantists (IPE), which existed in parallel to SAT.[17]

As these new ideas filtered into Japan, they not only began to influence the ways in which the left-wing Esperantists understood the language, but they also changed the ways in which they organized themselves. A variety of groups formed in the early to mid-1920s, as explicitly left-wing Esperanto began to take a more organized form. The first ones included student groups, such as the "watermelons," who emerged out of the Gakuren cross-university student federation in 1924, and the Esuperanto Seinen Dōmei (Esperanto Youth League), which was created the following year.[18] Another influential group from the same period with strong left-wing ties was the Kurara-Kai (named after L. L. Zamenhof's wife, Clara), an association for female Esperantists. This was founded by Sasaki Matsue, an important activist in her own right and the sister of the left-wing writer Yamakawa Kikue.[19]

However, the most significant group in terms of the development in Japan of explicitly proletarian linguistic theory and Esperanto was the Kashiwagi Rondo. This was a group of young Esperantists with a shared interest in socialism and Marxism who began to study together. The five core members of the group were Higa Shunchō, an Okinawan native who worked for the publishing house Kaizō; Nakagaki Kojirō, a Kyushu-born teacher who had learned Esperanto in Korea; and three ex-Waseda students, Ōshima Yoshio, Nagahama Torajirō, and Kiyomi Rokurō.[20] The group took its name from the site of their meetings: Higa's home in Western Tokyo. It started as an informal study group but gradually became more seriously organized.[21]

By the late 1920s, the Kashiwagi Rondo became seen as the de facto Japanese wing of the SAT, organizing SAT subgroups at the annual JEI Esperanto congresses. Members of the group (in particular, Ōshima Yoshio, writing under the pseudonym Takagi Hiroshi) worked to translate Soviet texts, bringing the proletarian theory of language to a Japanese audience,[22] while Sasaki Matsue, the leader of the Kurara-Kai, in turn wrote for the SAT magazine *Sennaciulo*.[23]

These groups represented a progression from the loose affiliations of left-wingers within the broad Japanese Esperanto organizations of the first generations of the language movement, and an intermediate step toward the more formal, separate proletarian Esperanto organizations that would emerge at the end of the decade, discussed later in this chapter. The development of a more concrete theory of socialist language and Esperanto's place within the full proletarian movement and the development of this distinct proletarian Esperanto movement occurred side by side.

Akita Ujaku in Moscow

One concrete proof of the sympathy between Esperanto and socialism, at least at a personal level, was Akita Ujaku's trip to the Soviet Union. The journey took place in 1927 and 1928, the tenth anniversary of the October Revolution, as the tensions between centrists and socialists within Japanese Esperanto were becoming apparent. While it was, in the first instance, a chance to experience firsthand the realities of Soviet life and society, it was also to prove a vital encounter with other overseas progressive Esperantists. Moreover, his time in the Soviet Union was proof to Akita of the realities of a Marxist state and of Esperanto as a means of bringing people together—partial realizations of the utopias that the two movements promised.

Akita's trip was meticulously planned over the course of the spring and summer of 1927: arranging visas, lining up newspapers to print his writing, and liaising with the Tokkō special police in advance of his departure.[24] In addition, Akita arranged to travel with a colleague and friend from Kuroishi, the Russian specialist Narumi Kanzō, to help with any language issues. Akita's excitement grew, becoming more and more apparent until the two men set off, by train, across Manchuria. As they traveled west, through Chinese towns "like beautiful paintings," Mukden, Harbin, and beyond, the Chinese influence gradually gave way to Russian: a stand of birch trees by a station platform, the endless stretch of Lake Baikal, and then the first snow, on the outskirts of Moscow.[25]

Once in Moscow, Akita and Narumi were hosted by VOKS, the All Union Society for Cultural Relations with Foreign Countries, which coordinated the activities of many foreign delegates at the celebrations of the October Revolution.[26] The formal events involved a series of congresses and committees, visits to political and literary sites, as well as meetings with a range of different figures. It was a chance to meet not only Soviet Russians, but also many of the other nations' delegates, including Europeans who were influential in Japan, such as Henri Barbusse.

However, right from the outset language was an issue in the formal events. Despite being provided with an interpreter, Mary, and both the presence of Narumi Kanzō and a reunion with Vasilii Eroshenko, Akita recorded a simple "language problems" as his sole comment about the first meeting of the centerpiece of foreign delegates' part in the celebrations, the Congress of Friends of the Soviet Union.[27] There were many Esperantists among the foreign delegates in Moscow.[28] They came together to put a motion in support of Esperanto to the main congress—Akita was lined up to propose the motion, with Henri Barbusse due to second it, but in echoes of events at the League of Nations, proponents of Esperanto's rival language, Ido, protested hard enough that in the end the motion was never formally made.[29]

However, if the formal events proved something of a disappointment (in addition to linguistic issues, Akita found the main parade through Red Square too militaristic for his tastes), by contrast the opportunities to meet regular Russians proved the highlight of his trip.[30] What is more, Esperanto proved central to his ability to make contact with them. On the train across Asia, Akita and Narumi made friends with some Russian passengers and they sang the unofficial Esperanto anthem "La Espero" as they crossed the border from China into Siberia.[31] This was just the beginning: Esperanto opened the door to a range of everyday experiences in the Soviet Union—as Akita recalled, "once I made some Esperanto friends, I was able to use their linguistic aid to enter the real life of Moscow . . . to make contact with workers' daily home, factory, and club life."[32]

As a result of his friendship with Vasilii Eroshenko in the Taishō era, Akita Ujaku's experience of speaking Esperanto (with non-Japanese natives) was greater than most of his fellow Japanese Esperantists. Nevertheless, it was still limited to those few foreign residents of Tokyo and very occasional visitors. The trip to Moscow, then, was a transformative experience: a series of encounters through Esperanto that would otherwise not have been possible, concrete proof of the potential of the language. He met students and workers, men and women, foreign delegates and local residents; he visited clubs such as that at the Department of Post, Telegraph, Telegram, and Radio (PTTR); he made a number of radio broadcasts about his interest in Esperanto; and in turn these encounters led to invitations to visit Esperantists further afield, in Minsk and the Caucuses.

The trip, all told, fulfilled Akita's hopes both of socialism's potential to transform society and of Esperanto's potential to bring people together—exactly the blend of future promise and already existing reality that united Esperanto and socialism. At one meeting of Esperantists, Akita wrote a poem to a fellow foreign delegate: "While you are the son of the West and I am the son of the East, some day we shall stand in the same field, and surely see the same sun."[33] He extended his visa from the end of November through the new year and to the May Day celebrations of 1928, eventually getting home to Tokyo on May 18.[34] On the last stretches of his return journey, Akita had one final reminder of the power of language to unite and to divide. Traveling back across Siberia, he fell in with a number of Chinese students—all ardent reformers, several drawn to ethnic nationalism (*minzoku-shugi*)—and despite their common interests, he reflected on "the absurdity that, while we were the same humankind, with the closest relationships of interest, due to the constraints of language we could not freely share those intents."[35] Despite this barrier, for a moment in Moscow at least, Esperanto had demonstrated to Akita that another world was possible.

Organizing Red Esperanto

Arriving back in Tokyo, Akita Ujaku was met by his wife and friends. His experiences in Moscow were of wide interest to young progressive Japanese, and so he gave a number of talks and went on to write up his thoughts in a book, *Wakaki Souēto Roshia*.[36] He was also instrumental in founding an organization, the Kokusai Bunka Kenkyūjo (International Culture Research Institute, reconfigured a year later as the Puroretaria Kagaku Kenkyūjo, or Puro-Kagaku, the Proletarian Science Research Institute). Its goals were "to introduce widely to the Japanese proletariat and their allies the ways in which proletarian culture, centered upon the Soviet Union, is and is becoming, superior to bourgeois culture."[37]

The timing of Akita's arrival back in Japan coincided with the transition from a socialist faction that was subsumed within the main body of Japanese Esperanto to its emergence as a separate and distinct movement, with its own institutions, publications, and apparatus. This was the coming together of, on the one hand, the growing sense of independence felt by the left-wing Esperantists and, on the other hand, a growing profile for Esperanto within the existing proletarian arts movement.

At the same time as this strain of Esperanto was developing in Japan, the Japanese proletarian literature and arts movement had been coming into being. The connections between these two movements can be traced as far back as the start of the 1920s and the *Tane Maku Hito* magazine discussed in chapter 4.[38] While Akita Ujaku was in Moscow, the main proletarian literature organization, JPAL (Nihon Puroretaria Geijutsu Renmei, Japan Proletarian Arts League) had ruptured into three rival groups: the Rōnō Geijutsuka Renmei (WPAL, Worker-Peasant Artists' League), the Zen'ei Geijutsuka Dōmei (VAL, Vanguard Artists League), and the remaining rump of JPAL. However, in the wake of the March 15 incident in 1928, in which a wave of arrests rocked the Japanese left, these groups came back together in a new organization. The Zen-Nihon Musanasha Geijutsu Renmei (All-Japan Proletarian Arts League) came to be known as NAPF, after its Esperanto translation, the Nippona Artista Proletaria Federacio. The creation of NAPF proved the stimulus that prompted the left-wing Esperantists such as the Kashiwagi Rondo and those working with Akita Ujaku and the Puro-Kagaku Kenkyūkai to shift from organizing beneath the Esperanto-centered JEI umbrella to doing so within the proletarian arts and science framework—from red within green to green within red. The year 1930 saw the creation of the Puroretaria Esuperanto Kyōkai (PEA, from the Esperanto translation, Proleta Esperanto-Asocio), an organization under the umbrella of NAPF and in effect the Esperanto wing of the proletarian arts movement.

The central challenge faced by the participants in PEA, as with NAPF and the wider proletarian movement, was one of adhering to the changing guidance emanating out of Moscow and the Comintern as to the theoretically right objectives and activities of the proletarian movement while at the same time remaining legal and able to avoid suppression at the hands of the domestic authorities.[39] As the committee themselves wrote: "PEA acts in a specific field of proletarian culture, according to the cultural plan of the revolutionary party . . . PEA is not itself a political body, but as far as possible its members must individually and in groups engage in organized political movements."[40] This was neither straightforward nor entirely within the control of the participants themselves: Moscow was rarely consistent in its guidance for long, and the Japanese authorities were proactive in their pursuit of domestic communism. In 1931, NAPF was refounded as KOPF (Federacio de Proletaj Kultur-Organizoj Japanaj, Proletarian Culture-Organizations of Japan); PEA was also recreated, in parallel, this time as PEU, the Proletarian Esperanto Union.[41] This reflected a change in overall outlook, drawn from the fifth congress of Profintern, communicated by Kurahara Korehito, an attendee of the congress, and member of both PEA and NAPF. The change in aims was partially successful—*Kamarado*, the magazine of PEU, reached a circulation of some two thousand, a multiple of the sales of the PEA's magazine, *Avangado*.[42]

However, this success brought with it more sustained scrutiny from the police. PEU's AGM in March of 1932 was met with a hostile reception. As Akita Ujaku recorded in his diary:

> A mass of PEU people was gathered. A gang of some 20 plain clothes police had also come. We members were speculating as to whether we'd be dissolved or not . . . the optimists were in the majority. The meeting opened, Mutō-kun gave an opening welcome, I stood up as the chair of the meeting, and no sooner had Makishima begun the announcements than we were shut down. Nakadai [Ichirō] was arrested. The police maintained that the agenda was banned. But the real reason can only be seen as a premeditated plan to suppress left wing cultural organizations.[43]

Although the committee managed to reconvene in private later that night, it was reflective of a more confrontational approach by the police and thus an increased risk to the participants over what had previously been the case for the proletarian arts movement (as distinct from the Japanese Communist Party). Over the following days, Akita reflected on the meeting, expressing relief at having, even if somewhat unsatisfactorily, completed a phase of the organization's work, and undertaking to reassert PEU's legal status and nature.[44]

However, this was to prove unsuccessful: the next couple of years saw a succession of arrests that included members of PEU and in particular no fewer than four secretaries-general between August 1933 and September 1934.[45] Akita himself was arrested in 1930, 1931 (twice), 1932, and 1933, the last of which saw him held for more than twenty days before reportedly issuing a statement of *tenkō*, a repudiation of his socialist beliefs.[46] By the time of this final arrest, Akita was fifty-one years old and very much an elder statesman of the proletarian movement, but it was hard to give too much credence to his claim, as the *Asahi Shinbun* reported, to be "a progressive liberal, not a Marxist," given his long history of activism, from Waseda Bungaku to the Nihon Shakaishugi Dōmei, his trip to the Soviet Union, three years as head of Kokusai Bunka Kenkyūjo/Puro Kagaku Kenkyūjo, as well as membership of the Nihon Puroretaria Sakka Dōmei, and the Sovieto Tomo no Kai.[47] Akita's exhaustion was not unique: under the state's sustained suppression and unable to operate legally, the PEU, and with it centrally organized proletarian Esperanto, effectively ground to a halt.

Learning and Using Left-Wing Esperanto

While the collapse of the PEU represented the end of the last centrally coordinated proletarian Esperanto body, it did not spell the end for the Japanese proletarian language movement as a whole. What remained from the arrests of the early 1930s reemerged in different forms: some of the older participants who had prior ties moved back toward the JEI-led mainstream, whereas other, younger survivors began to organize on a more localized basis. A number of smaller groups emerged under a general umbrella of "progressive Esperanto," by and large operating independently.[48] These included Marushu-sha in Kobe, Amiiko in Okayama, Furāto in Osaka, Poporo in Nagoya, and the Kyōtō Puroretario Esuperanto Kenkyūkai. This was a pragmatic response to the situation, as an editorial in Marushu-sha's magazine argued:

> In the current conditions, [a PEU-style] proletarian movement cannot exist legally, and this means it cannot become a mass movement; further, to operate illegally is effectively impossible. Moreover, today, where we face both tangible and intangible forms of suppression simply for being liberals (even though the language of progressivism does not mean the language of proletarianism), we cannot escape suppression, and so the pains of running a centralized organization would be large.
>
> Because of these reasons, we have selected a regional structure . . . Those comrades operating across the nation in each region should build groups along the correct lines for that region. In one region it may be right for an explicitly progressive group to unreservedly oppose the neutral groups, in another region it might be necessary to exist within the

> neutral organizations. And more, in one region a group may publish an independent magazine aiming at mass participation, whereas another may be able to do no more than publish their views within the JEI (neutral) groups' publications.[49]

This move, toward a more localized, cellular set of groups, was both a necessary response to the state's ongoing aggression and again the implementation of some of the guidance that had come from Profintern in Moscow.[50] However, while they might no longer be able to coordinate on a national scale, the move to subnational groups did not mean an end to the transnational dimension of the movement. This situation reiterates the central point of chapter 4, that small groups in the Japanese regions were as keen and as able to think and even act transnationally as were national bodies. These progressive Esperanto groups continued to interact with their overseas comrades as a fundamental part of their practice.

From the very outset, the socialists within the Esperanto movement had been notable for their hands-on use of the language, for example Ōsugi Sakae's experiences with Chinese students and Yamaga Taiji's trips to China. In the late 1920s, the first proletarian Esperantists sought to broaden this practice, focusing on language learning and on letter writing among students and workers.

In 1929, the Kashiwagi Rondo successfully argued a motion at the JEI congress seeking to send Esperanto materials to prisoners—targeting those swept up in the 1928 wave of anti-Marxist arrests—and funded through a collection at one of the congress's events.[51] According to Higa Shunchō, religious and language-learning texts were the only ones the prisoners were allowed; over one hundred inmates took the JEI up on the offer, mostly receiving beginners' texts.[52] This recalls the experiences of Ōsugi Sakae, studying Esperanto while in prison back in the first years of the century—one poem, published by Saitō Eizō and Ōda Ryūichirō suggests that Esperanto became a daily practice for some of the prisoners, much as it had for Ōsugi some twenty-five years earlier:

> Singing daily has become a habit; Esperanto song sings the dawn.[53]

There appears to have been some unevenness or tension in the spread of this practice however: one inmate described all Korean prisons as Esperanto schools, while elsewhere inmates experienced difficulties in obtaining study materials.[54]

As proletarian Esperanto became formalized and more organized, language study remained a central plank of its objectives. Akita Ujaku's Kokusai Bunka Kenkyūjo organized a summer school for languages in 1929, teaching Esperanto alongside a range of European languages.[55] When it reconfigured itself as the Puroretaria Kagaku Kenkyūjo, it continued to hold a regular Esperanto study group, and then in 1930 held a series of courses for new learners. In March, two groups studied in parallel—one for students and intellectuals, the other for workers—and then in July or August, the groups were split instead into beginners and intermediate learners. This was followed the following year by another summer school.[56]

The experiences of running these courses led to the development and publication of a set of specifically proletarian textbooks, *Puroretaria Esuperanto Kōza*, issued as a series of six volumes. The volumes mixed essays on the materialist theory of language and sociolinguistics with a course based around a series of proletarian themes—scenarios in a factory, letters from correspondents within the Soviet Union, and the like.[57] Priced at eighty *sen* per volume, the series was reportedly highly successful, recording sales in the thousands.[58]

Learning the language formed a base, but the next step was to actually use it. As suggested above, the transnational networks formed by proletarian Esperantists helped to share news and strategy, and to embody the solidarity and comradeship of the international workers' movement. While some of this practice took the form of publishing in magazines—for example, Ōsugi Sakae's earliest works of Esperanto, which were reports on the nature of the socialist movement in Japan—for the majority, letter writing formed the backbone of these networks and their own personal practice.

Correspondence networks were by no means unique to the socialists—they were one of the major planks of pre-Second World War Esperanto practice. Esperantists in a place like Japan, especially those outside of Tokyo and the other major port cities, had limited opportunity to speak their language with foreign practitioners, but they could make use of written language. Many Esperanto magazines carried "correspondents wanted" columns—a single advertisement taken out in one of these might prompt a huge number of replies, and each reply might be the start of a relationship that lasted decades. For example, the JEI archives house a file of over 120 letters from at least twenty-five countries—mostly European, but including Rhodesia, Argentina, Uruguay, China, the United States of America, Mexico, Australia, and the Soviet Union—all relating to a single advertisement taken out in the April 1925 edition of the international magazine *Esperanto*, by a Waseda University student, Yanagi Kojirō.[59] George Edward Gauntlett's experiments with letter writing led to the receipt of seven hundred letters from seventy-five countries—this in the early 1900s at the very start of organized worldwide Esperanto.[60] Later, a local Sunday school in Wakayama received over a thousand replies on both occasions that they sought

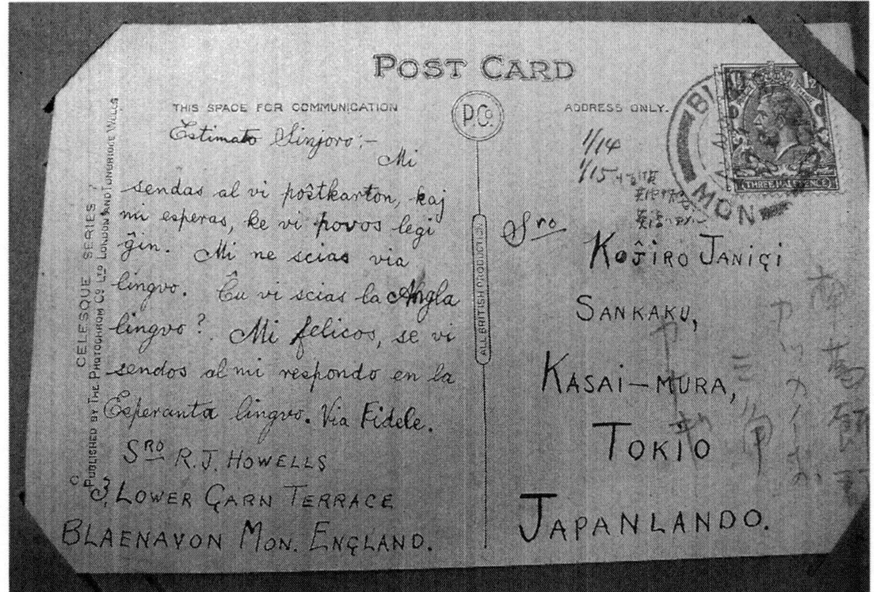
POST CARD

THIS SPACE FOR COMMUNICATION

ADDRESS ONLY.

Estimata Sinjoro:—
Mi
sendas al vi poŝtkarton, kaj
mi esperas, ke vi povos legi
ĝin. Mi ne scias via
lingvo. Ĉu vi scias la Angla
lingvo? Mi felicos, se vi
sendos al mi respondo en la
Esperanta lingvo. Via Fidele.
Sro R.J. Howells
3, Lower Garn Terrace
Blaenavon Mon. England.

Sro Koĵiro Janiĝi
Sankaku,
Kasai-Mura,
Tokio
Japanlando.

CELESQUE SERIES
PUBLISHED BY THE PHOTOCHROM Co LTD LONDON AND TUNBRIDGE WELLS

ALL BRITISH PRODUCTION

Figure 5.1. Postcard from Wales, 1926. Image courtesy of the Japanese Esperanto Institute.

correspondents in the early 1930s.[61] In 1994, a chance encounter led to the discovery of some 1,300 letters and cards received by Nishimura Isamu, another student from the 1920s, charting ongoing relationships between 1928 and his death in 1954.[62] From its outset, and throughout the period up to 1945, letter writing formed an important part of Japanese Esperanto.

While no doubt much of this correspondence was somewhat formulaic in nature—personal and family introductions—the scale of the network and the longevity of some relationships make them a notable phenomenon. And they demonstrate prewar Esperanto as a popular non-state activity—building from bottom-up networks and practices, forming decentralized informal channels, and representing a personal but tangible manifestation of a cosmopolitan ethos, one that appealed to many without other avenues for transnational encounter. Indeed, the practice of writing letters is important because it also demonstrates that for most Esperantists, at least in East Asia, Esperanto was a written rather than a spoken language. Magazines and letters were words traveling where and when people could not.

All of these characteristics held true for the left-wing Esperantists too: a few socialists had the chance to visit Europe or China to interact directly with other like-minded progressives, and some visitors (most notably Chinese students)

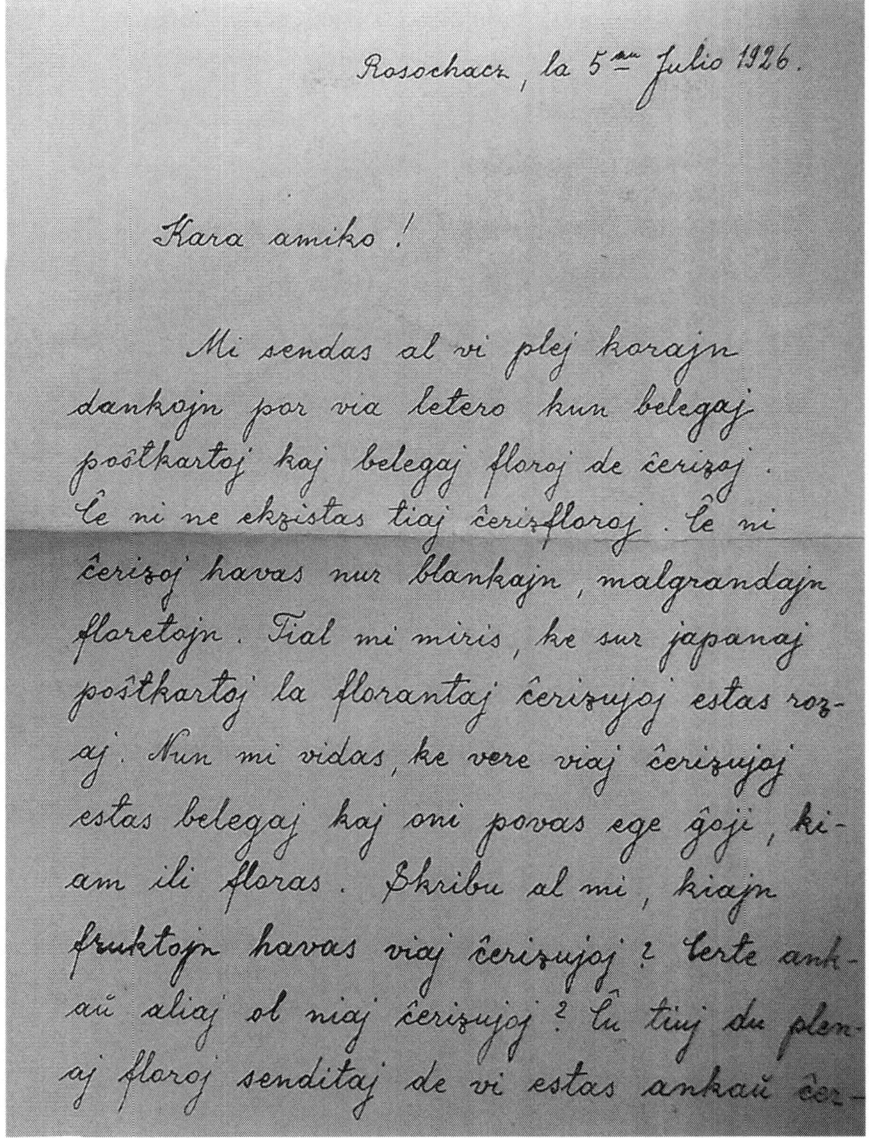

Rosochacz, la 5an Julio 1926.

Kara amiko!

Mi sendas al vi plej korajn
dankojn por via letero kun belegaj
poŝtkartoj kaj belegaj floroj de ĉerizoj.
Ĉe ni ne ekzistas tiaj ĉerizfloroj. Ĉe ni
ĉerizoj havas nur blankajn, malgrandajn
floretojn. Tial mi miris, ke sur japanaj
poŝtkartoj la florantaj ĉerizujoj estas roz-
aj. Nun mi vidas, ke vere viaj ĉerizujoj
estas belegaj kaj oni povas ege ĝoji, ki-
am ili floras. Skribu al mi, kiajn
fruktojn havas viaj ĉerizujoj? Certe ankaŭ aliaj ol niaj ĉerizujoj? Ĉu tiuj du plen-
aj floroj senditaj de vi estas ankaŭ ĉer-

Figure 5.2. Letter from Poland, 1926. Image courtesy of the Japanese Esperanto Institute.

came to Japan, but for the most part Japanese socialists and workers were not able to travel and so the international solidarity of which socialism spoke was proven more through the written word than it was in person. The *Proletaria Esuperanto Kōza* textbooks included letters from foreign workers in their study materials, alongside essays on Marxist theory, the Paris Commune, and the history of Esperanto's development, demonstrating this appeal.[63] Writing in Marushu-sha's magazine, *Marushu*, the young proletarian Esperantist Takaragi Yutaka spoke of the joys of Esperanto correspondence and how rapidly he had taken up Esperanto correspondence—"while [he] was still memorizing the grammar."[64] This stresses the value of these encounters, not only in terms of strategy and international politics, but also in terms of personal experience. The impact of contacts from socialists struggling abroad was a powerful symbol of the internationalism inherent within the (Esperanto) proletarian movement. Yutaka went on to recommend *Marushu*, as well as other socialist magazines, such as *Surposteno* (Leningrad?) and Shanghai's *La Mondo*, as ideal places to advertise for correspondence partners, and advocated sending photos or swapping books and stamps to cement burgeoning friendships.

These activities continued throughout the proletarian Esperanto movement. In 1931, activists opened a Japanese branch of Proleta Esperanto Korespondado (PEK, Proletarian Esperanto Correspondence), an organization of Russian origin that sought to encourage the building of networks, connecting groups as well as individuals "factory to factory, farming village to farming village, nation to nation."[65] For the Soviets, PEK represented an attempt to control the sort of bottom-up networks of contact that had been developing, in order to better manage the flow of information through Esperanto, but their recommendation of group letter writing was also noted as a good way of offsetting the challenges that one individual learner with limited Esperanto ability faced in writing letters.[66]

The authors of the *Proletaria Esuperanto Kōza* suggested that "the most important meaning of Esperanto for the world proletariat comprises its practical use for the class struggle—just as the proletariat's struggle is not limited by race or borders or language, Esperanto ignores national borders and linguistic difference."[67] Putting aside the materialist theory of a universal proletarian language to come, this focused on the practicalities of a common language in the present struggle against capitalism and fascism. Esperanto could be a powerful tool for sharing news, strategy, and Comintern guidance. Edwin Michielsen demonstrates that the language's practical potential was felt by proletarian writers across East Asia, imbuing it with an anticolonial power to breach boundaries.[68]

Perhaps the most notable example of the use of Esperanto networks for the flow of information into Japan was the translation of the "Dimitrov thesis" resulting from the seventh Comintern Congress in 1935. This congress marked the official turning point toward a united front approach in the struggle against fascism, in which communists worldwide were advised to work together with social democrats and other progressive political groups that hitherto had been rejected. Georgi Dimitrov's speech to the Congress came to be seen, in Japan at least, as the key analysis for the need for this policy.

However, the first versions of the speech to reach Japan were only a summary of Dimitrov's words, and a full script of the speech remained elusive.[69] It was only in 1936, when a number of the remaining proletarian Esperanto organizations received Esperanto-language translations of the text, that a full Japanese version could be produced. A number of different groups worked in secret on a translation—one in Kobe, one in Nagoya, and one in Tokyo.[70] However, the key effort was undertaken by Takaragi Yutaka, then only twenty years old, in Osaka. Takaragi, the key figure in the local Puro-Esu group Furāto (Frato, or Brother), was introduced to a local JCP organizer, Fujii Hideo, by a mutual friend, Kurisu Tsugunoshin. By then, the Esperanto texts had been joined by English and German versions, so the two men collaborated on a full translation, working in secret and taking great precautions to avoid being linked by the authorities.[71] The final translation was completed in the spring of 1936, and two illegal pamphlets were published that summer: one the full text, and the other a set of excerpts.[72]

Individual Efforts

While the practice of letter writing formed a continuity through the history of proletarian Esperanto, the years of the PEA and the PEU especially saw competing interests in the form of a focus on revolutionary theory. In the words of one PEU secretary, Sakai Matsutarō: "I didn't participate because I especially liked Esperanto, but because I was attracted by the revolutionary movement . . . this was, perhaps, true of most of us at the time."[73] By contrast, he described how Nakagaki Kojirō, one of the Kashiwagi Rondo founders, had been criticized by his younger, more theoretically inclined comrades as "technicalist" (技術的) or "politically blockheaded" (政治的鈍感) because of his refusal to get involved with the theoretical discussions.[74] The end of the PEU and the move toward regional groups operating on a smaller scale acted to weed out these more instrumental participants, leaving only those who were deeply interested in the language in its own right.

Faced with ongoing state suspicion, and with many of the key participants laboring under the shadow of suspended prison sentences, the smaller-scale organizations of the post-PEU era could not hope to produce magazines or textbooks with the professionalism or the sales volume of the PEA and PEU. Their publications were much less accomplished, mimeographed magazines with much smaller distributions, and their most notable achievements tended to be centered more upon individual initiative rather than groups and organization.

Takaragi's translation of the Dimitrov speech was one example; three others are considered here: Nakagaki Kojirō's work with Chinese expatriates, Saitō Hidekatsu's work on "linguistic imperialism," and Hasegawa Teru's move to China. All four of these grew out of what remained when the proletarian arts movement and PEU ceased to be able to operate, making use of the personal connections built through those structures. And significantly, they all retained important transnational connections to other nations' proletarian Esperantists—which meant that all continued to attract the suspicion of the state.

Nakagaki Kojirō was one of the members of the Kashiwagi Rondo, which had first bridged the gap between JEI-centered Esperanto and the distinct proletarian Esperanto movement. It was he whose lack of interest in the political niceties of the Comintern guidance had earned the criticism of other, less linguistically inclined members of the PEU. In the wake of the collapse of the PEU, he joined another former Kashiwagi Rondo member, Ōshima Yoshio, in setting up the Esperanto Bungaku Kenkyūkai (Esperanto Literature Research Association) together with a number of other Esperantists from both sides of the neutral/progressive divide. This represented a side step away from politics to focus more on explicitly linguistic issues, seeking to "raise the linguistic level of Esperantists as a whole," although their work on translation included a large number of proletarian writers.[75]

In 1936, Nakagaki rejoined the JEI. This was motivated by his growing involvement with a small group of Chinese expatriate students. In December 1935, *La Revuo Orienta* had reported the creation of the Chūka-Ryūnichi Sekaigo Gakkai (Sekaigo Institute for Chinese in Japan).[76] This group was created in recognition of the barriers to full participation within the usual JEI classes experienced by aspiring Chinese Esperantists, as a result of their poor Japanese skills.[77] The number of Chinese students resident in Japan had grown steadily after a dip in the aftermath of the Manchurian Incident, and just like the Chinese students taught by Ōsugi Sakae thirty years before, many of them found themselves drawn to the idea of Esperanto.[78]

JEI member Okamoto Yoshitsuku was the first person to act as a teacher for the group (about forty or so people), while Nakagaki began to participate in early 1936.[79] After two successful cycles of classes, organization of a third cycle stalled, and Nakagaki decided to host the interested students at his own house. Some ten or so of the original forty Chinese expats continued, including some who Nakagaki became close to, such as Deng Keqiang and Huang Nai. In the summer of 1937, after the group had been active for more than a year, the authorities stepped in to break it up. Nakagaki was arrested and several of the Chinese students were expelled from Japan.[80]

In arresting Nakagaki and his Chinese friends, the authorities described the group as representing "the shoots of a reestablishment of red Esperanto."[81] They pointed to the use of banned texts and Nakagaki's ties to the proletarian Esperanto movement, but significantly also to the students' contact with communist Esperantists in Shanghai who were "under the guidance of the Soviet Esperanto League in Moscow."[82]

While Nakagaki came from the generation of young Esperantists who had made the break from JEI-centered neutral Esperanto into the proletarian arts movement, by contrast Saitō Hidekatsu was younger. The son of a Sōtō Zen priest based in rural Yamagata, Saitō took up Esperanto in 1928 while studying at Komazawa University.[83] Although he did join the JEI as he became involved in the Esperanto movement, the bulk of his interest rapidly centered on more radical analyses of language, and so he had become involved in the PEU by the time he graduated in 1931.

Saitō's engagement with Esperanto was a part of a wider interest in what we would now term sociolinguistics—the interplay between (written) language and society, including the rōmaji movement and studies of dialects. During the early 1930s, Saitō worked as a *kokugo* teacher, also forming a rōmaji study group in the rural primary school at which he taught.[84] These interests stood out in his rural village—in his diary he recorded talk of being shunned by other villagers—and he had a bad relationship with his headmaster.[85] This all came to a head while Saitō was away visiting his parents in September 1932. The headmaster entered his quarters, taking stock of Saitō's reading matter and the various drafts he had littered around. Alarmed at what he saw, the headmaster fired Saitō the moment the young man returned to the village, then reported him to the police as a suspected radical. Saitō was arrested a few days later along with two colleagues as part of a group alleged to be using the cover of a rōmaji study group to engage in a "left-wing culture war."[86] This proved to be the end of Saitō's teaching career.

Saitō was arrested two more times in 1932 for distributing left-wing material such as the magazines *Senki* (Battle flag) and *Musan Shōnen* (Proletarian youth).[87] However, his most significant activity was writing and producing his own magazines. Between 1932 and 1938, Saitō published three different magazines—*Rōmaji no Kikansha* (1931–1932), *Moji to Gengo* (1933–1936), and *Latinigo* (1937–1938).[88] The content of these magazines reflected Saitō's interests: Esperanto and global language, script reform, and research on dialects.[89] Throughout the 1930s, in his own magazines and others, he wrote widely—publishing on his own native Shōnai dialect and on Tokyo dialect (important for its role as the base of the national standard *hyōjungo*), but also responding to articles in the wider press in what became a broad critique of Japan's language policies in Korea, Taiwan, and elsewhere, policies he explicitly labeled "linguistic imperialism."[90]

Throughout this, Saitō retained foreign links to others with a mutual interest in transnational language issues and questions of equitable reform. His final magazine, *Latinigo* (Romanization), was an Esperanto-language magazine published in rural Shōnai on a mimeograph machine, just like the other magazines of the post-PEU era. Yet it retained a scale and ambition that marked it out: the two issues ran articles on scripts and Romanization experiments in Japan, China, Mongolia, Indochina, the British Malay States, Germany, and the Soviet Union as well as an advertisement for the Korean Esperanto Association and a "correspondence wanted" item from Siam, with a similarly international list of authors.[91]

Saitō's interest in materialist linguistics and the social impact of language and language policy, as well as his ties to foreign linguists, meant he was of ongoing interest to the police. After an interview in 1933 in which the authorities displayed a knowledge of the contents of his diary, Saitō took to writing it in code.[92] In 1938, by then working in the library at Tōhoku University, police scrutiny of Saitō snowballed into a larger investigation into proletarian politics within linguistic studies. The "Left Wing Language Movement Incident" involved the arrest and interview of a number of Esperantist and rōmaji proponents who had written for Saitō's magazines over later 1938 and 1939. Saitō was charged with violation of the Peace Preservation Law and held for more than a year. A poem he wrote while incarcerated reveals something of the authorities' suspicions of Saitō's blend of transnational activism and language reform:

> "Making the Roman alphabet the national script? It's a dream!" says the assistant inspector with apparent confidence.
> Joining force with my rōmaji friend in China; He's fanning the flames of anti-Japanese feeling, they say.[93]

In 1940 Saitō contracted tuberculosis and was released home, where he died six months later.[94]

The final and best-known example of post-PEU individual transnational activities is the case of Hasegawa Teru. Her antiwar and anti-imperial efforts have attracted attention in the academy and beyond, focusing on her as a rare voice against the Japanese war effort, or as an advocate of women's rights.[95]

Hasegawa was born in 1912 in Tokyo; she became involved with Esperanto in 1931 as a student at a teacher training school in Nara. Like Saitō and Nakagaki, she rapidly joined the left-wing Esperanto movement, was arrested in the early 1930s, and, as the movement fractured, looked to pursue smaller-scale projects, such as the post-PEU magazine *Esuperanto Bungaku* with Nakagaki Kojirō and Ōshima Yoshio. Also like Nakagaki, she came into contact with the left-wing Chinese Esperantists, writing for the Shanghai journal *La Mondo* in 1935, and then in 1936 meeting another of the expatriate Chinese student Esperantists, Liu Ren, whom she married in secret the following year.[96]

Liu returned to China in early 1937, and Hasegawa followed him shortly afterward. The two arrived in Shanghai just before the Marco Polo Bridge Incident and the outbreak of full war between their two countries: as the war spread, Hasegawa elected to lend her efforts to the Chinese anti-Japanese resistance, abandoning thoughts of returning to Japan. The war merged personal and political for Hasegawa and Liu—she responded by writing (under the pseudonym Verda Majo, "Green May") antiwar propaganda for the Esperanto journal *Ĉinio Hurlas* (China screams), such as a translation of a letter written to her parents by a Japanese woman married to a Chinese man.[97] By 1938, the two made it into Chinese-controlled territory, to Hankou, where they continued to produce propaganda—Hasegawa now broadcasting in Japanese over the radio.[98] Eventually the Japanese authorities discerned the identity of "Verda Majo," and one of the national newspapers published it, together with an interview with Hasegawa's father, brandishing her as a "treasonous woman."[99]

By the late 1930s, the proletarian Esperanto movement was almost fully dead in Japan: national-level organizations and smaller, regional ones were broken up, and various individuals were dead (notably Takaragi Yutaka and Saitō Hidekatsu, both of tuberculosis), forced into inactivity or nonpolitical endeavors, or, in the case of Hasegawa, fled to China. Proletarian Esperanto, as a distinct entity in Japan, therefore had a life of a decade or thereabouts. Even within that period, the relationship between Esperanto and communism, or more broadly world language and the left, varied over time, reflecting both theory and context: proletarian Esperantists organizing in different ways, engaging in different activities, and articulating different visions in response to both their own ideas of what Esperanto represented to the proletarian struggle and the changing landscape of national and international politics. Yet through it all, the central truth of Esperanto as a language of practical use remained—permitting effective communication and exchange across national and linguistic borders. While this had much in common with the "bourgeois" Esperantists from whom the proletarian Esperantists sought to distinguish themselves, it was also one of the key ways in which those proletarian movements linked the language and the politics: symbolically through the sense of transnational solidarity, theoretically through the idea of a language that could overcome nationalism, and practically through the sharing of information. And, no less significantly, it helps explain why red Esperanto remained a central danger in the eyes of the state—the language permitting the introduction of foreign guidance, directly from Moscow, or via other proletarian groups in other nations.

If the proletarian Esperanto movement represented a break from what became known as the "neutral" or mainstream movement, those Esperantists still faced their own challenges during the 1930s. The first challenge was to avoid being tarred by the same brush as the proletarian movement—something that remained a cause of concern for them as the decade continued. A second challenge was to reconcile their visions of world language to a context that was increasingly nationalistic at home and combative abroad. The ways in which the mainstream Esperantists faced Japan's move toward militarism and imperial war form the subject of the next chapter.

CHAPTER 6

Imperial Language

On November 28, 1936, Eugène Lanti, the French anarchist founder of the "non-national" Esperanto organization SAT, arrived in Yokohama. Lanti had been advised not to come to Japan: the JEI was concerned his presence would reflect badly upon them and upon Esperanto, so had written to Lanti in Portugal to tell him that they would be passing on his travel plans to the authorities.[1] Nevertheless, he made his way through entry checks with no real incident, delayed only when officials decided to confiscate a book titled *The Japanese Danger*.[2] Lanti believed that he was allowed into the country only because by disembarking at Yokohama rather than his ticketed destination of Kobe, he encountered immigration officials who were not aware that the innocuous-seeming French pensioner Eugène Adam and the dangerous radical Lanti were in fact one and the same.

Lanti was on an expedition to visit Esperantists across the world. The year he spent in Japan was uneven: by 1937 there were essentially no proletarian Esperanto organizations left; nevertheless, he was visited by police in his first days in the country and warned to avoid association with anyone who had been a member of one of those groups. Based at first in Tokyo, his relationship with the politically neutral JEI was very uneasy.[3] He eventually moved on from the capital to places where the police presence proved less overbearing: spending the summer of 1937 in rural Ishikawa Prefecture with a Buddhist Esperantist, Takeuchi Tōkichi, before moving to Osaka, where the atmosphere also proved to be more relaxed than Tokyo.

In Osaka, Lanti fell in with the Esperanto circles based around the monthly magazine *Tempo*.[4] *Tempo* was an all-Esperanto magazine, issued by the publishing house Kaniya and its owner, Nakahara Shūji. Kaniya was a publisher specializing in books for students, but it had been involved in Esperanto publishing since at least 1921. In 1934 Nakahara had launched *Tempo*, which featured articles on current affairs as well as popular science, poetry, and the Esperanto scene.[5] Lanti never met Nakahara. When the Frenchman was in Osaka, the Japanese publisher was in Europe attending the UEA Congress as a part of an attempt to secure a later congress for Japan; by the time he returned, Lanti had moved on to Australia.[6]

The 1930s in Japan was a time typically characterized by the rising tide of nationalism and militarism. Looked at one way, the experiences of Lanti and Nakahara reflect that narrative: ongoing police suspicion of Esperanto's ties to the left and an understandable reluctance by many to risk police involvement. However, looked at another way, the view of an increasingly repressive society is less comprehensive: Esperantists remained active in the major cities and in rural backwaters, they were acting in increasingly sophisticated ways (such as supporting an all-Esperanto magazine of high publishing standards), and they remained active in the global movement, visiting Europe and arguing to bring the main international congress to Japan.

While it is tempting to assume that the early 1930s, marked by Japan's aggression in Manchuria and subsequent exit from the League of Nations in 1933, would prove antithetical to the sort of internationalist stance that motivated the Esperanto movement, the reality is more complex. Jessamyn Abel has shown that the Manchurian Incident did not mark the end of the Japanese government's desire to collaborate and cooperate in international activity.[7] The same is true of the Japanese Esperantists: many of them found new purpose in the "time of crisis," and new uses to which they could put their language. Moreover, the international language problem remained, taking on different stresses as Japan's position in the world was increasingly focused less on the West and more on a regional Asian framework.

In arguing that Japan's linguistic history has an international dimension, I have hitherto chiefly considered Japan in a national context. However, particularly in the first half of the twentieth century, it also had an important imperial one. The early boundaries between the Japanese nation and the Japanese Empire are somewhat ambiguous: while the Ryukyu Islands and Hokkaido were included within the borders of the nation-state, their development and incorporation had imperialistic dimensions. Language policy is a case in point: the use of the education system to spread the standardized language to Japan's national peripheries was the model for later strategy in Taiwan, Japan's first formal colony.[8] Indeed, these developments took place alongside the creation of the concept of *kokugo*. That is, Japanese was becoming an imperial language at the same time as it was becoming a national one.

There is a direct parallel between the Japanese language and the idealized Japanese emperor—between *kokugo* and the *kokutai*. In the context of the Japanese nation-state, this was relatively straightforward: to be Japanese was to be a subject of the emperor, and it was also to speak the Japanese language. The twin myths of the imperial line and the common Japanese language represented a connection both in space and time—bringing together all the existing subjects of the Japanese state with their ancestors in ages past. This ideological equation was both produced by and necessitated the processes of linguistic reform and spread that mark much of the modern history of the Japanese language.

However, in the context of the Japanese Empire, things were more complicated. There was a tension at the heart of the Japanese Empire between impulses to help integrate or assimilate colonial peoples and the need to retain a hierarchical distinction between them and the Japanese themselves. Here, too, language was central. Clause 4 of the 1911 Imperial Rescript on Education in Korea stated that the Japanese language was the *kokugo* of Korea.[9] Ensuring that colonial subjects in Korea and Taiwan were able to speak the Japanese language would help to assimilate them under the umbrella of the emperor's rule. However, the use of Japanese also marked boundaries. The distinction between the Japanese people and their colonial subjects was articulated in different ways, of which language was one: distinguishing between "those who habitually use[d] the national language" and those who did not.[10] Over time, efforts to spread Japanese language use throughout Taiwan and Korea were augmented by bans on the use of native languages within schools.[11] Linguistically, as well as politically, the Taiwanese and Korean people found themselves denied their own linguistic identity, but also prevented from full equality with the Japanese.

Japanese had thus been an imperial language since the beginnings of the Meiji period; by 1930 it had had status in Taiwan and Korea for thirty-five and twenty years, respectively. Nevertheless, the creation of Manchukuo in 1932 marked a new phase of Japanese imperialism again and, by extension, a new phase of Japan's imperial language problem. Whereas, prior to the creation of Manchukuo, the state policies of the Japanese language only had to distinguish between the *naichi* (Japanese home islands) and the *gaichi* (the colonies—essentially Korea and Taiwan), the full inclusion of Manchuria into the Japanese orbit, and then other parts of China, and eventually also the Southeast Asian territories captured in 1942, each with its own linguistic profile, history, and political status, made for a broad and complex problem, with practical and ideological dimensions.

Just as in the previous iteration a generation earlier, the Japanese language was motivated to knit together the Greater East Asia Co-Prosperity Sphere through processes of imperialization (*kōminka*).[12] However, how to effect this in practice, and to establish a lingua franca for easy practical communication across multilinguistic, multiethnic territory, under the conditions of war and at short notice, was much less clear.

While the literal translation of *kokugo* as "national language" perhaps obscures the international nature of the Japanese language's presence across East Asia, ideas of transnational and transcultural communication were central to the problems and debates experienced during the period. The Japanese Empire of the 1930s was a multiethnic and multinational region in which ideas of cooperation and collaboration ran, once again, into issues of communication and common language.

This chapter examines the history of international language during the period of the fifteen-year war (1931–1945) in three ways: by looking at how Esperanto and Esperantists adapted to the changing international and domestic context, by looking at how they sought to use their language beyond the Japanese Empire in order to communicate Japan's position, and by outlining their contributions to the debates surrounding language and language policy within the Japanese Empire itself.

In the face of a changing context, Japanese Esperantists continued to practice their language, advocate for it, and try to find common cause with prevailing national policies. Thus, even as the violence inherent in Japan's presence in continental Asia became starker, they continued to work in ways that cannot simply be characterized as collaboration with the militarists, resistance against them, or withdrawal. Ulrich Lins portrays the Esperantists of 1930s Japan as seeking to navigate a narrow path, disavowing association with the radical left but also avoiding "go[ing] to the other extreme by aligning themselves with the military government." Rather, he argues that they stuck to "the principle [of neutrality] . . . in resisting the pressure to commit to the prevailing ideology."[13] I argue that relations were more complicated: while in hindsight we see a contradiction inherent in the idea of internationalist cooperation with the Japanese continental policy of the 1930s, we must also recognize that at the time, many saw things differently. Rather than pick apart what appear in the present day to be inconsistencies or contradictions within historic actors' thinking and actions, my aim here is to seek to understand their perspectives and to recognize the genuine difficulties of navigating the different perspectives of such a tumultuous period. Esperanto, as a language, as a model, and as a cluster of ideas about international language, remained salient even during the 1930s and early 1940s. That the idea of a patriotic Esperanto movement made sense to many Japanese Esperantists of the 1930s makes it a phenomenon that warrants close examination.

Peak Esperanto: Japan in the Early Shōwa Era

The end of the First World War and the resultant "Wilsonian moment" represented the most favorable tailwind for both global and Japanese Esperanto. It was then that the second wave of the movement in Japan began and practice of the language grew the fastest. However, while the international and domestic contexts of the early 1930s were less obviously conducive to calls for an international language, nevertheless in many respects this was the period in which the prewar movement was at its most active and its most sophisticated.

Membership of the JEI peaked in the late 1920s, but attendance at its congresses continued to grow beyond then, into the next decade. Hatsushiba argues that the true peak of prewar Esperanto in Japan was the early 1930s—a period when everyday awareness of the language was at its highest, major bookstores maintained Esperanto shelves, and general activity was at its most diverse.[14] The decline in JEI membership in the late 1920s and early 1930s is likely reflective not only of the hiving off of the socialist wing of the movement, but also Esperanto's general diversification and the growth of other subsidiary associations. By the Shōwa era, an increasing number of clubs were devoted to promoting Esperanto in more specialist contexts—not only regional subgroups but also specific professions, religions, and the like. Rather than join the JEI, a young Esperantist in 1932 would be increasingly likely to join instead the Japan Buddhist Esperanto League, the association of Japanese Railway workers, the Clara-Kai (of women Esperantists), or their local club.

The 1932 Japanese Esperanto congress, held in Tokyo, had meetings of twelve separate subgroups. Many of these had origins in the 1920s or even earlier, but as they grew, they also grew more sophisticated and organized. For example, Esperantists were active in Buddhist circles (including Otani and Ryūkoku Universities) from at least the early 1920s, but the Japana Budhana Ligo Esperantista (Japanese Buddhist League of Esperantists, the JBLE) was not formed until 1931.[15]

Likewise, while scientists had been well represented in Esperanto circles since at least as early as the meteorologist Nakamura Kiyō's assumption of a leading role in the 1910s, they only formed a distinct identity in 1935, with the formation of the Nihon Esuperanto Kagaku Kyōkai (Japanese Esperanto Science Association). This group had ninety-four members by 1936, although it published a list of Esperantists active in science and technology that ran to 350 names (increased to over five hundred by 1938), reiterating the idea of different circles of Esperanto membership and activity. The association also published a magazine, *Scienco*, from 1936 until 1939.[16] By contrast, the medical profession had organized somewhat earlier, forming the Hipokratida Klubo in 1923 (later renamed the Eskulapida Klubo).

Nathan Shockey notes that the *Nihon-shiki* style romanization of Japanese scripts appealed to many scientists as "rational and efficient."[17] To a large degree there was a similar appeal to Esperanto, through the rational conception of a modernizing language discussed in chapter 1, but many scientists were also drawn to it by more mundane experiences of the difficulty of communicating with scientific peers overseas, and the allure of easier alternatives. Both general scientists and medical doctors engaged in a series of similar activities: participating in a global effort to standardize the Esperanto versions of their specialized vocabularies, writing Esperanto summaries of their work for a general audience, and also publishing more detailed versions of their work in Esperanto in the hope of reaching a wider audience.[18] In doing so, they were not alone: Michael Gordin's work on the international languages of science shows that scientists worldwide were drawn to the idea of a systematized, regular, rational language of international communication.[19]

A number of scientists made even more substantial efforts to use Esperanto to further their work. One example was Murata Masataka, a medical doctor and researcher. Murata had caused some controversy while at university in the 1920s, refusing to take one of his exams in German, as the unwritten norm demanded, and going on to argue that Japanese was the only language that Japanese medicine should use (a view that he later admitted proved highly unpopular among his colleagues and mentors).[20] But when he was drawn to Esperanto, he became a very active advocate, seeking to promote it among the medical community, publishing his research into diagnosis of syphilis in the language, and presenting in it at the fourth Far-Eastern Conference on Tropical Medicine.[21] Later, as the head of the Sotojima hospice for Hansen's disease, Murata introduced Esperanto classes for patients as one of a number of liberalizing measures.[22]

Another scientist who sought to use Esperanto to further the reach of his research, albeit one whose experience shows the limits of it as a strategy, was Ōishi Wasaburō. Ōishi was another of the meteorologist Esperantists who traced their involvement in the language to Nakamura Kiyō (and indeed another who went on to occupy a senior role in the language movement, instrumental in the creation of the JEI before becoming its president in the 1940s).[23] He was trained in the 1910s in France and Germany before returning to Japan to run a high-altitude observation station. From the mid-1920s onward he published the station's annual reports and other publications in Esperanto. These included his observations of the high-altitude, high-speed winds that came to be known as the jet stream. While the publications led to little if any wider awareness of Ōishi's work (the jet stream's discovery has been traditionally traced to Chicago in the immediate postwar period, following the experiences of military pilots during World War II), they nevertheless demonstrate the extent to which the language had become not just an object of study but also an object of practical use for some Japanese scientists by the 1930s.[24]

Developing infrastructure and technology also helped the spread and scale of Japanese Esperanto activity. The growth of radio from JOAK in Tokyo and JOBK in Osaka in 1925 to a nationwide network of stations including Taiwan, Korea, and Manchuria was rapidly picked up on by Esperantists, who participated in programs introducing the language to listeners and even short courses. The first course—spanning three months, twice weekly on JQAK in Dairen—was as early as 1926, while the first one in the Japanese mainland was on JOCK in Nagoya in 1927. They continued to run into the 1930s, culminating in a month-long course in 1932 that ran simultaneously nationwide, across ten different stations.[25] The courses seem to have proven popular: one course (Tokyo in 1927) reportedly sold fifteen thousand copies of its supporting textbook, five times the initial print run of three thousand.[26]

In 1931, the JEI launched a new monthly magazine, *Shotō Esuperanto*, that ran alongside *La Revuo Orienta* and was designed specifically for students of the language. Running to about two thousand copies per issue, the JEI launched a push in 1933 to make it available in bookstores nationwide.[27] The study of Esperanto, too, developed, with an increasing interest in the *parola metodo* (the spoken method) of learning.[28] Originally pioneered by André Cseh in Europe during the mid 1920s, the *parola* method focused on the spoken language rather than the written.[29] Coinciding with the rapid growth in Esperanto on the radio and the availability of vinyl discs of Esperanto conversation, this marked a further example of the growing maturity of the Japanese movement: a rounding-out of Esperanto experience and practice to include a more balanced understanding of the language as both spoken and written.

Esperanto in a Time of National Crisis: Toward a Patriotic Language Movement

The sophistication and volume of all this activity serve to show that Esperanto was increasingly a mature phenomenon in 1930s Japan, one with a reach across the country and society. However, it was also one that had intellectual work to do in order to adapt to the changing context. The first part of this was arguing for the clear distinction between socialist Esperanto and the mainstream (when the JEI surveyed its members in 1934 about their most pressing concerns, this was the one most commonly articulated). However, the general international context also mattered: one respondent to the survey argued that "the time of crisis for [Japanese] society is one for us Esperantists, too."[30] Japanese Esperantists, as Japanese subjects like any other, faced the crisis of Japan's increasing isolation. But at the same time, they worked to reconceptualize their language and movement as a part of the crisis's solution, through the emergence of a "patriotic" strain of Esperanto that sought to find common ground between the movement's vision of a united world and national objectives of regional dominance.

In repositioning Esperanto as a language and movement congruent with the changing wider environment, Esperantists looked to previous articulations of the relationship between nation and international language: "True Patriotism is never in opposition to a love of mankind . . . Esperantism is deeply filled with the love of mankind; however, it must not be forgotten that it is also steeped in this true meaning of patriotism."[31]

Indeed, Japanese Esperantists argued that Zamenhof himself had argued that "Esperantismo, which preaches love, and patriotism, which also preaches love, can never be hostile to one another."[32] This view was repeated in various different forms, arguing, for example, that "were one to abandon one's own national language to use another's national language, it might be thought of as unpatriotic, but the use of an international, unaffiliated language is unobjectionable,"[33] and cautioning that "if we Esperantists have forgotten this, how can we expect non-Esperantists to know it."[34]

This was not a new set of ideas; rather it was the movement of a hitherto marginal view toward the center. One example of this was the debates of 1919–1921 surrounding the nature of Esperantism as explored in chapter 2, with Chifu Toshio seeking to articulate a patriotic perspective that was out of step with the weight of opinion. The shift can perhaps be seen even more clearly in the reception to an essay by the Japanese Esperanto pioneer Kuroita Katsumi. Kuroita wrote the essay for the magazine *Taiyō* in 1915, when it seemed somewhat counter to prevailing sentiment; by 1932 things had changed, and the JEI revisited the essay, printing it as a part of a pamphlet outlining their basic stance.[35]

Kuroita's essay laid out a three-part structure: placing the Japanese language in a framework of national unity, critiquing Japanese approaches to foreign languages, and arguing that Esperanto was the answer to these problems. Stressing the importance of the Japanese language to national unity was a familiar position; connecting it to a critique of the presence of foreign languages in Japanese daily life was more unusual. While Kuroita argued that Japan's linguistic unity was more successful than, say, China with its geographic variation, he suggested that the incursions of foreign languages represented a threat to the unifying power of Japanese, undermining the country's linguistic vitality. It was English, in particular, that was the key threat: English was increasingly indispensable in daily life, appearing in newspapers, in government documents, on tobacco papers, on railway tickets, and at post offices, and worse, was integrally embedded within the middle school curriculum. Kuroita argued that only the adoption of Esperanto, in its guise of a neutral third language, could Japan ensure a buffer between *kokugo* and the incursions of English and others.

In stressing Esperanto as an auxiliary language—a second language with no presumption of replacing or interfering with people's primary tongues—it could be positioned as no threat to national prestige, and even capable of a patriotic contribution. It is tempting to see this vision of Esperanto as a patriotic barrier to foreign incursions as paradoxical or contradictory, to see Kuroita as either blinded to the nature of "true" internationalism or cynically manipulating it. However, Jessamyn Abel cautions us to resist the impulse to fall back on reductive ideas of internationalism's innate nature.[36] Instead, we can take Kuroita's argument at face value and seek to understand it, and perceive in the activities of Japanese Esperantists of the 1930s a genuine attempt to navigate the political currents of that most turbulent of decades. Rather than read their activities as wrong or misconstrued, we should read them to learn more about the ways in which the national and the global interact and relate to one another.

This mode of understanding of both the concept of internationalism and the 1930s as a moment does lead to some additional difficulties: in taking the internationalism of 1930s Japan seriously, we face problems of interpretation. If internationalism cannot be treated as innately progressive, then we have to recognize that it becomes hard to discern which actors and organizations were making use of internationalist (and relatedly Pan-Asian) rhetoric for instrumental reasons and those who were sincere. Indeed, this is not simply a problem of historical analysis: contemporary actors themselves had to wrestle with how to understand developments in international and regional politics and different actors' claims about contested motivations.

Rather than representing a death blow to calls for the establishment of a common international language and international understanding, the diplomatic crisis of 1931–1933 reprioritized the aims and objectives of the Japanese Esperanto movement and the ways in which people thought about their project. Just as Abel demonstrates that "the Japanese government continued to participate in ostensibly non-political League activities . . . supported the promotion of Japanese culture abroad, and experimented with regional forms of international organization," so too Japanese Esperantists continued to interact with the major international Esperanto organizations, used their language to press the Japanese case abroad, and increasingly thought about regional Asian problems of language.[37]

Citizens' Diplomacy

Kuroita's fear was that Japan's dysfunctional relationship with foreign languages represented a threat to its linguistic purity and to national unity as a result. By the early 1930s, others were arguing that the relationship was also influencing Japan's foreign position in more prosaic ways. One key Japanese claim in the wake of the Manchurian scandal was that the Western criticism of Japan's actions was the result of a failure of understanding of both Japan's nature and the regional situation, not least because of the success of Chinese propaganda (and the corresponding failure of Japanese): "Through the Chinese people's inherent language ability and traditional skills of propaganda, they have worked vigorously in the field of international propaganda such that they are gaining the sympathies of small countries with little contact with the orient and distant from events, and even created a mistaken understanding of our nation among foreigners with insufficient knowledge."[38] This provided Japanese Esperantists with a singular position to fulfill what the translator Nohara Kyūichi called their "duty as Japanese Esperantists"—to make use of their language abilities and networks of transnational contacts to promote the Japanese perspective on events in East Asia in order to correct this mistaken perspective.[39] Japan had won the military conflict but was losing the international war of opinions in the Esperanto sphere as well as others: "Despite it being well known that Chinese Esperantists of every region are, without exception, sending out false manifestos, appealing for the support of our fellow Esperantists [samideanoj] of all nations, our country's Esperanto organizations are without a plan."[40] Rectifying this was not just a national priority; recall that the central premise of Zamenhof's vision was that linguistic confusion was a barrier to true understanding and thereby peace. If one accepted the claim that Japanese actions and East Asian affairs were being fundamentally misunderstood internationally, then this was a transparent proof of Zamenhof's vision: "Taking up our Esperanto to make clear our nation's position and to explain to foreigners the traditional Japanese spirit, based upon justice and humanity, is not only our duty as Japanese, it is the only path in union with Dr Zamenhof's Homaranismo."[41]

Japanese Esperantists' efforts to explain their nation's expansion grew out of a prior body of writing about the Japanese presence on the continent. From the outset, Japanese Esperantists had been connected to China and elsewhere, professionally and through their language. Writers such as Fujisawa Chikao had written about their personal experiences, increasingly exploring the Japanese colonial possessions (as much for a domestic audience as an overseas one, in the first instance), while the whole area had been one in which Esperantists of varying nationality had met and interacted.[42] Later, the JEI also made use of sympathetic foreigners to produce accounts of the Japanese Empire, by translating an *Asahi Shinbun* article written by the Frenchman Claude Farrère and through a mirroring effort of their own involving a Hungarian Esperantist, Istvan Mezey.[43]

Another example of these efforts to promote a Japanese perspective through Esperanto networks was that of Ogasawara Yoshio, a businessman and local politician based in Wakayama. Ogasawara, born in 1868, had been involved in the Freedom and People's Rights movement and later became a Unitarian Christian.[44] In 1929 he formed what he called the Kokusai Nichiyō Gakkō (International Sunday School), linked to the Wakayama branch of the Japanese League of Nations Association, the quasi-official organization designed to promote the League and its activities.[45] Membership in the Sunday school grew to over one hundred, and the association's membership to two hundred; particular events such as the visit of an American missionary H. H. Guy, and later of fifteen students from Shantung Christian University drew even larger attendance.[46] However, the events of 1931–1933 hit activity hard. Ogasawara removed the League of Nations from the organization's title, but still attendance fell significantly. In his ongoing efforts to promote transnational activity and intercultural understanding, Ogasawara discovered Esperanto. The school's first attempts at studying the language, in 1931, were not successful, but in 1933–1934 they had more luck, building a more sustainable program. Notable among their activities was a pair of advertisements for pen pals placed in the European magazine *Heroldo de Esperanto*, which reportedly received more than one thousand replies on each occasion, from more than forty countries.[47]

In 1934, Ogasawara launched a small, self-published Esperanto-language magazine, *La Suno*. Building upon his previous work attempting to build connections between different nations (and particularly their children), the magazine's motivating philosophy was in direct accordance with the perspective that common language could enhance mutual understanding: aiming to communicate Japan, Japanese culture, and a Japanese perspective to the wider world in order to correct what Ogasawara saw as mistaken views of Asia. He funded the printing costs himself and offered to send the magazine free to anyone who requested a copy: although it was short and irregularly published (only running to nine issues between 1934 and 1939), he reportedly sent it to two thousand recipients in more than fifty nations.[48]

The consistent message of *La Suno*, reflecting the context of its publication, was an attempt to rectify "a constant error regarding the nation of Japan, which regrettably is reproached for its militarism."[49] Ogasawara sought to argue that the contemporary events within China were part of a Japanese effort to maintain peace and stability in the region, and to place them within a two-thousand-year-long history of Japanese peace. Ogasawara's stance can be seen as a part of the broader set of discourses citing a mistaken understanding of Japanese character and motivation, the distorting effect of Chinese propaganda, and frustration at Western hypocrisy within the League of Nations.

La Suno was not solely devoted to contemporary international relations. The misunderstanding that Ogasawara diagnosed in the West was not just framed in terms of Japanese actions; as suggested above it was a wider misunderstanding of Japanese character and civilization. Thus, the magazine sought to introduce other topics of wider Japanese culture and history to its audience.[50] It was not alone in doing so. Early magazines, such as *Orienta Azio*, focused on providing Esperanto-language introductions to Japanese arts and folktales. There was a parallel history of Japanese-to-Esperanto translation, focusing on poetry and short stories drawn from ancient and modern literature. The 1930s context placed these efforts into a more political light: efforts at articulating Japanese arts and literature within a conception of the creation of a world culture became a cultural dimension of the struggle to correct the "mistaken understanding of Japan."

The most significant single effort at translation as cultural communication was the work of Nohara Kyūichi. Nohara worked throughout the 1930s, translating Japanese classics into Esperanto. He started with short works such as the *Hōjōki*, but culminated in *Kroniko Japana*, a five-volume version of the *Nihon Shoki*, one of the foundational Japanese myths/histories. As a result, in 1939, Nohara was the first recipient of what became (and remains) an annual prize for contributions to Japanese Esperanto, the Osaka Prize.[51] In establishing the prize, JEI president Ōishi Wasaburō was explicit that it would recognize efforts that were part of a wider patriotic movement: "Today, a time of emergency for the nation-state, Esperantists are using the international language as a weapon, making clear Japan's righteous position, or working at advancing our national culture."[52]

With these efforts, the Esperantists were contributing to what came to be called people's diplomacy (*kokumin gaikō*), a term associated with the Nagata Hidejirō, the retired mayor of Tokyo.[53] Nagata, a firm proponent of Esperanto, was also instrumental in the successful campaign to host the 1940 Olympic Games. The campaign, which began in 1936, is a principal example of the ongoing Japanese internationalism explored by Jessamyn Abel and its complex meanings/readings. The 1936 Berlin Olympics represented a powerful example of the use of the international Games to further national objectives, and a similar desire was one dimension of the Japanese bid. The Olympic movement itself, far from "transcending politics," represents a format almost perfectly designed to permit the insertion of nationalism into internationalism: "by combining the internationalism of the Olympics with the imperial project, the campaign and subsequent preparation for the Tokyo Olympics expressed a kind of imperialist 'internationalism': an ostensibly internationalist activity deployed toward imperialist goals."[54]

The Olympic bid was timed to coincide with the 2,600th anniversary of the claimed origins of the Japanese imperial family; Japanese Esperantists likewise saw this anniversary and the coming of the Olympics as a chance to host the annual Universal Esperanto Association congress, the central global meeting of Esperantists. The campaign was not successful—despite support from the JEI and direct campaigning by Nakahara Shūichi at the Warsaw congress in 1937, the UEA responded that the distance was an insurmountable problem. They argued that as few as perhaps ten European Esperantists would be able to attend a Tokyo congress, and so it was not a viable proposal.[55]

While this problem was no doubt valid, it did risk the perception that the global Esperanto movement remained more interested in Europe than elsewhere. Japan, as the country with the largest non-European Esperanto community, represented a powerful potential proof of Esperanto's global ambition, and yet it was unable to host even one global congress. The European origins of Esperanto were embedded within the language, in the origins of its vocabulary. The Japanese had accepted that this meant the language was relatively more difficult for them to learn than it was for native speakers of Romance languages, even making a virtue of this—arguing, for example, that their efforts would serve as a powerful demonstration of commitment and call for wider adoption.[56] However, the outright refusal to countenance Japan hosting the UEA congress was a point of some frustration. "We still will not have a *universal* congress in Esperanto-land: we must call the current state 'the universal congress in the West' and we must organize on our side a 'universal congress in the East.'"[57] Rebuffed by the UEA and seeing the suspension of the Tokyo Olympics, the 1940 Japanese Esperanto congress celebrated the 2,600th anniversary in a different way, moving the national congress to Miyazaki, home to the main shrine to the first emperor, Jinmu, and a monolithic *Hakkō ichiu* monument.[58]

Japanese Esperanto, then, was a mature and ongoing phenomenon in the early 1930s. Far from a contradiction in terms, the notion of patriotic Esperanto represented a continuation of the movement's previous history. Rather than seeking to navigate a "neutral" path between the radical left on one side and Japanese militarism on the other, the nonradical Japanese Esperantists continued to operate and act in a setting that, while clearly different from that of ten years before, they did not see as precluding the promotion of international cooperation and understanding.

Imperial Language

Esperanto, then, was one medium through which Japanese citizens and groups might hope to communicate their perspectives and culture, and in doing so they formed a part of a wider phenomenon of informal internationalism, or citizens'

Figure 6.1. Poster for the Twenty-Eighth Japanese Esperanto Congress. Image courtesy of the Japanese Esperanto Institute.

diplomacy. However, this was not the only major role that Esperanto and Esperantists were to play in the major issues of the 1930s and early 1940s. The efforts considered thus far have mostly been focused on Japan's connections and communication with the West and within a global frame. The other frame, which was of fundamental importance to early Shōwa Japan, was regional: the Japanese Empire and/or East Asia as a whole. While not global in scale, this was innately international and indeed transcultural and translinguistic. As a result, the international (or perhaps imperial) language problem was a pressing one in this context, too. Indeed, the ideas and practices that made up the Esperanto vision of international language played a role in the debates that arose while thinking about language use in the Japanese Empire.

The first manifestation of this debate in the 1930s was one with a focused scope: the question of the common language of Manchukuo. Manchukuo's creation was cast in terms of a harmonious union of the "five races" (referring to the major ethnicities in the state: Japanese, Korean, Chinese, Manchurian, and Mongolian). This revealed not only the ethnic but also the linguistic diversity of the territory. In the terms of *kokugo*, this was a serious problem to be overcome: Kuroita Katsumi had pointed to the scale of dialectal variation as a cause of national disunity in China, while the leading *kokugogaku* scholar, Hoshina Kōchi, looked to the Austro-Hungarian Empire as an example of a state whose multilinguistic character had helped cause it to fail.[59] In the words of Arakawa Kanjirō, a longtime resident of Manchuria: "Beyond the languages of each of the peoples, a fixed common language for official use is not only vital from the point of view of governing or of uniting the people, I believe that for the execution of national affairs, it cannot be delayed for a single day."[60]

Japanese Esperantists had been connected to Manchuria since the start of the twentieth century, when Takahashi Kunitarō had first picked up the language there. Over the years it proved to be a space of ongoing Esperanto activity and innovation. A Japanese Esperanto society was created in Dalian in 1922, and the South Manchuria Railway Company (SMCR) also had an internal Esperanto club from the early 1920s. While the Japanese dominated this activity, Chinese, Russian, and other Esperantists also took part. Over the decade a series of courses were run by Japanese Esperantists in various towns along the railway lines, building a community of Esperantists numbering in the hundreds who were pioneers in, for example, the use of the radio to promote the language.[61] By the 1930s, they received support from the SMCR, which published an Esperanto guidebook to the region, *Gvidfolio por Vojaĝanto en Manĉŭkŭo*.[62]

Experienced in both the specific space of northeastern China and in the terms of the linguistic issues at hand, Esperantists were keen to contribute to the solution to the problem of what language to choose for Manchukuo, a debate that would be ongoing throughout the 1930s. A roundtable in 1939 featuring four Esperantists with experience of life in Manchukuo revealed that even then, the linguistic diversity of the region was bewildering and problematic: Japanese and Chinese were used as quasi-official languages, but there were far more than the languages of the five recognized peoples of Manchukuo evident in daily life, and even the Japanese on display revealed widespread variation depending on the origins of the expatriate communities there.[63] Even these four discussants, however could not agree on the solution: Yamagata Mitsue argued that a simpler clearer Japanese was an urgent issue; Fujieda Ryōei argued that it was really an issue of Chinese dialects and so a simplified and unified form of Chinese was needed; and Takagi Teiichi suggested that a general principle should developed such that "where the Hinomaru [the Japanese Rising Sun flag] flies, use Japanese; beyond there, use Esperanto."

It was generally accepted that a real barrier to East Asian integration was a perceived wider range of linguistic diversity than the European case, such that a common language (and as urgently, a common script) were issues of concern to many. A few different scripts were proposed, such as a Mango Kana, purportedly in preparation in Manchukuo, or a "new East Asian Esperanto kana alphabet" created by a librarian in Tokyo in 1938.[64] In 1934, preparations for a Pan-Asian conference, organized in part by Ōkawa Shūmei, the Pan-Asian writer later tried

Figure 6.2. Meeting of an Esperanto club, Dairen, 1930s. Image courtesy of the Japanese Esperanto Institute.

at the Tokyo War Crimes Trials, proposed the development of a common Asian language:

> It is a long-term project, requiring surveys and research, but to unify the peoples of all Asia, mutual linguistic unity is essential. For this we would establish something akin to an Asian Esperanto: the grammar will be taken from the world Esperanto, and in the manner of taking 1000 words from European languages, 1000 words from Chinese and 1000 words from Japanese, we will establish something Asian that is simple for Asians to learn.[65]

Even where Esperanto itself was not proposed directly as a solution to these problems, it remained a key reference point as a language, as a model, or as a metaphor for alternatives proposed (even by non-Esperantists). The universal linguistic vision of Esperanto was reformulated somewhat, on a more regional basis than it had been previously—for example, Ishiga Osamu's proposal for the development of an "oriental" Esperanto that drew more thoroughly on Asian languages. This, he mused, might lead to the establishment of two distinct but mutually intelligible variants of universal language akin to the differences between British and American English.[66] Nevertheless, the idea of the need for a transnational language to facilitate communication across the Japanese Empire, and possibly beyond, drew heavily upon the foundations of international language thinking.

Especially as time went on, and in particular in the early 1940s, it became more widely accepted that Japanese was to be the solution to the East Asian language problem in some form or other: "Japanese has become not only the Japanese of Japan alone, but has taken on the size of the continent," as one writer commented.[67] Or, in the words of the Korean writer Yi Hyosŏk, Japanese had become a *sekaigo*.[68]

Not all necessarily celebrated this outright: Esperanto's model of an auxiliary language retained influence. The businessman and official Inoue Masuzō, in the same breath as celebrating the "globalization of the Japanese language," argued that this should mean "not the elimination of native languages and their replacement by Japanese," but rather its adoption by regional leaders as the common international language.[69] Some even stuck hard to the concept of linguistic neutrality—Takeuchi Tōkichi arguing that the replacement of English by Japanese in international conferences across Asia could not be considered real progress.[70]

There were indeed problems to be solved and different proposals to be had. The extension of the older *naichi/gaichi* division between Japan's main islands and its direct colonies to include even further peripheries—Manchukuo, Chinese territory, and eventually even the colonies in Southeast Asia—took in increasing levels of linguistic variation. Linguists' debates centered around how to teach Japanese under the rapidly increasing complexity. Some scholars advocated degrees of reform to *kokugo* (similar to Yamagata Mitsuei's conclusion regarding Manchukuo)—for example, a move to phonetic *kana* usage, rather than historic forms.[71] Elsewhere, proposals drew on ideas tied to Charles Ogden's 1930 Basic English, a restricted form of English designed for foreign learners: first Kiso Nihongo, proposed for Manchukuo by Doi Kōchi (a scholar at Tohoku Imperial University) in 1933, and then in 1942 Nippongo, with a vocabulary of three hundred words and a restricted grammar, which was translated into various Southeast Asian languages.[72]

These were examples of a policy of multiple Japaneses: *kokugo* within Japan and the original colonies, with a simplified *nihongo* to be taught in the further territories. However, moves to reform or restrict the Japanese language were open to charges of undermining the power of *kokugo*: if one plank of the *kokugo* ideology was its power to convey the Japanese spirit to other Asian subjects and thereby to truly unify the Japanese Empire, then reforming the Japanese language to make it easier to learn risked losing the very characteristics that made language more than just a pragmatic tool.[73] There was an internal catch here: to reform the *kokugo* would be to lose the *kotodama* (the soul of the language), but to refuse to reform it would prevent its real spread throughout the empire.[74]

In the maelstrom of the Pacific and Asian War, few of these ideas made it far beyond the pages of magazines and newspapers. Comments by educators and *kokugo gakusha* in the post-1931 period, even prior to Pearl Harbor and the expansion of the scale of conflict, expressed frustrations with the complexity of the Japanese language, the limited progress with efforts to reform it, and the consequences for language policy and planning. The influence of even the more highly esteemed linguists' and scholars' views on the language policy of the Japanese Empire seem to have had little impact.[75] As an Esperantist and expert in language teaching, Ishiguro Yoshimi suggested, "together with the growth in our national power, recently *Kokugo*'s international spread has continued, from Manchuria, to China, to Asia, and to the rest of the world; however, the failure of these plans to take hold is of course down to the complexity of our characters and the extreme confusion of the *Kokugo*."[76]

Nevertheless, while it is perhaps unsurprising that, under the extreme conditions of the war, the extreme nationalist ideology, and the rapid expansion of the empire, there was limited ability to develop a fully fledged language and education policy, the preoccupation with these language problems of empire serves to illustrate the extent to which the Japanese Empire faced a major linguistic issue, to stress that the Japanese language had a distinct entity as imperial (and international) language, and finally, to show that in the search for a policy to mirror in an imperial context the national impact of *kokugo*, the ideas of international and auxiliary languages retained influence.

In the spring of 1938, only a few months after Eugène Lanti had been in Japan, the *Yomiuri Shinbun* carried the announcement of the creation of the Esuperanto Hōkoku Dōmei (the Patriotic Esperanto League).[77] The aim of the league was "to work towards the publication and distribution to foreign Esperantists, both individual and group, of Esperanto language works essential for informing the world of the legitimacy of our country's true actions in relation to the current incident."[78] In this regard, the organization was much like several other efforts outlined in this chapter: seeking to make use of Esperanto as a part of a national effort at propaganda. The Japanese Foreign Ministry, together with the Rotary Club, teamed up with the League to produce a pamphlet titled *Prudento Kaj Nuna Ĥina Afero* (Understanding and the current China affair), which represented itself as a "plea for understanding by the people of Japan."[79]

Its founders included the translator Nohara Kyūichi and the longtime Esperantist Takahashi Kunitarō, but perhaps most strikingly, also Fujisawa Chikao, the one-time member of the Secretariat of the League of Nations. In the early 1920s, Fujisawa had been an ardent Homaranismo-inspired Esperanto internationalist and advocate of the language at the League. However, during the later 1920s and 1930s, he underwent a "return to Japan," retaining his interest in Esperanto but becoming increasingly drawn to the more nationalistic articulations of Japanese culture.[80] By 1934 he was arguing for the adoption of Esperanto as the connecting language between Japan and Manchukuo using Pan-Asian rhetoric, such as the argument that its use would be nothing less than the manifestation of the "kingly way."[81]

Fujisawa's journey from strong-willed internationalist to (Esperanto-embracing) nationalist was notably extreme. However, what one might consider the center of mass of the Japanese Esperanto movement underwent a parallel move, if less dramatic, over the same time period. In arguing (after Jessamyn Abel) that we should take seriously the internationalism of the Esperantists of the 1930s and the language proposals for the Japanese Empire from both Esperantists and others influenced by international language considerations, I have sought to argue that characterizing the internationalist impulse of those in the 1930s as hypocritical, paradoxical, or deluded misses the opportunity to see more complexity and nuance within our conceptions of both internationalism and language.

That said, especially around 1941 and the expansion of the war with China into the Pacific against the Western allies, it did become increasingly hard to maintain much in the way of genuine, outward-looking Esperanto activity. Three hundred people had attended the 1940 Esperanto congress in Miyazaki, marking the 2,600th anniversary of imperial rule; by 1942 that figure was only sixty (in Tokyo, where attendance has typically been higher than in the regions).[82] Some activity did continue, but where it did it showed evidence of a turn inward: for example, Nohara Kyūichi's translations of the Japanese classics were written with the express intention of disseminating Japanese literary and cultural production overseas, whereas a 1940s effort to produce translations of the *Aikoku Hakunin Isshu* (Patriotic hundred poems by a hundred poets), a wartime reinvention of a classic Japanese poetry form, was more of an inward-looking exercise in patriotic symbolism.[83] In a sense, this final turn inward in the most heightened period of conflict serves to highlight the persistence of the outward-facing engagement—the "real" internationalist impulse—for so much of the 1930s, even as militarism was becoming overwhelming.

Epilogue

In the summer of 2015, I was in Japan conducting archival research. On the TV and in the newspapers, controversy raged over attitudes toward the seventieth anniversary of the end of World War II. It was a strikingly hot summer, and I often had the archive or library largely to myself, trying to remain focused alone in a stuffy room with little or no air-conditioning. One weekend, my family and I fled out to Bōze in the Setō Inland Sea to find some respite from the heat. On the way back, we paid a visit to Mine Yoshitaka, a Japanese Esperantist who had helped me in my first years of research. He, together with his wife, picked us up at the rusty port at Himeji, as we got off the ferry. They took us for lunch and then dropped us off at Himeji Castle. Already sick with the cancer that would kill him two years later, Mine was unrecognizable from the first time I had met him, almost a decade before: frailer, and yet with his face seemingly rounder, a different shape. In the sweltering heat, he was too tired to join us in the castle, but still made the effort to come out to see us.

In many respects, Mine encapsulated a generosity that has defined my dealings with the Japanese Esperanto movement: when we first met he was willing to put me, a near perfect stranger, up in his house; to share his time, his knowledge, and his books with me; and later to make the effort to decipher the no doubt impenetrable Esperanto emails I sent him. He had been recommended to me as a valuable contact not only because of this generosity, but because he was an influential part of the notable postwar effort within the Japanese Esperanto movement to write their history. More an editor than a writer himself, Mine was nevertheless a vital actor in the production of a series of books and articles that have recorded much activity that might otherwise be lost.

Even before 1945, the Japanese Esperantists had a sense of their own past—expressed, for example, in a 1936 commemoration of the first Japanese Esperanto boom, or in the efforts to record Oka Asajirō's creation, Zilengo. Nevertheless, the postwar period built upon these prior foundations, demonstrating a sense of self-awareness of Esperanto as a subject of historical significance and the movement as having its own internal history and importance within Japan and the wider world.

The most influential of the postwar historians—Miyamoto Masao, Kurisu Kei, and Takasugi Ichirō—had been themselves participants in the prewar movement, indeed all had been connected to the proletarian wing that faced suppression in the 1930s. In the first instance, much of the writing focused on left-wing Esperanto, reflecting the extent to which the outcome of the war cast these activities in a more positive light than those that did not explicitly resist the war effort. However, as time has gone on, this work has diversified to include right-wing figures such as Kita Ikki, Fujisawa Chikao, and (arguably) Deguchi Onisaburō, as well as microhistories of various individuals and regional groups.

The postwar phase of Esperanto in Japan began almost immediately after the war had ended. Indeed, the organized movement had persisted right to the last days of the war. Only in March 1944 was printing suspended of *La Revuo Orienta*, citing paper shortages and the need for labor to be reallocated to more urgent activities.[1] Moreover, this suspension was short-lived: discussions about how and when to resume issuing the magazine began the day after the announcement of Japan's defeat, August 16, 1945, and the first postwar issue came out in October.[2]

The shortness of this gap is striking—evidence of the urgency Esperanto's advocates in Japan felt about their language. The persistence of Japanese Esperanto between 1905 and the present day, unbroken save for that yearlong rupture of the end of the war, is strong evidence for the continuation of the factors that prompted people's interest in the language. The widespread desire for peer-to-peer transnational engagement remains as true today as it did in 1905. So too, does the significance of language as a barrier to or facilitator of widening global interaction, and for some at least, the idea of a neutral medium for communication.

While the international language problem remains, much has changed over the intervening decades, and thus how it manifests has also changed. Particularly from the 1960s onward, international travel became cheaper and more readily achievable, with the result that the number of people able to make overseas trips themselves grew dramatically. Thus, for Esperantists and for others, spoken language rose in salience relative to written language. The impact of these changes was, if anything, more extreme for East Asian Esperantists than their colleagues in Europe, because they had been more isolated beforehand.

In 1962, Yagi Hideo, a longtime Kyoto Esperantist and medical doctor, became the first non-European president of the Universal Esperanto Association. Then, in 1965, Japan finally hosted the UEA congress. The contrast with Nakahara Shūji's failed attempts to secure the UEA congress for Japan in the late 1930s is obvious: the changing nature of international travel as well as rising living standards meant that more Europeans and Americans could afford the expense of visiting Asia, and so, increasingly, networking could take place in person rather than by mail. Always an important symbolic part of the global Esperanto movement precisely because it was not European, Japanese Esperanto became more fully integrated within a more complex network in the postwar period. This trend has only continued into the twenty-first century and the internet age.

Despite these postwar developments, worldwide Esperanto never again experienced a high point akin to its consideration at the League of Nations in the early 1920s. Looked at as a global phenomenon, many postwar trends have been sympathetic to Esperanto's cause. The United Nations and global discourses such as those of human rights and decolonization, as well as late twentieth-century efforts to preserve and promote minority languages, have been natural partners for the Esperanto movement's idea of linguistic neutrality. However, the dominant role of the United States of America at the heart of trends of postwar globalization meant that English has become increasingly dominant in an international and transnational context.

Thus, while the international language problem remains, and Esperanto has consistently attracted advocates in Japan and elsewhere, the second half of the twentieth century has seen a shift in emphasis within the global Esperanto movement away from the potential for universal adoption to focus on the community of speakers that exists. While some older Esperantists perhaps regretted the retreat of that imagined future, the increased prominence of the realized present brought with it new dimensions. Increasingly able to meet fellow Esperantists from around the world in person and concentrating more on concrete connections, global Esperanto, and the Japanese with them, began to focus more on what Lins characterizes as "amusement and pleasure": tourism, friendship, and even romance fostered through planned language.[3]

It is too simple to divide the twentieth-century history of Esperanto in Japan between pre-1945 history making and post-1945 history writing; however, the 1945 break and the dramatic changes that developed subsequently form a useful way to reflect upon how the historical actors considered in this book confronted the international language question. They lacked the material developments in travel and electronic communications that have become so important in the twenty-first century, but nevertheless they forged dense transnational networks—traveling in person where they could, at other times sending letters and magazines, or "thinking . . . beyond the nation."[4] And while the *fun* that has perhaps come to define postwar Esperanto was certainly not alien to the young students of the 1920s, for example, the prewar movement in Japan was certainly *serious*.

The early twentieth century saw a wide spectrum of expressions of the urge to reach out beyond Japan's borders: in Esperanto they ranged from essays written in elite magazines to debates in the assembly hall of the League of Nations and discussions in villages scattered throughout Japan; from thinking about the nature of the problem to practical activities, letters written, and conversations conducted in Esperanto. The participants ranged from the intellectuals of the Meirokusha in the early Meiji period to an ever-widening range of people: students, scholars, monks, villagers, socialists, nationalists, soldiers, men and women, old and young, unified by a common desire to reach out beyond Japan's borders and to make contact with the people they found there.

Glossary

Shibata and Gotō's *Nihon Esuperanto Undō Jinmei Jiten* contains comprehensive details of most participants in the Japanese Esperanto movement.

Rōmaji	Japanese	Esperanto	English
Chihō shugi	地方主義		Regionalism
Chūka-Ryūnichi Sekaigo Gakkai	中華留日世界語学会		Sekaigo Institute for Chinese in Japan
		Deklaracio de Boulonja	Boulogne Declaration
Esuperanto Bungaku Kenkyūkai	エスペラント文学研究会		Esperanto Literature Research Association
Esuperanto Fukyūkai	エスペラント普及会	Esperanto-Propaganda Asocio	Esperanto Propaganda Association
Esuperanto Hōkoku Dōmei	エスペラント報告同盟		The Patriotic Esperanto League
Esuperanto Seinen Dōmei	エスペラント青年同盟		The Esperanto Youth League
Esuperanto shugi	エスペラント主義	*Esperantismo*	Esperantism
Gakuren	学連 (full name 学生社会科学連合会)		
Homaranisumo	ホマラニスモ	Homaranismo	"Human being"–ism

Rōmaji	**Japanese**	**Esperanto**	**English**
Ichihan Ichigo	一犯一語		One crime, one language
		Interna ideo	Internal idea
Kokusai-go	国際語		International Language
Kokusai-hojogo	国際補助語		International Auxiliary Language
Kokusai Bunka Kenkyūjo (later Puroretaria Kagaku Kenkyūjo)	国際文化研究所; プロレタリア科学研究所		The International Culture Research Institute, later Proletarian Science Research Institute
Kotodama	言霊		
Kurarakai	クララ会		Clara Kai
Kyōdokai	郷土会		Local Studies Association
Kyōdo Bungei Undō	郷土文芸運動		Local Arts Movement
Nihon Esuperanto Gakkai (later Nihon Esuperanto Kyōkai)	日本エスペラント学会（日本エスペラント協会）	Japana Esperanto-Instituto	Japanese Esperanto Institute
Nihon Esuperanchisuto Kyōkai	日本エスペランチスト協会	Japana Esperantisto Asocio, JEA	Japanese Association of Esperantists
Nihon Puroretaria Geijutsu Renmei	日本プロレタリア芸術連盟		The Japan Proletarian Arts League, JPAL
Puroretaria Bunka Renmei (alt. Koppu)	プロレタリア文化連盟 (コップ)	Federacio de Proletaj Kultur-Organizoj Japanaj, KOPF	Japanese Federation of Proletarian Culture Organizations
Puroretaria Esuperanto Kōza	プロレタリアエスペラント講座		

Rōmaji	Japanese	Esperanto	English
Puroretaria Esuperanchisuto Kyōkai	プロレタリアエスペラチスント協会, ポエウ	(Japana) Proleta Esperantista-Asocio, PEA, JPEA	(Japanese) Proletarian Esperantist Assocation
(Nihon) Puroretaria Esuperanchisuto Dōmei	(日本)プロレタリアエスペランチスト同盟, ポエウ	(Japana) Proleta Esperantista Unio, PEU, JPEU	(Japanese) Proletarian Esperantist Union
Puroretaria Esuperanto Tūshin, Pēku	プロレタリアエスペラント通信, ペーク	Proleta Esperanto Korespondado, PEK	Proletarian Esperanto Correspondence
Rasu Chijinkai	羅須地人会		Rasu Farmers' Association
Rōnō Geijutsuka Renmei	労農芸術家連盟		The Worker-Peasant Artists' League, WPAL
		Sennacia Asocio Tutmonda, SAT	The Global Non-National Association
Shakaishugi Dōmei	社会主義同盟		Socialist League
Shinjinkai	新人会		
Shirakaba-ha	白樺派		White Birch Society
Tane Maku Hito	種蒔く人		The Sower
Tōhoku Shinkōkai	東北振興会		Society for the Advancement of Tōhoku
Zen'ei Geijutsuka Dōmei	前衛芸術家同盟		The Vanguard Artists' League, VAL
Zen-Nihon Musanasha Geijutsu Renmei (Nappu)	全日本無産者芸術連盟; ナップ	Nippona Artista Proleta Federacio, NAPF	The All-Japan Proletarian Arts League

Notes

Introduction

1. This account is based upon Williams's own account of the mission, *A Journal of the Perry Expedition to Japan.*

2. Tao, "Negotiating Language in the Opening of Japan."

3. See Howell, "Foreign Encounters and Informal Diplomacy in Early Modern Japan."

4. There is a considerable ambiguity between terms such as "international," "transnational," and "global." Insofar as we need to define them analytically, I use "international" to refer to institutional and official activities within the network of states; "transnational" to refer to non-state activities that cross, or are not contained within, national borders; and "global" as a frame of analysis for anything that is broader than the nation. However, I am also conscious that in everyday English, "international" often acts as a catch-all for these sorts of phenomena, and in the interests of readability I am keen to avoid being doctrinaire about these terms except where the distinction matters.

5. Planned languages are also often known as *artificial* languages. The semantic difference between the two terms is slight, but using "planned" (or sometimes "constructed") implies that the majority of languages, be they national languages, dialects, or other, are *unplanned* rather than, in the case of artificial, *natural.* Given the tendency of human societies toward mythologizing their own cultural markers, "planned" is therefore preferable.

6. For an introduction to the history of planned languages see either Eco, *The Search for the Perfect Language*, or Okrent, *In the Land of Invented Languages.*

7. For the most part, Zamenhof used only the initials L.L. as an author. These corresponded to names that have been rendered most commonly in English as Ludwig Lazar, but with considerable variance depending on the choice of transliteration or Anglicization, as well as whether to start from a Russian or Yiddish version of the original.

8. See Forster, *The Esperanto Movement*, or Schor, *Bridge of Words*, for more details.

9. Konishi, *Anarchist Modernity*; Stalker, *Prophet Motive*; Michielsen, *Assembling Solidarity*; Shockey, *The Typographic Imagination*; Lins, *Kiken Na Gengo*; Müller-Saini and Benton, "Esperanto and Chinese Anarchism 1907–1920"; O'Keeffe, *Esperanto and Languages of Internationalism in Revolutionary Russia*; Li, *Nihon Tōchika ni okeru Taiwan Esuperanto Undō Kenkyū.*

10. See Gordin, *Scientific Babel*, for a discussion of the narrowing of international languages in another setting (science).

11. I term Japanese Esperanto a "popular" movement by which I would suggest that it was a largely grassroots endeavor that achieved a consistent, diverse, nationwide level of activity that perhaps did not quite rise to the scale that one might describe as a "mass" movement. Just

how popular Esperanto was is somewhat difficult to pin down, and what constitutes an Esperantist proves tricky to define. Scholars of interlinguistics, the study of planned languages, have suggested that it is valuable to conceive of concentric rings of activity—people who have mastered the language and use it regularly form the central and smallest circle, but moving out beyond this are growing pools of people who have looser relationships to Esperanto—who are members of clubs, who have studied it, or who have other relationships to it (Lindstedt, "Esperanto as a Family Language," 69–80). The main Japanese Esperanto group, the JEI, had a membership between two and three thousand during the late Taishō / early Shōwa period, but studying local Esperanto activity suggests that there were many members of local town clubs who were not members of the JEI. For example, the Esperanto activity of Kuroishi, Aomori, analyzed in chapter 4, took place at a time when the JEI membership of the entire prefecture was recorded as only five people. Throughout this book I am keen to focus wherever possible on broad Esperanto activity, rather than a narrower focus on Esperanto organizations. A 1928 survey of global Esperanto activity estimated the Japanese community of Esperantists at 6,900, two to three times the JEI membership, and on a par with all but the largest Esperanto movements in European nations (Dietterle, "Tutmonda statistiko esperantista," quoted in Forster, *The Esperanto Movement*, 20–22).

12. Clark, *The Kokugo Revolution*; Gottleib, *Language and the Modern State*; Heinrich, *The Making of Monolingual Japan*; Lee, *The Ideology of Kokugo*.

13. For example, see Eurtürk, *Grammatology and Literary Modernity in Turkey*, or Zhong, *Chinese Grammatology*.

14. Jacobowitz, *Writing Technology in Meiji Japan*, 99; Eurtürk, *Grammatology and Literary Modernity in Turkey*, x. See the appendices to Liu, *Translingual Practice*, for examples of the complex origins of neologisms in the Chinese language.

15. Howland, *Translating the West*; Liu, *Translingual Practice*.

16. It is, of course, the conceit of the modern historian to often assume that the historical phenomena that they study are unique to their period. None of these processes—cross-border communication, transnational influences on language change and reform, and so on—were unique to the last two hundred years. Japanese writing was a transnationally shaped practice from its very outset, as Lurie, *Realms of Literacy*, shows, while "brushtalk"—live written exchanges based upon the shared heritage of Chinese language and characters—was an important medium for communication across East Asia for a long span of time (Clements, "Brush Talk as the 'Lingua Franca' of Diplomacy"; Howland, *Borders of Chinese Civilization*, chap. 2, "Civilization as Universal Practice").

17. Cheah and Robbins, *Cosmopolitics*.

Chapter 1: *Sekaigo*

1. Ōsugi, "Gokuchū Shōsoku," 390. "Albert" is perhaps the French anarchist Joseph Albert, also known as Albert Libertad, although I have been unable to track down exactly what text this refers to. Ludwig Feuerbach's *On Religion* is most likely his *Das Wesen der Religion*.

2. Nihon-Esuperanto-Gakkai, *Nihon Esuperanto Undō-Shiryō*, 10–13.

3. Shibukawa Genji, "Kanjimoku," *Asahi Shinbun*, October 2, 1906. The other *ōzeki* was *naniwabushi*, a style of folk singing. This was a nod to the practice of organizing categories into rankings modeled on *sumo banzuke*, a tradition spanning the transition from Tokugawa to Meiji that ranged over such subjects as rabbit breeders, Chinese and Western doctors, and

photography studios. The *yokozuna*, the current highest rank in sumo wrestling, was not formally recognized by the Sumo Association until a few years later; see Thompson, "The Invention of the Yokozuna and the Championship System," 177.

4. Gottlieb, *Language and the Modern State*; Lee, *The Ideology of Kokugo*. The phrase "unified style" is from Jacobowitz, *Writing Technology in Meiji Japan*, p. 5.

5. Shimoda, "Tongues-Tied."

6. See, for example, Lee, *The Ideology of Kokugo*, pp. 7–8.

7. Mori, *Education in Japan*, lvi.

8. See the introduction to Lee, *The Ideology of Kokugo*, and chapter 1 of Heinrich, *The Making of Monolingual Japan* (146) for discussion; Heinrich points out that, according to Kobayashi Toshihiro ("Mori Arinori No 'Datsu-a, Nyu-Ō Cho-Ō' Gengo Shisō No Shosō (2)," 45–46), Baba Tatsui was instrumental in establishing the general assumption that the adoption of English in Mori's work implied the abolition of Japanese.

9. Letter from Mori Arinori to William D. Whitney, May 21, 1872, quoted in Griolet, "Language, Script, and Modernity." I have chosen to quote these works at length, in order to fully see the nature of Mori's comments in context.

10. Mori, *Education in Japan*, lv–lvi.

11. One potential line of analysis might be that the influence of the classical Chinese tribute system and the close control over foreign contact had rendered the three archetypes effectively merged during the Tokugawa *sakoku* era (see, for example, Hellyer, *Defining Engagement*), and thus one impact of the opening of Japan to greater Western contact and influence was the gradual separation of them into more distinct spheres.

12. Tao, "Negotiating Language in the Opening of Japan."

13. These issues are explored in Liu, "Translingual Practice," and Howland, *Translating the West*.

14. Sakatani Shiroshi, "A Certain Question," *Meiroku Zasshi* 10, 1874; translation from Braisted, *Meiroku Zasshi*, 136.

15. Braisted, *Meiroku Zasshi*, 137.

16. *Peke* and *sarampan* were words common in other Asian port languages, apparently of Malay origin (Daniels, "The Vocabulary of the Japanese Ports Lingo"). I'm indebted to Sven Osterkamp for pointing out that on at least two previous occasions, 1874 and 1887, these two specific words were used as indicative of the sort of language used in the ports. It's interesting, but ultimately secondary to my purposes here, to wonder why these two Malay words seem to have emerged as symbolic of a port pidgin that was mostly based on Japanese and English.

17. Anon., "Exercises in the Yokohama Dialect."

18. "Pidgin Japanese," in Chamberlain, *Things Japanese*.

19. These patterns of influence continue to shape the languages spoken across the Pacific to the present day. See, for example, "Hawaiian Pidgin English," in Tryon and Charpentier, *Pacific Pidgins and Creoles*.

20. Williams, *A Journal of the Perry Expedition to Japan*, and Beasley, "The Language Problem in the Anglo-Japanese Negotiations of 1854," are both illuminating on the subject of the realities of language in a diplomatic setting.

21. See, for example, Han, "Tragedy in China-Town." The term "contact zone" is from Pratt, *Imperial Eyes*.

22. Gordin, *Scientific Babel*, 114–117.

23. Forster, *The Esperanto Movement*, 46–47.

24. Nihon-Esuperanto-Gakkai, *Nihon Esuperanto Undō-Shiryō*, 3; Fujima, *Kindai Nihon Ni Okeru Kokusaigo Shisō No Tenkai*, 27.

25. There were at least forty articles and grammar inserts in the *Yomiuri Shinbun* between the first mention in December 1887 and December 1888.

26. Heyden and Sasaki, *Wayaku Sekaigo Jirin*.

27. Another noteworthy figure who learned Volapük was Takusari Kōki. Takusari, as the originator of Japan's first Western-inspired shorthand system, is a significant actor in Seth Jacobowitz's work on the technological prompts to Meiji-era language reforms, again tying together the twin threads of national and international language debates (Jacobowitz, *Writing Technology in Meiji Japan*).

28. "Kokusaigo Zilengo no Chōsha Oka Asajirō ni Kiku," *La Revuo Orienta*, April 1940, 142–145.

29. Oka Asajirō, "Omoide," *La Revuo Orienta*, June 1936, 202–203.

30. As a rare example of an early Japanese planned language project, Zilengo attracted the attention of the Japanese Esperanto movement in later years—especially from the 1930s onward, when Japanese Esperantists began to consider their own history. Oka claimed that he created it before encountering Esperanto, but given the grammatical and lexical similarities between the two, over and above those inevitable given their similar intellectual origins, it seems likely that Oka continued to develop Zilengo after beginning to study Esperanto.

31. S. Gauntlett, "Edward Gauntlett (1868–1956)."

32. G. E. L. Gauntlett and Maruyama, *Sekaigo Esperanto*, 2.

33. G. E. L. Gauntlett and Maruyama, *Sekaigo Esperanto*, 4, emphasis in original.

34. G. E. L. Gauntlett and Maruyama, *Sekaigo Esperanto*, 9.

35. Regarding the number of Gauntlett's correspondence students, a figure of 677 is often quoted, although I have been unable to ascertain the original source for it. The introduction to G. E. L. Gauntlett and Maruyama, *Sekaigo Esperanto* (1), claims he had taught 823 students.

36. Oka, *Okayama No Esuperanto*, 9–27.

37. Yoshino, "Esuperanto to Watashi." Yoshino confessed that he was not very diligent in his studies and soon gave up, although he later encountered the language again during the Taishō era, when the student group Shinjinkai, with which he was associated, became interested in it. The June 1936 issue of *La Revuo Orienta* celebrated thirty years of Japanese Esperanto activity with a series of personal memories from early Esperantists. Many of them are used in this chapter.

38. Katō Misao, "Yokosuka ni Nihon Esuperanto Kyōkai wo Sōritsu shita Tōji no Omoide," *La Revuo Orienta*, June 1936, 191–196.

39. According to one account, the NES was apparently not even the first group to take the name Nihon Esuperanto Kyōkai—Abiko Teijirō having created a short-lived club in 1905 (Nihon-Esuperanto-Gakkai, *Nihon Esuperanto Undō-Shiryō*, 8).

40. *La Revuo Orienta*, June 1936, 193.

41. Tomimatsu Masao, "Meiji Jidai Nagasaki de Esu-go wo Yatta Hito," *La Revuo Orienta*, June 1936; also see Nihon-Esuperanto-Gakkai, *Nihon Esuperanto Undō-Shiryō* (7), although the source for this is likely also Tomimatsu.

42. Heiminsha, *Chokugen*, March 19, 1905 (reprinted in Rōdō Undō-shi Kenkyūkai, *Meiji Shakai-shugi Shiryō-shū*); *Yomiuri Shinbun*, May 17, 1906.

43. Muramoto worked in his family printing firm, which did a moderate amount of rōmaji-based business with the foreign residents of Okayama. In March 1906 he brought out

one of the first Japanese domestic Esperanto publications—an English-Esperanto dictionary designed to support Gauntlett's correspondence course (Oka, *Okayama No Esuperanto*, 18–22).

44. Both of these are available in digital format from the National Diet Library. See details in the bibliography: G. E. L. Gauntlett, *Sekaigo Esperanto*, and Katō Misao, *Esuperanto Dokushū Zensekaitsūyōgo*.

45. The given authors of the book, *Esperanto-Japana Vortaro*, were Kuroita, Asada Eiji, and Abiko Teijirō, but it is suggested that Kuroita completed the project more or less single-handedly during a weeklong holiday in Hakone (*La Revuo Orienta*, March 1947).

46. Fujima, *Kindai Nihon Ni Okeru Kokusaigo Shisō No Tenkai*, 40.

47. Itō, "Futabatei to Esuperanto," in *Takaku Takaku, Tōku No Hō E*, 251.

48. Fujima, *Kindai Nihon Ni Okeru Kokusaigo Shisō No Tenkai*, 43.

49. Futabatei, *Seikaigo—Esuperanto*.

50. Itō, *Takaku Takaku, Tōku No Hō E*, 253.

51. Fujima, *Kindai Nihon Ni Okeru Kokusaigo Shisō No Tenkai*, 45.

52. Ryan, *Japan's First Modern Novel*.

53. Fujima, *Kindai Nihon Ni Okeru Kokusaigo Shisō No Tenkai*, 50.

54. Various essays from *La Revuo Orienta*, June 1936.

55. One final intriguing possible early link between Esperanto and Japan came in the person of Richard Geoghagen. The Irishman Geoghagan was an early Esperantist who produced some of the first English texts on the language by a native English speaker. He worked for the Japanese consulate in Seattle for some time roughly between 1893 and 1900, reportedly visiting Japan on at least one occasion. Some have speculated that it is hard to imagine such an enthusiastic Esperantist not trying to spread the language while in a foreign country, but no concrete evidence has been found (Nihon-Esuperanto-Gakkai, *Nihon Esuperanto Undō-Shiryō*, 6).

56. Koyama Eigo, "Nihon de Saisho no Esuperanto-go Gakkō," *La Revuo Orienta*, June 1936. This level of intense study with a fairly high dropout rate seems to have been not particularly unusual for early twentieth-century Esperanto courses in Japan.

57. Nihon-Esuperanto-Gakkai, *Nihon Esuperanto Undō-Shiryō*, 48.

58. Müller-Saini and Benton, "Esperanto and Chinese Anarchism 1907–1920," 47–48. The other main origin of Chinese Esperanto and anarchism was a parallel group studying in Paris in the same period.

59. The Chinese title of the magazine was *Mingshen*, 民聲; *Voĉo de la Popolo* was the Esperanto alternative title.

60. Müller-Saini and Benton, "Esperanto and Chinese Anarchism 1907–1920," 55; "Biografio de Sinjoro Sifo," *Orienta Azio*, December 1915, 12.

61. Mukai, *Anakizumu to Esuperanto*, 221. Shifu died in 1916; *Voĉo de la Populo* ceased publication in that year, too (Müller-Saini and Benton, "Esperanto and Chinese Anarchism 1907–1920," 58).

62. Müller-Saini and Benton, "Esperanto and Chinese Anarchism 1907–1920," 56; *Orienta Azio*, November 1913, December 1914; Mukai, *Anakizumu to Esuperanto*, 36; see also Ōsugi, "Gokuchū Shōsoku."

63. Mukai, *Anakizumu to Esuperanto*, 27, 61. In this period too, Yamaga became acquainted with Kita Ikki, eventually marrying a woman who worked in his household (63–64).

64. *Yomiuri Shinbun*, January 3, 1888.

65. *Chokugen*, March 19, 1905.

66. *Yomiuri Shinbun*, December 30, 1887.

67. *Yomiuri Shinbun*, February 24, 1888. The quote came from a letter to the (London) *Times* from a Charles Jonas of Prague.

68. *Yomiuri Shinbun*, February 18, 1888.

69. Katō, "Introduction," in *Esuperanto Dokushū Zensekai-Tsūyōgo*.

70. Higuchi, *Kokka-Shakai Shugi Shin Kyōiku Gaku*, 327.

71. For example, *Chokugen*, March 19, 1905; or Higuchi, *Kokka-Shakai Shugi Shin Kyōiku Gaku*, 326. Futabatei Shimei also made reference to the pre-Esperanto history of planned languages in his article in *Fujin Sekai*, while Kuroita placed planned languages within a history of general language development ("Sekaigo," *Yomiuri Shinbun*, May 16–17, 1906), and Higuchi (*Kokka-Shakai Shugi Shin Kyōiku Gaku*, 317–335, 333) drew upon the history of national language creation, in particular the case of Norwegian.

72. Jacobowitz, *Writing Technology in Meiji Japan*; Shockey, *The Typographic Imagination*, especially chapter 5.

73. Jacobowitz, *Writing Technology in Meiji Japan*, 11.

74. Deklaracio Bolonja, http://en.hades-presse.com/languages/declaration-boulogne.shtml.

75. Halliday, "Three Concepts of Internationalism," 190.

76. Miyamoto and Ōshima, *Hantaisei Esuperanto Undō-Shi*, 24–27.

77. Scalapino and Yu, *The Chinese Anarchist Movement*, 31, cited in Konishi, *Anarchist Modernity*, 280.

78. Katō, "Introduction," in *Esuperanto Dokushū Zensekaitsūyōgo*.

Chapter 2: A Portrait of the Blind Russian

1. The two paintings are reproductions; the original of Nakamura's painting is in the National Museum of Modern Art, and Tsuruta's is owned and exhibited at the Nakamuraya museum in Shinjuku.

2. "Eroshenko-shi no Zō," Bunka Isan Onrain, Bunkachō, https://bunka.nii.ac.jp/heritages/detail/96693.

3. Just as with the terms "international" and "transnational," for most of this book I will use the terms "internationalism" and "cosmopolitanism" in a nontechnical fashion, rather than adhere to a specific analytic definition. I tend to regard the relationship between the two concepts, at least in most manifestations, as rather more like that between a cappuccino and a café latte (similar ingredients, but blended in a different fashion) than that between a coffee and tea (more fundamentally different). The major exception to this comes in chapter 5, where it is important to be aware of the socialist conception of internationalism (or at least its usual Japanese translation, *kokusaishugi*) as fundamentally tied to the bourgeois nation-state system.

4. "Kare wa Naita," *Asahi Shinbun*, May 29, 1921, 5.

5. "Nichi-Futsu Bijutsu Kōkan Tenrankai ga iyoiyo Myōshū kara Jitsugen," *Yomiuri Shinbun*, May 29, 1921.

6. The most thoroughly researched account of Eroshenko's life was undertaken by Takasugi Ichirō, who compiled two timelines of his life, one *Yoake Mae No Uta* (397–402), the other in *Eroshenko Zenshū* (281–287).

7. Takasugi, *Yoake Mae No Uta*, 61–63.

8. Shibata and Gōtō, *Nihon Esuperanto Undō Jinmei Jiten*, 86.

9. Shibata and Gōtō, *Nihon Esuperanto Undō Jinmei Jiten*, 362; Ōi Manabu, "Omoide no Nakamura Kiyō Sensei," *La Revuo Orienta*, February 1930.

10. Shibata and Gōtō, *Nihon Esuperanto Undō Jinmei Jiten*, 63–64, 344–345.

11. For example, Yagi Hideo and Torii Tokujirō (trans.), *Mōjin Esuperanto Kōshū Dokuhon* (Kaniya Shoten, 1922); Osaka Kenji and Kishimoto Jūtarō, *Tenji Esuperanto Kyōkasho* (Kaniya Shoten, 1922); Torii Tokujirō, *Tenji Esu-Wa Jiten* (Kaniya Shoten, 1923); Nakanishi Yoshio, *Jiten Esuperanto Kōgi* (Bukkyō Zaiyogun Jiten-bu, 1929); and Ishiguro Yoshimi, *Mōjin'yō Esuperanto Dai-Ippō* (Kibō-sha, 1931).

12. Kataoka, *Yami Wo Terasu Mō Hitotsu No Hikari*, 76–77.

13. Akita Ujaku, *Ujaku Jiden*, 50.

14. The Bahá'í religion has produced a number of works on the early history of their mission in Japan, such as Alexander and Sims, *History of the Bahá'í Faith in Japan*, and Sims, *Unfurling the Divine Flag in Tokyo.*

15. Their original store was in Hongō, near Imperial University, although they soon relocated to Shinjuku and the site on which the store still operates.

16. The Nakamuraya maintains a rich online resource about the history of the business and its coterie of artists: http://www.nakamuraya.co.jp/pavilion/founder/index.html.

17. Akita Ujaku, *Akita Ujaku Nikki*, 1: 38. Eroshenko's relationship with Kamichika Ichiko seems to have been unusually close and passionate, even for the notably charismatic Russian. Eroshenko and Akita were there to pick Kamichika up when she was released from prison (at the end of her sentence for stabbing her lover, Ōsugi Sakae), bringing her her favorite fruit, a banana ("Sabishii Egan wo Misetsutsu," *Asahi Shinbun*, October 4, 1919), and when Eroshenko was eventually expelled from Japan, he assigned the royalties for his forthcoming works to Kamichika ("Mōshijin E-shi no Ureishiki Ai no Katami," *Yomiuri Shinbun*, June 23, 1921). One contemporary recalled rumors that the two might have been going to marry ("Shinjinkai no Zō ni Nijimu Kodoku no Gakka no Musō," *Asahi Shinbun*, May 7, 1990). For her part, Sōma Kokkō thought that the two were not in love: "Kamichika [and Eroshenko] seemed unusually close, but by my reckoning Kamichika was [romantically] indifferent to Eroshenko, whereas for Eroshenko this was not true. When the two came together, an argument like fireworks would always break out. One evening, their voices became so loud that the bakery staff were drawn upstairs, thinking they might be fighting. Far from the soft voices of lovers, these were harsh words" (Sōma, *Mokui*, 277).

18. The magazine *Atarashiki Mura* featured an introduction to Homaranismo (see later in this chapter) in volume 2, issue 3 (March 1919); *Kaizō* ran a special issue on Esperanto in August 1922; for the Shinjinkai, see Miyamoto and Ōshima, *Hantaisei Esuperanto Undō-Shi*, 115ff.

19. Eroshenko and Takasugi, *Eroshenko Zenshū*, 338.

20. See, for example, Silverberg, *Erotic Grotesque Nonsense*; Smith, *Japan's First Student Radicals*; Tipton, *Society and the State in Interwar Japan*; Tipton and Clark, *Being Modern in Japan.*

21. "Esperanto for Koreans," *Japan Advertiser*, February 22, 1920, quoted in Gotō, "Esperanto tsuita Yanagita Kunio."

22. Tim Harper's *Underground Asia* includes an extensive discussion of Bose's place within the underground Indian resistance movement. See Hotta, "Rash Behari Bose and His Japanese Supporters," for an extended analysis of Bose's time in Japan.

23. Hatsushiba, *Nihon Esuperanto Undō-Shi*, 34.

24. Russell and Einstein were brought to Japan by the magazine *Kaizō*, whereas Tagore's sponsor was the *Asahi Shinbun*.

25. Hay, *Asian Ideas of East and West*, 62; Akita Ujaku, *Akita Ujaku Nikki*, 1: 59.

26. *Asahi Shinbun*, June 12, 1916.

27. See for example, Hay, *Asian Ideas of East and West*, 89.

28. Akita Ujaku, *Akita Ujaku Nikki* 1: 57ff.

29. Tagore, *A Visit to Japan*, 67.

30. Tagore, *The Spirit of Japan*, 4–5.

31. Tagore, *The Spirit of Japan*, 12–13.

32. Hay, *Asian Ideas of East and West*, 83.

33. "Sanjō no Tagōru," *Waseda Bungaku*, July 1916, quoted in Hay, *Asian Ideas of East and West*, 89.

34. The main source for this disagreement is Takasugi Ichirō's *Yoake Mae No Uta* (142), although Akita Ujaku recorded debating Tagore's views with Eroshenko in his diary (*Akita Ujaku Nikki*, 1: 60). While I have not discovered a direct source outlining his views of Tagore's work, Eroshenko elsewhere was critical of views of divided humanity (e.g., "Ima Tane Maku Toku de, Kiri Ire Toki dewanai," in Eroshenko and Takasugi, *Eroshenko Zenshū* (511), and Takasugi was a contemporary of many of Eroshenko's friends and associates, so had access to firsthand accounts. While Eroshenko was not present for the photo of Tagore meeting the Bahá'í group (https://bahai-library.com/images/s/sims_traces_that_remain_35.big.jpg) and Tagore's visit to the Nakamuraya appears to have been a more private occasion (a photo of that features only Tagore, Bose, and family members), it's far from fanciful to imagine that the two men might have met directly, given the closeness of the circles they were moving in in Tokyo.

35. See Eroshenko's letters, in Eroshenko and Takasugi, *Eroshenko Zenshū*, 2: 330–401.

36. This correspondence took place variously in Esperanto and Japanese (including Braille), depending on Eroshenko's partner (Eroshenko and Takasugi, *Eroshenko Zenshū*, 2: 330). The surviving letters are chiefly those Eroshenko sent to Torii Tokujirō, but it is clear from those that Eroshenko was also writing to a number of other Japanese colleagues and friends: Agnes Alexander, Nakamura Kiyō, Kamichika Ichiko, and others.

37. This wasn't a trouble-free approach—in Bangkok Eroshenko fell in with a Russian community that his host (a Siamese who had previously worked at the Tokyo School of Foreign Languages) considered to be highly questionable.

38. Eroshenko and Takasugi, *Eroshenko Zenshū*, 2: 391.

39. Eroshenko and Takasugi, *Eroshenko Zenshū*, 2: 334.

40. Eroshenko and Takasugi, *Eroshenko Zenshū*, 2: 334.

41. Eroshenko and Takasugi, *Eroshenko Zenshū*, 2: 98, 3: 284.

42. IEroshenko and Takasugi, *Eroshenko Zenshū*, 3: 284.

43. Craig Calhoun suggests that low points of on-the-ground action in social movements are often the phases in which key ideological and conceptual work is done ("Social Movements and Social Change," LSE Public Lectures, 2012, http://www.lse.ac.uk/lse-player?id=1673).

44. "Declaration of Esperantism," announced at the First Universal Congress of Esperanto, Boulogne-sur-Mer, 1905.

45. Mukai, *Anakizumu to Esuperanto*, 59–60.

46. Hatsushiba, *Nihon Esuperanto Undō-Shi*, 35. Chifu was a graduate of the Ōsugi Sakae Esperanto night school who worked in the post office and Ministry of Communications and Transportation, including a spell as a censor. He was a significant organizer in the

JEA in the early years of Esperanto in Japan. (Shibata and Gotō, *Nihon Esuperanto Undō Jinmei Jiten*, 318).

47. Nihon-Esuperanto-Gakkai, *Nihon Esuperanto Undō-Shiryō*, 25.

48. Osaka and Ujaku, *Memlernanto De Esperanto*, introduction.

49. Editorial, *Verda Utopio*, January 1923.

50. Chifu, "La Esperantismo estas pura lingva movado," *La Movado*, January 1923, 14.

51. The prefix "Aĉ-" means "awful, terrible, ugly," and the stem "ulo" means "person." The group wrote a hymn to the Aĉuloj including the chant "Aĉa Aĉuloj Aĉe Aĉas," which would be more literally "the awful awfuls are awfully awful" (Ishiguro Yoshimi, "Esuperanto 60nen," 46).

52. Nihon-Esuperanto-Gakkai, *Nihon Esuperanto Undō-Shiryō*, 41–43.

53. Nihon-Esuperanto-Gakkai, *Nihon Esuperanto Undō-Shiryō*, 44–45; "Arata ni Gakkai wo Setsuritsu," *Yomiuri Shinbun*, December 21, 1919.

54. "Arata ni Gakkai wo Setsuritsu," *Yomiuri Shinbun*, December 21, 1919.

55. Nihon-Esuperanto-Gakkai, *Nihon Esuperanto Undō-Shiryō*, 24.

56. Figures from issues of the occasional JEI annual, *Jarlibro de JEI*.

57. Torii Tokujirō, *Orienta Blindularo*, 1928, quoted in Kataoka, *Yami Wo Terasu Mō Hitotsu No Hikari*, 83–84.

58. Asano, "Nihon Ni Okeru Bukkyō Esuperanto Undō Koshi."

59. One noteworthy point is that Ōmoto and Bahá'ism never seem to have formed significant links, the mutual interest in Esperanto notwithstanding. I suspect that this is likely because both religions' international perspective, perversely, made it harder to find a comfortable relationship. By contrast, most of the other religions that Ōmoto partnered with in continental Asia seem to have been still largely domestic in outlook (Stalker, *Prophet Motive*, chap. 5).

60. Stalker, *Prophet Motive*, outlines in detail the full spectrum of Deguchi's "paradoxical internationalism" (chap. 5). She also makes the key point that, given the size of Ōmoto's apparent following, the impact of Deguchi advocating Esperanto to the faithful likely had a dramatic impact on overall levels of Esperanto learners and practitioners in Japan, even if few Ōmoto Esperantists necessarily became members of the central organization, the JEI, or other clubs.

61. Stalker, *Prophet Motive*, chap. 5.

62. The term is from Manela, *The Wilsonian Moment*.

63. See Tokubetsu Yōshisatsujin Jōsei Ippan #6, a watchlist of foreigners in Japan deemed worthy of special attention by the police (Gendai Shiryō Shussei [hereafter GSS], *Zoku Gendaishi Shiryō* 7: 487; also discussed in Fujii Shozo, *Eroshenko No Toshi Monogatari*, 8–9). During the first phase of Eroshenko's time in Japan, the police noted his links to Ōsugi Sakae and prior contact with Piotr Kropotkin while in London. Subsequent notes included his ties to Kamichika Ichiko and information provided by the British representatives in Japan regarding Eroshenko's time in India (GSS, *Zoku Gendaishi Shiryō* 7: 699).

64. Fujii, *Eroshenko No Toshi Monogatari*, 13.

65. Akita Ujaku, *Akita Ujaku Nikki*, 1: 247.

66. Akita Ujaku, *Akita Ujaku Nikki*, 1: 248.

67. "Mōshijin Kensoku Saru," *Asahi Shinbun*, May 2, 1921.

68. Akita Ujaku, *Akita Ujaku Nikki*, 1: 248.

69. "Sakujitsu Kensoku sareta Ro Mōshijin," *Yomiuri Shinbun*, May 2, 1921.

70. "Shakaishugi Attō Saru," *Asahi Shinbun*, May 10, 1921.

71. "Omou koto ga shaberareta" *Asahi Shinbun*, May 10, 1921. The *Asahi* perhaps sardonically observed that "seeing the meeting done and dusted without incident and cleared away by 10pm, was truly an amazing event."

72. "Rokoku Tsuihō Shobun ni kansuru ken," quoted in Fujii, *Eroshenko No Toshi Monogatari*, 16.

73. "Mōshijin E-shi wo Taikyo sasu wake," *Asahi Shinbun*, May 29, 1921.

74. "Kare ha Naita," *Asahi Shinbun*, May 29, 1921.

75. "Nakamuraya E-shi wo Rachi shita Yodobashi Shochō wo Uttaeru," *Yomiuri Shinbun*, June 8, 1921.

76. Akita Ujaku, *Akita Ujaku Nikki*, 1: 251ff.; Fujii, *Eroshenko No Toshi Monogatari*, 26.

77. "Sasurai Mōshijin," *Asahi Shinbun*, June 3, 1921.

78. "Yami kara Yami ni," *Asahi Shinbun*, June 4, 1921.

79. Akita Ujaku, *Ujaku Jiden*, 82.

80. "Tsuihō saruru Eroshenko yo," *Asahi Shinbun*, June 2, 1921; Fujii, *Eroshenko No Toshi Monogatari*, 29

81. Fujii, *Eroshenko No Toshi Monogatari*, "Mōshijin' no tanjō."

82. Fujii, *Eroshenko No Toshi Monogatari*, 26.

83. Kisaki was later a police chief in Nihonbashi, celebrated by the Kokumin Shinbun as the "chief who speaks Esperanto," and after that a politician in Tokyo city politics (Shibata and Gotō, *Nihon Esuperanto Undō Jinmei Jiten*, 163).

84. Kisaki Hiroshi, "Eroshenko-kun wo Okuru," *Yomiuri Shinbun*, June 2, 1921.

85. "Shakaishugi wo Niramu," *Yomiuri Shinbun*, May 30, 1921.

86. Official quoted in "Mōshijin E-shi wo Taikyō sasu wake," *Asahi Shinbun*, May 29, 1921.

87. Fujii, *Eroshenko No Toshi Monogatari*, 29.

88. "Sakunichi Kensoku sareta Ro-Mōshijin," *Yomiuri Shinbun*, May 2, 1921.

89. Ward, *Thought Crime*. Ward demonstrates how the wording of the 1921 bill was replaced in the 1925 bill by references to threats to the *kokutai*, that vaguely articulated presence of imperial sovereignty within the prewar Japanese polity and society.

90. Eguchi Kan, "Eroshenko Washirii wo Omou," *Yomiuri Shinbun*, June 21, 1921.

91. Miyamoto and Ōshima, *Hantaisei Esuperanto Undō-Shi*, 115–124, and Fujii, *Eroshenko No Toshi Monogatari*, 37.

92. Vasili Eroshenko wrote his own account of his attempts to return home, "Nihon Tsuhōki," reprinted in Eroshenko and Takasugi, *Eroshenko Zenshū*, 2: 5–29.

Chapter 3: Language and Diplomacy

1. The term is from Manela, *The Wilsonian Moment*.

2. Glenda Sluga (*Internationalism in the Age of Nationalism*) stresses that to imagine the opening of a new age of internationalism required the forgetting of a prewar history of internationalist organizations and movements.

3. Baigorri-Jalón, *From Paris to Nuremberg*, 19.

4. Baigorri-Jalón, *From Paris to Nuremberg*, 23.

5. For a fuller account of Esperanto as considered by the League of Nations, see Forster, *The Esperanto Movement*, chap. 6.

6. Nitobe, "Esperanto and the Language Question at the League of Nations," 9. Nitobe remarks that English and French were not explicitly official languages of the League, as such, but their use in the founding covenant gave them quasi-official status.

7. Draft resolution, League of Nations, document number 20/48/194, December 1920 (via Japan Center for Asian Historical Records [hereafter JACAR] document B06150936600, Foreign Ministry file on International Language Problems).

8. Report presented to the assembly by Committee II, "International Language," League of Nations, document 20/48/253. The report suggested that the third paragraph of the draft resolution regarding the hopes of the assembly that Esperanto teaching be spread be dropped.

9. League of Nations 1st Assembly Plenary Meetings, 31st Plenary meeting, December 18, 1920, 753–754.

10. The only significant difference was a footnote remarking that "by international language is understood a practical auxiliary language which will in no way prejudice the rights and traditional prestige of the French tongue as the international language of diplomacy" (document A/74/1921).

11. Nitobe, "Esperanto and the Language Question at the League of Nations."

12. Forster, *The Esperanto Movement*, 177.

13. "The League of Nations: Esperanto Spurned," *Time*, August 13, 1923; League of Nations Committee on Intellectual Cooperation, Report of the Second Session (document A/31/1923.XII), 12–13.

14. Forster, *The Esperanto Movement*, 177.

15. Harlow, *The Esperanto Book*, chap. 7.

16. See Shimazu, *Japan, Race, and Equality*, for further details.

17. For example, see Barshay, *State and Intellectual in Imperial Japan*, 72–73.

18. Burkman, *Japan and the League of Nations*, xiv.

19. Burkman, *Japan and the League of Nations*, 29–59, contains a more detailed outline of bureaucratic responses to the emergence of the League of Nations movement and its subsequent creation.

20. Burkman, *Japan and the League of Nations*, xiii, 139.

21. Forster, *The Esperanto Movement*, 170.

22. One partial exception to that is the interest in Esperanto shown by Hayashi Tadasu, two-time foreign minister, during the 1906 boom.

23. *La Revuo Orienta*, October, November, and December 1920.

24. Usui, "Kokusaiha Kara Okkuruto Nashonarisuto He," 5.

25. Usui, "Kokusaiha Kara Okkuruto Nashonarisuto He," discusses a number of different accounts.

26. Nihon-Esuperanto-Gakkai, *Nihon Esuperanto Undō-Shiryō*, 44.

27. It is possible that Nitobe Inazō was instrumental in Fujisawa's employment at the League—Nitobe was headmaster at the first higher school in Tokyo while Fujisawa was a student there, so they had some prior history (Usui, "Kokusaiha Kara Okkuruto Nashonarisuto He," 6–7).

28. *La Revuo Orienta*, January 1921, 2.

29. *La Revuo Orienta*, January 1921, 2.

30. *La Revuo Orienta*, February 1921, 1. The verbatim record of the plenary session makes no reference to Japan, but Fujisawa Chikao's on-the-spot account makes it clear that, if the Japanese delegation was not particularly instrumental in preventing the Esperanto motion from being passed, they were nevertheless opposed to it.

31. *La Revuo Orienta*, January 1921, 8.

32. *La Revuo Orienta*, February 1921, 2.

33. *La Revuo Orienta*, June 1921; also "Kokusairenmei ni okeru Esperanto Mondai," *Asahi Shinbun*, March 16–22, 1923.

34. Quoted in Forster, *The Esperanto Movement*, 184.

35. Fujisawa: *La Revuo Orienta*, January 1921, 2; Yanagita: Yanagita, "Jenēbu No Omoide," 311; Nagata: "Nihon Kokumin to Esuperanto," *La Revuo Orienta*, December 1933, 342.

36. Nitobe, "Esperanto and the Language Question at the League of Nations," 9, Nitobe's own emphasis.

37. Nitobe, "Esperanto and the Language Question at the League of Nations," 1–2.

38. Nitobe, "Esperanto and the Language Question at the League of Nations," 5.

39. Nitobe, "Esperanto and the Language Question at the League of Nations," 2.

40. Biltoft, "Speaking the Peace," 90.

41. Howes, "Japan's New Internationalism and the Legacy of Nitobe Inazo," 8.

42. Nitobe, "Esperanto and the Language Question at the League of Nations," 10.

43. Nitobe, "Esperanto and the Language Question at the League of Nations," 6.

44. *La Revuo Orienta*, November 1921, 130.

45. *La Revuo Orienta*, September 1921, 100.

46. Forster, *The Esperanto Movement*, 175.

47. JACAR Document B04122523300, Foreign Ministry files on International Esperanto meetings.

48. Forster, *The Esperanto Movement*, 178; *La Revuo Orienta*, February 1922.

49. *La Revuo Orienta*, February 1922, 20.

50. Forster, *The Esperanto Movement*, 11.

51. Biltoft, *Speaking the Peace*, 100.

52. Biltoft, *Speaking the Peace*, 102.

53. Biltoft, *Speaking the Peace*, 29, 101.

54. Mayer, *The Yanagita Kunio Guide to the Japanese Folktale*, preface. See also Burkman, "Yanagita Kunio, Nitobe Inzaō, and the League of Nations."

55. Wright, *Mandates under the League of Nations*, 240. This view emerged in the PMC proceedings and was not universally endorsed.

56. Yanagita, "Jenēbu No Omoide," 313.

57. Yanagita, "Taishō 11 Nikki," 466, 477.

58. Yanagita, "Jenēbu No Omoide," 311.

59. Ishii Kikujirō, *Gaikō Yoroku*, 436. Also published in partial translation in 1935 as *Diplomatic Commentaries* (Johns Hopkins Press).

60. Yanagita, "Jenēbu No Omoide," 313.

61. Nitobe, *The Use and Study of Foreign Languages in Japan.*

62. Oguma, *A Genealogy of "Japanese" Self-Images*, 183.

63. Yanagita, "Taishō 11 Nikki," 475, 480.

64. Yanagita's "Suisu Nikki" and "Taishō 11 Nikki" contain details of his appointments and activities at home and in Geneva. Nara Hitoshi, "Yanagita Kunio to Esuperanto," features a thorough account of Yanagita's Esperanto-related entries.

65. *Asahi Shinbun*, January, 21 1921; *La Revuo Orienta*, February 1922.

66. *Minutes of the Permanent Mandates Commission 1922–1938*, League of Nations Publications 1: 279–286.

67. *Minutes of the Permanent Mandates Commission 1922–1938*, 1: 284–285.

68. See Manela, *The Wilsonian Moment*, for a history of the experience of Wilsonianism in colonial settings.

69. Fukuda, Katō, and Sakai, *Esuperanto Binran*, 72. The previous year a government official, Matsuoka Masao, had attended some Esperanto meetings and argued with an Esperantist of Taiwanese ethnicity, Su Bihui (蘇璧輝). Nakamura's visit was for professional (i.e., meteorological) reasons, but his high status meant that he was welcomed by officials in Taiwan. When he learned that the Japanese authorities in Taiwan were acting to oppose Esperanto, he reportedly threatened to attend only Esperanto meetings during his visit. For a full exploration of Taiwanese engagement with Esperanto, see Li, *Nihon Tōchika ni okeru Taiwan Esuperanto Undō Kenkyū*.

70. *Verda Ombro*, April 1922, quoted in Miyamoto and Ōshima, *Hantaisei Esuperanto Undō-Shi*, 94–95. Miyamoto and Ōshima note that, perhaps unsurprisingly, this passage attracted the attention of the censor.

71. See also chapter 6 in Tsu, *Sound and Script in Chinese Diaspora*, for discussion of Esperanto as an influence in native Taiwanese efforts at script and language reform.

72. Hara, "The Åland Settlement as a Resolution Model," 7.

73. Hara, "The Åland Settlement as a Resolution Model," 7.

74. Hara, "The Åland Settlement as a Resolution Model," 10; Heiskanen, "The Territorial Issue between Japan and Russia," 103.

75. Halén, *Biliktu Bakshi*, 212ff.

76. Heiskanen, "The Territorial Issue between Japan and Russia," 103.

77. Halén, *Biliktu Bakshi*, 257.

78. Hatsushiba, *Nihon Esuperanto Undō-Shi*, 51.

79. Heiskanen, "The Territorial Issue between Japan and Russia," 103; Halén, *Biliktu Bakshi*, 219–220.

80. Forster, *The Esperanto Movement*, chap. 6, esp. 182–183.

81. Lins, *Kiken Na Gengo*, 18.

82. Biltoft, *Speaking the Peace*, 101.

Chapter 4: Tōhoku Modern

1. Akita Ujaku, *Akita Ujaku Nikki*, 1: 389–390.

2. See Kawanishi, *Tōhoku*, for a fuller outline of the construction of Tōhoku as a region.

3. See Wilson, "Angry Young Men and the Japanese State," 100–101, for a discussion of this historiography.

4. Cohen, "Rooted Cosmopolitanism."

5. Cheah and Robbins, *Cosmopolitics*.

6. Long, *On Uneven Ground*, 23.

7. Satō Kentarō, "Taishō Jidai No Tōhoku Shinkō Undō," 326.

8. Long, *On Uneven Ground*, 19–20.

9. Satō Kentarō, "Taishō Jidai No Tōhoku Shinkō Undō," 372. See pages 324–325 for discussion of prior historiography and the perception that there was little response to the movement from the inhabitants of Tōhoku themselves.

10. Shibata and Gotō, *Nihon Esuperanto Undō Jinmei Jiten*, 290–291.

11. Narumi K, *Yasashii Sora*, 1932, quoted in Miyamoto, *Miyamoto Masao Sakuhin-Shū*, 4: 206. Narumi was one of the first Japanese poets to experiment with Romanization,

publishing *Tuti Ni Kaere* ("Return to the soil"—Romanization Narumi's own) in 1914. His ties to Otsuka Kōzan, a poet and critic of the 1911 Great Treason Trial, led to him being chased out of teaching. A full account of Narumi's life can be found in Takenami, *Hyōden Narumi Kanzo.*

12. Gotō, *Esuperanto Wo Sodateta Hitobito*, 7–8.

13. *La Revuo Orienta*, February 1923, 4.

14. See "Enlanda Kroniko," *La Revuo Orienta*, various issues 1920–1924.

15. Esperanto was not unique in this regard; see, for example, Crump, *Hatta Shūzō and Pure Anarchism in Interwar Japan*, 58–59, for an example of anarchists touring Tōhoku seeking to promote their movement.

16. The account of the trip is drawn from chapter 7 of Ishiguro's memoir, "Esuperanto 60nen." He was also one of the "wastrels" who celebrated the rise of the more idealistic expressions of Esperanto at the 1923 Sendai Congress.

17. JEI, *Jarlibro*, 1922.

18. "19,220 Auskultantoj," *La Revuo Orienta*, July 1923, 5–9.

19. Ōwada, "Komaki Ōmi 'Tane Maku Hito' He No Dōtei," 19–21.

20. Arkenstone, *The Clarté Movement in Japan and Korea*, 258ff.

21. Odagiri, "Komaki Oumi and Henri Barbusse," 8.

22. Arkenstone, *The Clarté Movement in Japan and Korea*, 61.

23. Arkenstone, *The Clarté Movement in Japan and Korea*, 60.

24. Komaki, *Aru Gendaishi*, 49.

25. Komaki, *Tane Maku Hitobito*, 42.

26. Racine, "The Clarté Movement in France, 1919–21," 201. Although the movement shared much common ground and indeed several members with the signatories of Romain Rolland's 1919 Declaration of Intellectual Independence, Rolland himself was not involved, having found several points of difference with Barbusse's manifesto (200).

27. Yi Sookyung, "Hansen Undo 'Kurarute Undo' Ga Nihon to Chosen Ni Utsutaeta Eikyo," 194.

28. Hokuju, *"Tane Maku Hito" Kenkyu: Akita No Dojin Wo Chushin to Shite*, 19; Imano and Sasaki, *Kajinroku*, 5.

29. Ōwada, "Tsuchizaki-Ban Sansatsu No Igi," 60, 64.

30. *Tane Maku Hito* 1 (February 1921): 18.

31. Curiously, *The Sower* was also the inspiration for the logos of two major publishing houses: Iwanami Shoten in Japan and Simon and Schuster in New York. In the case of Iwanami Shoten, the blank for the logo was designed in the early 1930s by the sculptor Takamura Kōtaro, who a decade earlier had been a participant in the Nakamura-ya bakery salon.

32. *Tane Maku Hito,* Issue 1, February 1921, 1.

33. Ōwada, "Tsuchizaki-Ban Sansatsu No Igi," 65.

34. Ōwada, "Tsuchizaki-Ban Sansatsu No Igi," 61, 67.

35. Ōwada, "Tsuchizaki-Ban Sansatsu No Igi," 63–64.

36. Imano Kenzō's diary entry for March 20, 1921 (Imano and Sasaki, *Kajinroku*, 191); Ōwada, "Tsuchizaki-Ban Sansatsu No Igi," 79.

37. Ōwada, "Tsuchizaki-Ban Sansatsu No Igi," 79.

38. The first issue was funded by a mix of advertising, Komaki's salary, and donations from the likes of Arishima Takeo, Sōma Aizō, and Sōma Kokkō, but it was almost immediately banned. Hokuju, *"Tane Maku Hito" Kenkyu*, 27–28; Fujita Fujio, "Sasaki Takamaru to Akita Ujaku," 185.

39. *Tane Maku Hito* 1, no. 1 (October 1921): contents.

40. "Kyukan ni Tsuite: Tane Maku Hito no Tachiba," pamphlet, *Tane Maku Hito*, October 1923.

41. Akita Ujaku, *Akita Ujaku Nikki*, 1: 266.

42. "Kyōdo Bungei ni tai-suru Taido," *Mutsu no Tomo*, March 15, 1919; reprinted in Aomori Ken, *Aomori Ken Shi*, document 634, 696–698.

43. Yanagita called his movement Kyōdo Bungei Undō. As will become clear, there were rival proposals, and so the difference between *Kyōdo* and *Chihō* is significant—I will translate them as "local" and "regional," respectively, in order to retain this distinction.

44. Details of the summer universities can be found through Akita Ujaku, *Akita Ujaku Nikki*, 1; Aomori Ken, *Aomori Ken Shi*; and Aomori Ken Rōseika, *Aomori Ken Rōdō Undōshi*.

45. Akita Ujaku Kenkyūkai, *Akita Ujaku*, 96; Matsumoto, *Aomori Ken Esuperanto Undō Shi*.

46. Aomori Ken Rōseika, *Aomori Ken Rōdō Undōshi*, photo pages.

47. Aomori Ken Rōseika, *Aomori Ken Rōdō Undōshi*, 656–658.

48. Matsumoto, "Aomori Ken Esuperanto Undō Shi."

49. Matsumoto, "Aomori Ken Esuperanto Undō Shi."

50. "Chihō Bunka Undō," *Tōoku Nippō*, January 16, 1924; reprinted in Aomori Ken, *Aomori Ken Shi*, document 638, 701.

51. "Chihō Bunka Undō," *Tōoku Nippō*, January 16, 1924; reprinted in Aomori Ken, *Aomori Ken Shi*, document 638, 701.

52. "Kyōdo Undō no Ryūsei," *Hirosaki Shinbun*, July 8, 1924; reproduced in Aomori Ken, *Aomori Ken Shi*, document 637, 700.

53. Aomori Ken, *Aomori Ken Shi*, document 699.

54. "Chihō Undō panfuretto no Hakkan," January 17, 1924; reproduced in Aomori Ken, *Aomori Ken Shi*, document 639, 703.

55. Shibata and Gotō, *Nihon Esuperanto Undō Jinmei Jiten*, 314.

56. Fukushi Kojirō, "Esuperanto no Byūkan," *Hirosaki Shinbun*, April 12, 1925 (Aomori Ken, *Aomori Ken Shi*, document 645, 711).

57. Fukushi Kojirō, "Esuperanto no Byūkan," *Hirosaki Shinbun*, April 12, 1925 (Aomori Ken, *Aomori Ken Shi*, document 645, 700).

58. Kuroishi Shi, *Kuroishi Shishi*, 584.

59. Shibata and Gotō, *Nihon Esuperanto Undō Jinmei Jiten*, 2.

60. Kuroishi Shi, *Kuroishi Shishi*, 561; Akita Ujaku Kenkyūkai, *Akita Ujaku: Sono Zenshigoto*, 100.

61. *La Revuo Orienta*, 1936, 409.

62. Tōno City Museum, *Nihon No Gurimu*, 85–92.

63. Figal, *Civilization and Monsters*. Chapter 4 contains an extensive consideration of the production of *Tales of Tōno*.

64. Sasaki, *Sasaki Kizen Zenshū*, 13, 28.

65. Yanagita, "Taishō 11 Nikki," *Teihon Yanagita Kunio Shū*, Appendix, 4: 466.

66. Sasaki, *Sasaki Kizen Zenshū*, 32 (letter dated December 20, 1924). This account is complicated somewhat by his diary entries from 1922, which continue to show mentions of his receipt of Esperanto pamphlets and journals.

67. Shibata and Gotō, *Nihon Esuperanto Undō Jinmei Jiten*, 227.

68. Sasaki, *Sasaki Kizen Zenshū*. See diary entries, for example, January 22, 1922; March 12, 1922; April 2, 1922; November 4, 1924; and pages 102–113 for a bibliography of Sasaki's essays and research.

69. Sasaki's ties to the rōmaji movement appear to have been through Mizuno Yōshū, another folklorist, who was the one who first introduced him to Yanagita Kunio, and who was a longtime proponent of rōmaji. It's conceivable, then, that Sasaki's essays in rōmaji were in effect a favor for another figure Sasaki looked to as a mentor.

70. Sasaki, "Sesso Kandan," *Tōhoku Hyōron*, January 1923; reprinted in Sasaki, *Sasaki Kizen Zenshū*, 418–422.

71. Sasaki, *Sasaki Kizen Zenshū*, 2: 419.

72. Tōno City Museum, *Nihon No Gurimu*, 85, 87, 91.

73. Tōno City Museum, *Nihon No Gurimu*, 86, 46.

74. Seki T, "Hayachinesan to Kizensan," *Iwate Nippō*, October 27, 1933, quoted in Ishii Masami, "Takuboku Ishikawa and Kizen Sasaki and Kenji Miyazawa," 180.

75. Scholars have speculated on the meaning of the association's name—"Chijin" refers fairly straightforwardly to farmers (地人, people of the earth), but the term "Rasu" (羅修) is more obscure. It has tended to be either seen as a reference to John Ruskin, the British arts and crafts pioneer—an inspiration for Mushanokōji Saneatsu and perhaps also Miyazawa—or as an inversion of Shura, a Buddhist hell that Miyazawa made reference to in his poetry collection *Haru to Shura* (Kikuchi, *Japanese Modernization and Mingei Theory*, 37).

76. Miyazawa Kenji, letter to his father, December 12, 1926, quoted in Satō Ryūichi, *Sekai No Sakka*, 115.

77. Najita and Harootunian, "Japanese Revolt against the West."

78. Miyazawa came from a family of relatively wealthy local traders, rather than farmers. This perhaps gave him a sense of dislocation—neither a member of the urban elite nor an integral member of those who worked the land—which helped motivate projects such as the Rasu Chijin Kyōkai.

79. "Ihatov" has been described as an Esperanto rendering of "Iwate." The reality is that it is more complicated: "Ihatov" predated Miyazawa's interest in Esperanto, but it is perhaps true to say that he adapted the name (which seems to come from an older formulation of "Iwate," "Ihate") to look more like an Esperanto noun—placing the stress on the penultimate syllable and adding an *o*- sound at the end: from "Iihatobu" to "Iihatōvo," although he used various versions in different stories (see the entry for Esperanto in Watabe, *Miyazawa Kenji Daijiten*, 271).

80. "Nōmin Geijutsu Gairon Kōyō," in Miyazawa, *Kōhon Miyazawa Kenji Zenshū*, vol. 13.

81. Clarke, "The Great Dialect Debate."

Chapter 5: Green on the Outside and Red Within

1. See, for example, Müller-Saini and Benton, "Esperanto and Chinese Anarchism 1907–1920," or Chan, "China and the Esperanto Movement."

2. See Duus and Scheiner, "Socialism, Liberalism, and Marxism, 1901–1931," for an analysis of the influence of the Soviet Union in shaping the trajectory of various forms of socialism within Japan.

3. Forster, *The Esperanto Movement*, 188.

4. Max Ward's *Thought Crime* draws a parallel between the Japanese response to Marxism-Leninism in the interwar period with contemporary states' stance toward radical Islamism.

5. Sho Konishi ("Translingual World Order") describes Esperanto as seen by the Taishō-era socialists explicitly as a "language without culture."

6. Nitobe, *The Use and Study of Foreign Languages in Japan.*

7. *Esperanto en Nipponlando*, May 1926, 85.

8. "Naze Puro-Esu Undō ha Hitsuyō Ka?," *Kamarado*, March 1932, 3.

9. Miyamoto and Ōshima, *Hantaisei Esuperanto Undō-Shi*, 119.

10. Miyake, *Tatakau Esuperantisuto-Tachi No Kisei*, 30.

11. Asada Hajime, "Akka to Midorika," *Asahi Shibun*, May 8, 1926.

12. Ward, *Thought Crime*, chap. 3.

13. For example "Hijōji-Kyoku to Esuperanto" (*La Revuo Orienta*, pamphlet published by the JEI, 1938), and "Hakkō Ichiū to Esuperanto" (*La Revuo Orienta*, speech given to the Manchurian Esperanto Association, 1939, January 1940, 41).

14. Sasaki Takamaru, "Sekai shugi Bungaku to Sekaigo," *Asahi Shinbun*, July 5, 1922.

15. Sasaki Takamaru, "Sekai shugi Bungaku to Sekaigo II," *Asahi Shinbun*, July 6, 1922.

16. Forster, *The Esperanto Movement*, 192

17. Forster, *The Esperanto Movement*, 198–203.

18. Miyake, *Tatakau Esuperantisuto-Tachi No Kisei*, 31.

19. Miyake, *Tatakau Esuperantisuto-Tachi No Kisei*, 32–33; After she died, aged only forty-seven, Sasaki's Esperanto writings were collected in *Vortoj De Macue Sasaki*, JEI, 1935.

20. Miyake, *Tatakau Esuperantisuto-Tachi No Kisei*, 37. Other key members included Miyake Hisano, a Clara-kai member and Labor activist, and a Taiwanese person identified only as Ii (Takeuchi, *Puroretaria Esuperanto Undō Ni Tsuite*, 157).

21. This gradual organization helps to explain an ambiguity within the sources as to when the group formed: anywhere from 1924 to 1928 depending on the source (Takeuchi, *Puroretaria Esuperanto Undō Ni Tsuite*, 150; Miyake, *Tatakau Esuperantisuto-Tachi No Kisei*, 36 n 37).

22. For example, Drezen, *Esuperanto Undō Shi.*

23. Miyake, *Tatakau Esuperantisuto-Tachi No Kisei*, 101.

24. The bulk of this account comes from Akita Ujaku's diary entries for 1927 and 1928 (Akita, *Akita Ujaku Nikki*, vol. 2).

25. Akita, *Akita Ujaku Nikki*, 2: 34–37.

26. For an explanation of the typical experiences of foreign visitors to the Soviet Union hosted by VOKS, see Stern, *Western Intellectuals and the Soviet Union, 1920–40.* There was a broad quid pro quo at play: in exchange for hosting and support in Moscow, visitors tended to supply positive coverage of their experiences in their home media.

27. Akita, *Akita Ujaku Nikki*, 2: 44. Akita recorded the interpreter's name in Katakana as Mary Tsuin—I have been unable to identify quite what Cyrillic that is equivalent to.

28. They met as a group—see photo in Akita Ujaku, *Wakaki Souēto Roshiya*, 102.

29. Akita Ujaku, "Sōbieto Roshia no okeru Esuperanto Undō," *Esuperanto*, August 1928, 138–141, 170–171. In his diary, Akita also mentioned a female worker harshly rebuking both him and the language (Akita, *Akita Ujaku Nikki*, 2: 45).

30. Akita, *Akita Ujaku Nikki*, 2: 44.

31. Akita, *Akita Ujaku Nikki*, 2: 44.

32. Akita, *Ujaku Jiden*, 33–35.

33. Akita, *Akita Ujaku Nikki*, 2: 98.

34. By contrast Narumi Kanzō remained in the Soviet Union until 1935 (Shibata and Gotō, *Nihon Esuperanto Undō Jinmei Jiten*, 370; Ohta, *"Roshia Modanizumu," Wo Ikiru*).

35. Akita, *Ujaku Jiden*, 151.

36. Akita, *Wakaki Souēto Roshiya*.

37. Hiraide, "Puroretaria Bunka Undō Ni Tsuite No Kenkyū," 242.

38. See Shea, *Leftwing Literature in Japan*, especially chapter 6, for the development of proletarian literature and arts in Japan.

39. Tatiana Linkhoeva, *Revolution Goes East*, is keen to stress that the Japanese communists developed their own interpretation of Japan's trajectory and appropriate strategy, which was not always in line with the Comintern's view. It think, however, it's still fair to stress the importance of Soviet guidance, even if its influence was not always straightforwardly followed.

40. Miyake, *Tatakau Esuperantisuto-Tachi No Kisei*, 53.

41. Miyake, *Tatakau Esuperantisuto-Tachi No Kisei*, 62; Bowen-Struyk, "Introduction: Proletarian Arts in East Asia," 259.

42. Takeuchi, *Puroretaria Esuperanto Undō Ni Tsuite*, 167, 183. There is some debate about how high and for how long the circulation was sustained—see also Hiraide, "Puroretaria Bunka Undō Ni Tsuite No Kenkyū," 310, and Miyake, *Tatakau Esuperantisuto-Tachi No Kisei*, 62.

43. Akita, *Akita Ujaku Nikki*, 2: 289–290.

44. Akita, *Akita Ujaku Nikki*, 2: 290.

45. Takeuchi, "Puroretaria Esuperanto Undō Ni Tsuite," 202–204.

46. "Ujaku-shi Kensoku," *Asahi Shinbun*, September 30, 1930, 392; "Akita Ujaku-shi Nado Kaihō saru," *Asahi Shinbun*, June 19, 1931; "Akita Ujaku-shi Nado 58-mei Kensoku," *Asahi Shinbun*, September 21, 1931; also Fujita Tatsuo, *Akita Ujaku Kenkyū*, 392; Ōzawa, *Fashizumu to Akita Ujaku*, 142.

47. "Puro Bundan no Genrō Akita Ujaku-shi mo Tenkō," *Asahi Shinbun*, September 13, 1933.

48. Miyake, *Tatakau Esuperantisuto-Tachi No Kisei*, 13.

49. Takeuchi, *Puroretaria Esuperanto Undō Ni Tsuite*, 211–212.

50. Tokkō Gaiji Geppō, August 1937, reprinted in GSS, *Zoku Gendaishi Shiryō*, 7: 502; Shea, *Leftwing Literature in Japan*, 207–208.

51. Akita, *Akita Ujaku Nikki*, 2: 164.

52. Shibata, *Nakagaki Kojirō: Nichi-Chū Esuperanchisuto No Shi*, 27; Takeuchi, *Puroretaria Esuperanto Undō Ni Tsuite*, 158. According to Miyake, *Tatakau Esuperantisuto-Tachi No Kisei*, 37, there were approximately three hundred prisoners held as a result of the arrests, so this represented a take-up of between one-third and one-half of the inmates.

53. *Gokuchū ni Utaeru*, quoted in Miyamoto and Ōshima, *Hantaisei Esuperanto Undō-Shi*, 149.

54. Michielsen, *Assembling Solidarity*, 183–184.

55. Miyamoto and Ōshima, *Hantaisei Esuperanto Undō-Shi*, 160.

56. Takeuchi, *Puroretaria Esuperanto Undō Ni Tsuite*, 159–160; Puroretaria Kagaku Kenkyūjo, *Puroretaria Kagaku* (October 1931), reprinted in Hōsei Daikgaku, *Ōhara Shakai Mondai Kenkyūjo* (1979), 114.

57. The textbooks were reissued in 1968 by the publisher Yōbunsha: Puroretaria Kagaku Kenkyūjo, *Puroretaria Esuperanto Kōza*.

58. Exact figures are hard to come by, but Miyamoto and Ōshima, *Hantaisei Esuperanto Undō-Shi* (161) suggests a figure of almost eight thousand, while Takeuchi, *Puroretaria Esuperanto Undō Ni Tsuite* (162) confirms it was said at the time to be several thousand,

suggesting that almost everyone involved in the proletarian Esperanto movement read them. Even if the figure was spread over six volumes, this seems to have been a successful publication.

59. JEI Archives, Waseda, Tokyo.

60. G. E. L. Gauntlett, "Kio Estas Esperanto," *La Japana Esperantisto*, September 1906; reprinted as a pamphlet by Okayama Esperanto-Societo in 2011.

61. Egawa and Fukumoto, *Wakayama to Esuperanto*, 9.

62. Yoshikawa, *Naka San'nin Okareta Hito*, introduction and p. 4.

63. "Hungaria no Puroretaria no Tegami," Puroretaria Kagaku Kenkyūjo, *Puroretaira Esuperanto Kōza*, 4: 84–85; "Letero de Sovetia Studento," Puroretaria Kagaku Kenkyūjo, *Puroretaira Esuperanto Kōza*, 5: 76–78.

64. Takaragi Yutaka, "Boku no Keiken," *Marushu*, 1935; reprinted in Takaragi, *Rejisutansu No Seishun*, 180–182.

65. Gendai Shiryō Shussei, *Zoku Gendaishi Shiryō*, 7: 504; Takeuchi, *Puroretaria Esuperanto Undō Ni Tsuite*, 133.

66. The extent of Soviet control over these exchanges seems to have been a mixed bag. One proletarian Esperantist, Kurisu Kei, received an old French Esperanto primer from one correspondent in the Soviet Union. Opening the book, he found notes in the margins that painted life in the Soviet Union in a very critical light (Lins, *Dangerous Language*, 2: 46–47).

67. "Esuperanto Tsūshin," Puroretaria Kagaku Kenkyūjo, *Puroretaria Esuperanto Kōza*, 69.

68. Michielsen, *Assembling Solidarity*, chap. 2, esp. 169–185.

69. The first text came via the United States of America, through Nosaka Sanzō's publication "Kokusai Tsūshin" (Takaragi, *Rejisutansu No Seishun*, 88).

70. Miyamoto and Ōshima, *Hantaisei Esuperanto Undō-Shi*, 222.

71. Takaragi, *Rejisutansu No Seishun*, 91–93.

72. Takaragi, *Rejisutansu No Seishun*, 192.

73. Miyake, *Tatakau Esuperantisuto-Tachi No Kisei*, 54.

74. Sakai Matsutarō, "1931-nen no Hibi," *Nova Rondo*, March 1966, quoted in Shibata, *Nakagaki Kojirō*, 37.

75. Ōshima Yoshio, "Esuperanto Bungaku ni tsuite," *Nova Rondo*, no. 20 (1971), quoted in Miyake, *Tatakau Esuperantisuto-Tachi No Kisei*, 75; Michielsen, *Assembling Solidarity*, 155.

76. *La Revuo Orienta*, December 1935, 351.

77. *La Revuo Orienta* also made brief mention of previous "misunderstandings by the police" related to Chinese participants in JEI-related activities, hinting at some form of at least suspected political engagement (December 1935, 351).

78. Shibata, *Nakagaki Kojirō*, 43.

79. Shibata, *Nakagaki Kojirō*, 46–47.

80. Shibata and Gotō, *Nihon Esuperanto Undō Jinmei Jiten*, 195, 349, 536, 551.

81. *Hōchi Shinbun*, June 29, 1937; reprinted in Shibata, *Nakagaki Kojirō*, 63.

82. Officials quoted in "Shina Ryūgakusei: Aka no Kengi," *Asahi Shinbun*, June 6, 1937.

83. Shibata and Gotō. *Nihon Esuperanto Undō Jinmei Jiten*, 218–219.

84. Satō Jisuke, *Fubuku Nozura Ni*, 323.

85. Satō Jisuke, *Fubuku Nozura Ni*, 152–160.

86. "Aka kyōin san-mei Kensaku," *Shōnai Shinpō*, September 16, 1932; quoted in Satō Jisuke, *Fubuku Nozura Ni*, 171.

87. Miyamoto and Ōshima, *Hantaisei Esuperanto Undō-Shi*, 218.
88. Satō, *Fubuku Nozura Ni*, 324–326.
89. Miyamoto & Ōshima, *Hantaisei Esuperanto Undō-Shi*, 119.
90. Satō Jisuke, *Fubuku Nozura Ni*, chap. 5, "Gari-ban no Zasshi wo Dasu," explores the full range of Saitō's writing.
91. *Latinigo*, no. 1 (1937); digitized by Kadoya Hidenori: https://www.academia.edu/37343450/Latinigo_1_2_1937_1938_.
92. Satō Jisuke, *Fubuku Nozura Ni*, 323.
93. Satō Jisuke, *Fubuku Nozura Ni*, 285–286.
94. Shibata and Gotō, *Nihon Esuperanto Undō Jinmei Jiten*, 218.
95. For example, see Hasegawa Teru Henshū Iinkai, *Hasegawa Teru*; Tone, *Teru No Shōgai*; Esselstrom, "The Life and Memory of Hasegawa Teru"; Müller, "Hasegawa Teru Alias Verda Majo"; Mitsui, "Longing for the Other."
96. Shibata and Gotō, *Nihon Esuperanto Undō Jinmei Jiten*, 398.
97. Müller, "Hasegawa Teru Alias Verda Majo," 8–9.
98. Hasegawa Teru Henshū Iinkai, *Hasegawa Teru*, 240–243.
99. Hasegawa Teru Henshū Iinkai, *Hasegawa Teru*, 228; Müller, "Hasegawa Teru Alias Verda Majo," 13.

Chapter 6: Imperial Language

1. Lanti, *Leteroj De E. Lanti*, 103.
2. This confusion was repeated by some of the first Esperantists he met, too (Lanti, *Leteroj De E. Lanti*, 135–136).
3. Lanti, *Leteroj De E. Lanti*, 136.
4. Nojima, *Nakahara Shūichi to Sono Jidai*, 72.
5. It is worth noting that even most magazines for Esperantists (*La Revuo Orienta* being the most obvious, but others, such as *Verda Mondo*, *Verda Utopio*, *Orienta Azio*, *Esperanto en Nipponlando*, and the like) were a mix of Esperanto-language articles and Japanese-language articles. *Tempo* is almost unique in Japan for the scale of its Esperanto-language production—monthly, with very few missed months, all in Esperanto, and published to a high standard. The magazine was liberal in outlook, but it was censored only once, in 1938. It ceased publication in 1940, however, in the wake of the arrest of both editor and publisher by the Tokkō (Nojima, *Nakahara Shūichi to Sono Jidai*, 265).
6. Lanti, *Leteroj De E. Lanti*, collects Lanti's during the final years of his life.
7. Abel, *The International Minimum*, chap. 1, "Leaving the League."
8. Heinrich, "Visions of Community."
9. Heinrich, "Visions of Community," 245.
10. Christina Yi, *Colonizing Language*, 14.
11. Heinrich, "Visions of Community," 244–246.
12. Christina Yi, *Colonizing Language*, 14. This can be linked to, but distinguished from, the previous effort at assimilation (Dōka), reiterating the extent to which the Manchurian Incident reflected the start of a new stage in Japanese imperialism.
13. Lins, "Esperanto as Language and Idea in China and Japan," 52–53.
14. Hatsushiba, *Nihon Esuperanto Undō-Shi*, 85; see also Kurosaki Makoto, *La Revuo Orienta*, January 1934, 16.
15. Asano, "Nihon Ni Okeru Bukkyō Esuperanto Undō Koshi."

16. Hatsushiba, *Nihon Esuperanto Undō-Shi*, 94.

17. Shockey, *The Typographic Imagination*, 160.

18. Yanagita Kunio, in a 1927 column, had advocated Esperanto as a medium for Japanese scholars of all stripes to reach a wider audience and participate in more global research activity ("Nihon ga Buntan subeki Ninmu," *La Revuo Orienta*, January 1927, 1).

19. Gordin, *Scientific Babel*, chaps. 4 ("Speaking Utopian") and 5 ("The Wizards of Ido").

20. Murata's life is documented in Gotō, "Esuperanto to Hansen-Byō."

21. Gotō, "Esuperanto to Hansen-byō."

22. *La Revuo Orienta*, October 1925, 202–205; Gotō, "Esuperanto to Hansen-Byō." This liberalization backfired in the 1930s when it prompted a red scare in his hospice, which led to Murata being drummed out of the position.

23. Shibata and Gotō, *Nihon Esuperanto Undō Jinmei Jiten*, 89–90.

24. Lewis, "Ooishi's Observation," 357–358. The prewar discovery was more widely known domestically and led to an experimental military operation that sought to make use of the winds to send balloon bombs across the Pacific (Mikesh, "Japan's World War II Balloon Bomb Attacks on North America").

25. *La Revuo Orienta*, September 1932, 350.

26. *La Revuo Orienta*, February 1937, 7; Hatsushiba, *Nihon Esuperanto Undō-Shi*, 76–78. The reported take-up rates for courses continued to be high throughout the late 1920s and early 1930s. The peak was a 1931 course, which reportedly saw applications for twenty thousand texts (*La Revuo Orienta*, August 1931, 251; *La Revuo Orienta*, February 1937, 7). While initial interest did not necessarily guarantee the completion of a course or ongoing interest in the language, this scale does indicate a wider and more comprehensive awareness and interest in Esperanto.

27. *La Revuo Orienta*, January 1933, 21. It was merged back into *La Revuo Orienta* in 1938.

28. "Eho de Parola Metodo," *La Revuo Orienta*, October 1932; "Ĉe-metodo ni tsuite," *La Revuo Orienta*, January 1933.

29. Grady, "La Cseh Metodo." Cseh stressed the need for classes to be fun—his courses were notable for often ending with more students than they started with. This is notably different from the usual report of Japanese Esperanto courses of the time, which typically suffered a high level of attrition given the long hours of study they tended to adopt.

30. Yoshida Taichi, *La Revuo Orienta*, January 1934, 12. The ongoing suspicion that Esperanto was innately socialist remained high on the respondents' consciousness—the need to correct "the mistaken perception of Esperanto" was a more common reply than references to the international situation.

31. Kitano, *Shisō-Kai No Taiyō Hakuai Jiyū Shugi*, 67.

32. *La Verda Mondo* 9, no. 9 (September 1933): 1. This came from a speech to the third Esperanto Congress, in London ("Parolado de L. L. Zamenhof en Guildhall"), which distinguished between true patriotism and "pseudo-patriotism."

33. *La Revuo Orienta*, December 1933, 342.

34. *La Revuo Orienta*, January 1934, 9.

35. Kuroita Katsumi, "Kokugo wo ronjite," *Kokugo no Yōgo wo Ronjite, Kokusaigo ni Oyobu*, JEI, 1932.

36. Abel, *The International Minimum*, introduction.

37. Abel, *The International Minimum*, 15.

38. Kawamura Rokurō, "Ni-shi Funsō ni Sai shite," *La Revuo Orienta*, April 1932, 3.

39. *La Revuo Orienta*, January 1934, 21–22.

40. Kawamura Rokurō, “Ni-shi Funsō ni Sai shite,” 3.

41. Kawamura Rokurō, “Ni-shi Funsō ni Sai shite,” 3.

42. Fujisawa Chikao, “Impresoj en Vladivostoko,” *La Revuo Orienta*, January–July 1920.

43. “Impresoj pri Japanujo sub la Konflikto,” JEI, 1938. Mezey, “Mia Impreso Pri Japanujo,” *La Revuo Orienta*, May 1938, 1–4. Farrère’s visit to Japan was sponsored by the Japanese government; he had long been a supporter of Japan and its colonial expansion, drawing direct parallels to European colonialism of a previous generation (Kawakami, *Travellers’ Visions*, 63–75).

44. Shibata and Gotō, *Nihon Esuperanto Undō Jinmei Jiten*, 108.

45. Egawa and Fukumoto, *Wakayama to Esuperanto*, 8. The Sunday School was later reconfigured as a youth wing of the League association branch.

46. Egawa and Fukumoto, *Wakayama to Esuperanto*, 9.

47. *La Suno*, no. 1 (October 1934): 7.

48. *La Suno*, no. 8 (July 1939): 8; Egawa and Fukumoto, *Wakayama to Esuperanto*, 14. The survival of copies of the magazine in European archives such as the Biblioteko Hector Hoddler in Rotterdam demonstrates that the magazine had at least some overseas reach.

49. *La Suno*, no. 1 (October 1934): 1.

50. *La Suno*, no. 2 (May 1935).

51. *Yomiuri Shinbun*, April 14, 1939; *La Revuo Orienta*, May 1939, 2. The prize was named after Osaka Kenji, the first president of the JEI.

52. *La Revuo Orienta*, December 1938, 17. It should be noted, however, that the other two wartime prizes (1940, 1941) were given for nonpolitical linguistic projects.

53. An article in *La Revuo Orienta* (January 1940, 18) noted that although Nagata was described by the *Kokumin Shinbun* as one of Japan’s leading Esperantists, his activity was limited to promoting the language’s spread, rather than studying and using the language himself. In this, he is much like Nitobe Inazō, as described in chapter 3.

54. Abel, *The International Minimum*, 111, 118.

55. “Parolas Membroj,” *La Revuo Orienta*, August 1936, 31; “Nefavora Respondo,” *La Revuo Orienta*, December 1936, 32; Nojima, *Nakahara Shūichi to Sono Jidai*, 44.

56. Nagata Hidejirō, “Nihon Kokumin to Esuperanto,” *La Revuo Orienta*, December 1933, 342. However, the Japanese were also robust in seeking to prevent the ongoing introduction of more vocabulary of European origin, passing a motion in 1933 that demanded that new words should be developed from the existing Esperanto word base, rather than by importing new stems from European languages (*La Revuo Orienta*, May 1934, 142).

57. Nojima, *Nakahara Shūichi to Sono Jidai*, quoting *Tempo*, June 1937.

58. *Hakkō ichiu* being the central imperial slogan meaning “eight corners of the world under one roof.” The complexity of the Games’s fusion of internationalism and nationalism can been seen in the way that the Tokyo Games of 1964 were hailed as a symbolic reentry of Japan into the community of nations, a direct mirror of the way in which the prewar use of the Games for national advertisement was decried. Moreover, the parallels between the Olympic Games and the UEA congress continued in the postwar period, when Tokyo finally did host the annual event in 1965, again closely influenced by the city hosting the Olympics.

59. Lee, *The Ideology of Kokugo*, 185–187.

60. Arakawa, “Manshūkoku Kōyō-Go Mondai,” 1.

61. “Manshū Esuperanto Undō Nenpyō,” *La Revuo Orienta*, April 1940, 32–40.

62. *La Revuo Orienta*, October 1935, 438–439. This was reprinted in 1937 as a result of successful orders coming from Europe (*La Revuo Orienta*, April 1940, 176). The SMCR also collaborated with *La Revuo Orienta* in a series of articles in 1936–1937 that gave basic details about Manchukuo and its geography and governance, while by 1940 the magazine was running a regular column on Manchurian affairs.

63. "Tairiku ni okeru Gengo no Mondai," *La Revuo Orienta*, 1939, 400–406. The gap between the uniform, standardized *hyōjungo* of the classroom and textbooks and the messy realities of colonial settlers' spoken Japanese was something recognized in occupied Korea as well (Christina Yi, *Colonizing Language*, 4).

64. Lee, *The Ideology of Kokugo*, 193–194; "Tōyō no Esuperanto Shin-Kanamoji Hatsumei," *Chūgai Shōgyō Shinbun*, August 5, 1938.

65. "Ō-Ajia no Reimei," *Kōbe Yūshin Nippō*, January 19, 1934.

66. "Kensetsu no Kadai: Orienta Esperanto," *La Revuo Orienta*, 1942, 174. This view proved controversial within Esperanto circles, given the way in which it undermined the universality of Esperanto.

67. Yamagata Mitsuei, "Tairiku ni okeru Gengo no Mondai—Tairiku to Nihongo," *La Revuo Orienta*, 1939, 401.

68. Yi, *Colonizing Language*, 53.

69. "Daitōa Kensetsu to Esuperanto," *La Revuo Orienta*, March 1942, 66.

70. "Wareware ha Niton no Ryōshin ni Saidai no Nozomi wo Kakeyou," *La Revuo Orienta*, October 1937, 360.

71. Lee, *The Ideology of Kokugo*, 199–203.

72. Yasuda, *Kokugo No Kindaishi*, 168–169.

73. Yasuda, *Kokugo No Kindaishi*, 169; Lee, *The Ideology of Kokugo*, 208–210.

74. Lee, *The Ideology of Kokugo*, 65.

75. Lee, *The Ideology of Kokugo*, 204–208.

76. Yasuda, *Kokugo No Kindaishi*, 160.

77. *Yomiuri Shinbun*, March 3, 1938.

78. *La Revuo Orienta*, January 1938, 46.

79. JEI, Prudento kaj Nuna Ĥina Afero, 1938, 1. Five thousand copies were produced, distributed between the Foreign Ministry, the Rotary Club, and the members of the JEI (*La Revuo Orienta*, March 1938, 39, 46).

80. Fujisawa dated the origins of this switch to an encounter in Europe with Henri Bergson, in which he revealed himself to be deeply ignorant and dismissive of his own national culture (Usui, "Kokusaiha Kara Okkuruto Nashonarisuto He," 9–11).

81. Fujisawa Chikao, *Manmō*, no. 14 (March 1933): 32.

82. JEI records, https://www.jei.or.jp/listo_de_jek.

83. Miyake Shihei, "Tanka no ESP-yaku no shikata," *La Revuo Orienta*, April 1943, 2–3; also "Utaoj" in the following months' issues.

Epilogue

1. "Kyūkan no Aisatsu," *La Revuo Orienta*, March 1944, 4–6.
2. *La Revuo Orienta*, October 1945, 2.
3. Lins, "Esperanto as Language and Idea in China and Japan," 54.
4. Cheah and Robbins, *Cosmopolitics*.

Bibliography

Abel, Jessamyn R. *The International Minimum: Creativity and Contradiction in Japan's Global Engagement, 1933–1964*. Honolulu: University of Hawai'i Press, 2015.

Akita Ujaku. *Akita Ujaku Nikki*. Tokyo: Mirai-sha, 1965.

———. *Ujaku Jiden*. Tokyo: Shin Hyōronsha, 1953 (reprinted 1987).

———. *Wakaki Souēto Roshiya*. Tokyo: Sōbunkaku, 1930.

Akita Ujaku Kenkyūkai. *Akita Ujaku: Sono Zenshigoto*. Tokyo: Kyōeisha, 1975.

Alexander, Agnes, and Barbara Sims. *History of the Bahá'í Faith in Japan*. Tokyo: Bahá'í Publishing Trust of Japan, 1977.

Anon. "Exercises in the Yokohama Dialect." Yokohama, 1879.

Aomori Ken. *Aomori Ken Shi, Shiryōhen, Volume 5: Kingendai*. Aomori: Aomori Ken, 2004.

Aomori Ken Rōseika. *Aomori Ken Rōdō Undōshi, Vol. 1*. Aomori: Aomori Ken Minseibu Rōseika, 1969.

Arakawa Kanjirō. "Manshūkoku Kōyō-Go Mondai." Self-published, 1932.

Arkenstone, Quillon B. "The Clarté Movement in Japan and Korea, 1919–1925." PhD thesis, University of Hawai'i at Mānoa, 2017.

Asano Sanchi. "Nihon Ni Okeru Bukkyō Esuperanto Undō Koshi." *Informilo de JLBE* 32 (1955).

Baigorri-Jalón, Jesús. *From Paris to Nuremberg: The Birth of Conference Interpreting*. Translated by Holly Mikkelson and Barry Slaughter Olsen. Benjamins Translation Library. Amsterdam: John Benjamins Publishing Company, 2014.

Barshay, Andrew E. *State and Intellectual in Imperial Japan: The Public Man in Crisis*. Berkeley: University of California Press, 1988.

Beasley, William G. "The Language Problem in the Anglo-Japanese Negotiations of 1854." *Bulletin of the School of Oriental and African Studies* 13, no. 3 (1950): 746–758.

Biltoft, Carolyn N. "Speaking the Peace: Language, World Politics, and the League of Nations, 1918–1935." PhD thesis, Princeton University, 2010.

Bowen-Struyk, Heather. "Introduction: Proletarian Arts in East Asia." *Positions: East Asia Cultures Critique* 14, no. 2 (2006): 251–278.

Braisted, William Reynolds. *Meiroku Zasshi: Journal of the Japanese Enlightenment*. Cambridge, MA: Harvard University Press, 1976.

Burkman, Thomas W. *Japan and the League of Nations: Empire and World Order, 1914–1938*. Honolulu: University of Hawai'i Press, 2008.

———. "Yanagita Kunio, Nitobe Inzaō, and the League of Nations." In *Yanagita Kunio and Folklore Studies in the Twenty-First Century,* 2nd ed. Edited by R. Morse and C. Goehlert, 35–52. Saitama: Japanime, 2021.

Chamberlain, Basil Hall. *Things Japanese: Being Notes on Various Subjects Connected with Japan*. Cambridge: Cambridge University Press, 1890.

Chan, Gerald. "China and the Esperanto Movement." *Australian Journal of Chinese Affairs* 15, no. 15 (1986): 1–18.

Cheah, Pheng, and Bruce Robbins. *Cosmopolitics: Thinking and Feeling beyond the Nation*. Minneapolis: University of Minnesota Press, 1998.

Clark, Paul. *The Kokugo Revolution: Education, Identity and Language Policy in Imperial Japan*. Berkeley: Institute of East Asian Studies, University of California, 2009.

Clarke, Hugh. "The Great Dialect Debate: The State and Language Policy in Okinawa." In *Society and the State in Interwar Japan*, edited by Elise K. Tipton, 206–230. London: Routledge, 2002.

Clements, Rebekah. "Brush Talk as the 'Lingua Franca' of Diplomacy in Japanese-Korean Encounters c. 1600–1868." *Historical Journal* 62, no. 2 (2019): 289–309.

Cohen, Mitchell. "Rooted Cosmopolitanism: Thoughts on the Left, Nationalism, and Multiculturalism." *Dissent* 39, no. 4 (1992): 478–483.

Crump, John. *Hatta Shūzō and Pure Anarchism in Interwar Japan*. Basingstoke, UK: Macmillan, 1993.

Daniels, Frank J. "The Vocabulary of the Japanese Ports Lingo." *Bulletin of the School of Oriental and African Studies* 12, no. 3–4 (1948): 805–823.

Drezen, Ernest. *Esuperanto Undō Shi,* translated by Takagi Hiroshi. Tokyo: Tettō Shoin, 1931.

Duus, Peter, and Irwin Scheiner. "Socialism, Liberalism, and Marxism, 1901–1931." In *The Cambridge History of Japan*, vol. 6: *The Twentieth Century*, 654–710. Cambridge: Cambridge University Press, 1988.

Eco, Umberto. *The Search for the Perfect Language*. Hoboken, NJ: Wiley, 1994.

Egawa Harukuni and Fukumoto Hirotsugu. *Wakayama to Esuperanto.* Tokyo: Japana Esperanto-Instituto, 2008.

Eroshenko, Vasilii. *Eroshenko Zenshū*. Edited by Takasugi Ichirō. Tokyo: Misuzu Shobō, 1959.

Esselstrom, Erik. "The Life and Memory of Hasegawa Teru: Contextualizing Human Rights, Trans/Nationalism, and the Antiwar Movement in Modern Japan." *Radical History Review* 2008, no. 101 (2008): 145–159.

Eurtürk, Nergis. *Grammatology and Literary Modernity in Turkey.* Oxford: Oxford University Press, 2011.

Figal, Gerald A. *Civilization and Monsters: Spirits of Modernity in Meiji Japan*. Durham, NC: Duke University Press, 1999.

Forster, Peter G. *The Esperanto Movement.* Contributions to the Sociology of Language 32. The Hague, Netherlands: Walter de Gruyter, 1982.

Fujii Shozo. *Eroshenko No Toshi Monogatari*. Tokyo: Misuzu Shobō, 1989.

Fujima Tsunetarō. *Kindai Nihon Ni Okeru Kokusaigo Shisō No Tenkai*. Toyonaka: Japana Esperanto Librokooperativo, 1978.

Fujita Fujio. "Sasaki Takamaru to Akita Ujaku." In Ōwada, ed., *"Tane Maku Hito" No Chōryū*, 181–202. Tokyo: Bunchido Shoten, 1999.

Fujita Tatsuo. *Akita Ujaku Kenkyū*. Hirosaki: Tsugaru Shobō, 1973.

Fukuda Masao, Katō Kōichi, and Sakai Matsutarō. *Esuperanto Binran*. Tokyo: Yōbunsha, 1967.

Futabatei Shimei. *Seikaigo—Esuperanto*. Tokyo: Saiunkaku, 1906.

Gauntlett, G. E. L., and Maruyama J. *Sekaigo Esperanto*. Tokyo: Yūrakusha, 1906.

Gauntlett, S. "Edward Gauntlett (1868–1956), English Teacher, Explorer and Missionary." In *Britain and Japan: Biographical Portraits, Volume VI*, edited by Hugh Cortazzi, 323–330. Folkestone, UK: Global Oriental, 2007.

Gendai Shiryō Shussei. *Zoku Gendaishi Shiryō, Volume 7: Tokkō to Shisō Kenji*. Tokyo: Misuzu Shobō, 1982.

Gordin, Michael D. *Scientific Babel: The Language of Science from the Fall of Latin to the Rise of English*. London: Profile Books Ltd, 2015.

Gotō Hitoshi. "Esperanto tsuita Yanagita Kunio." In *Yanagita Kunio to Tōhoku Daigaku*, edited by Suzuki Iwayumi and Kobayashi Takashi. Sendai: Tōhoku Daigaku Shuppan, 2018.

———. "Esuperanto to Hansen-Byō'." *La Movado* 2010–2011 (2010).

———. *Esuperanto Wo Sodateta Hitobito: Sendai No Rekishi Kara*. Sendai: Soei Publishing, 2008.

Gottlieb, Nanette. *Language and the Modern State: The Reform of Written Japanese*. Nissan Institute/Routledge Japanese Studies Series. London: Routledge, 1991.

Grady, D. Gary. "La Cseh Metodo." *La Usona Esperantisto* 1 (2001).

Griolet, P. "Language, Script, and Modernity." *Cipango* 2 (2013).

Halén, Harry. *Biliktu Bakshi, the Knowledgeable Teacher: G. J. Ramstedt's Career as a Scholar*. Helsinki: Finno-Ugrian Society, 1988.

Halliday, Fred. "Three Concepts of Internationalism." *International Affairs (Royal Institute of International Affairs 1944–)* 64, no. 2 (1988): 187–198.

Han, Eric C. "'Tragedy in China-Town': Murder, Civilization, and the End of Extraterritoriality in Yokohama." *Journal of Japanese Studies* 39, no. 2 (2013): 247–270.

Hara, Kimie. "The Åland Settlement as a Resolution Model for Asia-Pacific Regional Conflicts? Considering the 'Nitobe Settlement' for the 'Northern Territories' Problem as a Case Study." *Issues and Insights* 7, no. 4 (2007): 1–14 (Pacific Forum CIC: New Initiatives for Solving the Northern Territories Issue between Japan and Russia: An Inspiration from the Åland Islands, edited by Kimie Hara and Geoffrey Dukes).

Harlow, Don. *The Esperanto Book*. 1995. http://literaturo.org/HARLOW-Don/Esperanto/eaccess/eaccess.book.html.

Harper, Tim. *Underground Asia*. Cambridge, MA: Harvard University Press, 2021.

Hasegawa Teru Henshū Iinkai. *Hasegawa Teru*. Osaka: Seseragi Shuppan, 2008.

Hatsushiba, Takemi. *Nihon Esuperanto Undō-Shi*. Tokyo: Japana Esperanto-Instituto, 1998.

Hay, Stephen N. *Asian Ideas of East and West: Tagore and His Critics in Japan, China, and India*. Cambridge, MA: Harvard University Press, 1970.

Heiminsha. *Chokugen*. 1905. Reprinted by Rōdō Undō-shi Kenkyūkai. Tokyo: Meiji Shakai-shugi Shiryō-shū, 1960.

Heinrich, Patrick. *The Making of Monolingual Japan: Language Ideology and Japanese Modernity*. Multilingual Matters 146. Bristol: Multilingual Matters, 2012.

———. "Visions of Community: Japanese Language Spread in Japan, Taiwan and Korea." *Internationales Asienforum* 44, no. 3–4 (2013): 239–258.

Heiskanen, Markku. "The Territorial Issue between Japan and Russia; Inspiration from the Åland Islands Experience." *Issues and Insights* 7, no. 4 (2007): 101–109 (Pacific Forum CIC: New Initiatives for Solving the Northern Territories Issue between Japan and Russia: An Inspiration from the Åland Islands, edited by Kimie Hara and Geoffrey Dukes).

Hellyer, Robert I. *Defining Engagement: Japan and Global Contexts, 1640–1868*. Cambridge, MA: Harvard University Press, 2009.

Heyden, Willem van den, and H. Sasaki. *Wayaku Sekaigo Jirin*. N.p.: N.p., 1889.

Higuchi, Kanjirō. *Kokka-Shakai Shugi Shin Kyōiku Gaku*. Tokyo: Dōbunkan Zōban, 1904.

Hiraide Hiizu. "Puroretaria Bunka Undō Ni Tsuite No Kenkyū." N.p.: Justice Ministry Research Department, 1940.

Hokuju, Tsunehisa. *"Tane Maku Hito" Kenkyū: Akita No Dojin Wo Chushin to Shite*. Tokyo: Ofusha, 1992.

Hotta, Eri. "Rash Behari Bose and His Japanese Supporters: An Insight into Anti-Colonial Nationalism and Pan-Asianism." *Interventions* 8, no. 1 (2006): 116–132.

Howes, John. "Japan's New Internationalism and the Legacy of Nitobe Inazo: Sixty Years Later." Occasional Paper 5. Tokyo: Obirin University, 1993.

Howland, Douglas. *Borders of Chinese Civilization: Geography and History at Empire's End*. Durham, NC: Duke University Press, 1996.

———. *Translating the West: Language and Political Reason in Nineteenth-Century Japan*. Honolulu: University of Hawai'i Press, 2002.

Imano Kenzō and Sasaki Hisaharu. *Kajinroku*. Akita: Mumeisha Shuppan, 1982.

Ishiguro Yoshimi. "Esuperanto 60nen." Unpublished manuscript, n.d.

Ishii Kikujirō. *Gaikō Yoroku*. Tokyo: Iwanami Shoten, 1930.

Ishii Masami. "Takuboku Ishikawa and Kizen Sasaki and Kenji Miyazawa." *Bulletin of Tokyo Gakugei University Section 2 Humanities* 56 (2005): 157–182.

Itō Saburo. *Takaku Takaku, Tōku No Hō E*. Tokyo: Tettō Shoin, 1974.

Jacobowitz, Seth. *Writing Technology in Meiji Japan: A Media History of Modern Japanese Literature and Visual Culture*. Cambridge, MA: Harvard University Press, 2015.

Kataoka Tadayoshi. *Yami Wo Terasu Mō Hitotsu No Hikari*, vol. 6. Toyonaka: Riberoisha, Riberoi Sōsho, 1997.

Katō Misao. *Esuperanto Dokushū Zensekaitsūyōgo*. Tokyo: Okazakiya, 1906.

Kawakami Akane. *Travellers' Visions: French Literary Encounters with Japan, 1881–2004*. Liverpool: Liverpool University Press, 2005.

Kawanishi Hidemichi. *Tōhoku—Tsukurareta Ikyō*. Tokyo: Chūkō Shinsho, 2004.

Kikuchi, Yūko. *Japanese Modernization and Mingei Theory: Cultural Nationalism and Orientalism*. London: Routledge, 2004.

Kitano Chōgorō. *Shisō-Kai No Taiyō Hakuai Jiyū Shugi*. Osaka: Shōwa Kokunan Dakai Kisei-Kai, 1930.

Kobayashi, Toshihiro. "Mori Arinori No 'Datsu-a, Nyu-Ō Cho-Ō' Gengo Shisō No Shosō (2)— 'Eigo Saiyō Ron' Gensetsu No 'Godoku' No Keifu." *Seiyō Bungei* 178 (2002): 35–77.

Komaki, Ōmi. *Aru Gendaishi—"Tane Maku Hito" No Zengo*. Tokyo: Hosei Daigaku Press, 1965.

———. *Tane Maku Hitobito*. Kamakura: Kamakura Shunshu, 1978.

Konishi, Sho. *Anarchist Modernity: Cooperatism and Japanese-Russian Intellectual Relations in Modern Japan*. Cambridge, MA: Harvard University Press, 2013.

———. "Translingual World Order: Language without Culture in Post-Russo-Japanese War Japan." *Journal of Asian Studies* 72, no. 1 (2013): 91–114.

Kuroishi Shi. *Kuroishi Shishi*, vol. 2. Kuroishi: Kuroishi Shi, 1988.

Lanti, Eugène. *Leteroj De E. Lanti*. Paris: SAT, 1987.

Lee Yeounsuk. *The Ideology of Kokugo: Nationalizing Language in Modern Japan*. Translated by Maki Hirano Hubbard. Honolulu: University of Hawai'i Press, 2010.

Lewis, John M. "Ooishi's Observation: Viewed in the Context of Jet Stream Discovery." *Bulletin of the American Meteorological Society* 84, no. 3 (2003).

Li, Bichhin. "Nihon Tōchika ni okeru Taiwan Esuperanto Undō Kenkyū." PhD thesis, Hitotsubashi University, 2016.

Lindstedt, Jouko. "Esperanto as a Family Language." In *Lingua francas: La véhicularité linguistique pour vivre, travailler et étudier*, edited by F. Dervin, 69–80. Paris: L'Harmattan, 2010.

Linkhoeva, Tatiana. *Revolution Goes East: Imperial Japan and Soviet Communism*. Ithaca, NY: Cornell University Press, 2020.

Lins, Ulrich. *Dangerous Language, Volume 2—Esperanto and the Decline of Stalinism*. London: Palgrave Macmillan, 2016.

———. "Esperanto as Language and Idea in China and Japan." *Language Problems and Language Planning* 32, no. 1 (2008).

———. *Kiken Na Gengo: Hakugai No Naka No Esuperanto*. Translated by Kurisu Kei. Tokyo: Iwanamai Shoten, 1975.

Liu, Lydia H. "Translingual Practice: The Discourse of Individualism between China and the West." *Positions* 1, no. 1 (1993): 160–193.

———. *Translingual Practice: Literature, National Culture, and Translated Modernity—China 1900–1937*. Stanford, CA: Stanford University Press, 1995.

Long, Hoyt. *On Uneven Ground: Miyazawa Kenji and the Making of Place in Modern Japan*. Stanford, CA: Stanford University Press, 2011.

Lurie, David. *Realms of Literacy: Early Japan and the History of Writing*. Cambridge, MA: Harvard University Press, 2011.

Manela, Erez. *The Wilsonian Moment: Self-Determination and the International Origins of Anticolonial Nationalism*. Oxford: Oxford University Press, 2007.

Matsumoto Hiroshi. *Aomori Ken Esuperanto Undō Shi*. Hirosaki: Hirosaki Esuperanto Kai, 1971.

Mayer, Fanny Hagin. *The Yanagita Kunio Guide to the Japanese Folktale*. Bloomington: Indiana University Press, 1948.

Michielsen, Edwin. "Assembling Solidarity: Proletarian Arts and Internationalism in East Asia." PhD thesis, University of Toronto, 2021.

Mikesh, Robert C. "Japan's World War II Balloon Bomb Attacks on North America." Washington, DC: Smithsonian Institution Press, 1973.

Mitsui, Hideko. "Longing for the Other: Traitors' Cosmopolitanism." *Social Anthropology* 18 (2010): 410–416.

Miyake Eiji. *Tatakau Esuperantisuto-Tachi No Kisei*, vol. 1. Toyonaka: Riberoi-sha, Riberoi Sōsho, 1995.

Miyamoto Masao. *Miyamoto Masao Sakuhin-Shū*. Toyonaka: Japana Esperanta Librokoooperativo, 1994.

Miyamoto Masao and Ōshima Yoshio. *Hantaisei Esuperanto Undo-Shi*. Tokyo: Sanseido, 1973.

Miyazawa Kenji. *Kōhon Miyazawa Kenji Zenshū*. Tokyo: Chikuma Shobō, 1997.

Mori Arinori. *Education in Japan*. New York: D. Appleton, 1873.

Mukai Kō. *Anakizumu to Esuperanto: Yamaga Taiji Hito to Sono Shōgai*. Tokyo: JCA Shuppan, 1984.

Müller, Gotelind. "Hasegawa Teru Alias Verda Majo (1912–1947). A Japanese Woman Esperantist in the Chinese Anti-Japanese War of Resistance." Heidelberg: University of Heidelberg, 2013. Translated from Gotelind Müller, "Hasegawa Teru alias Verda Majo (1912–1947). Eine japanische Esperantistin im chinesischen anti-japanischen Widerstand." In *Cheng—All in Sincerity. Festschrift in Honour of Monika Übelhör*, edited by Denise Gimpel and Melanie Hanz, 259–274. Hamburg: n.p., 2001.

Müller-Saini, Gotelind, and Gregor Benton. "Esperanto and Chinese Anarchism 1907–1920: The Translation from Diaspora to Homeland." *Language Problems and Language Planning* 30, no. 1 (2006).

Najita, Tetsuo, and H. D. Harootunian. "Japanese Revolt against the West: Political and Cultural Criticism in the Twentieth Century." In *The Cambridge History of Japan*, vol. 6: *The Twentieth Century*, edited by Peter Duus, 711–774. Cambridge: Cambridge University Press, 1989.

Nara Hitoshi. "Yanagita Kunio to Esuperanto." In *Setsukan Yanagita Kunio Kenkyū*, vol. 4, 76–91. Tokyo: Hakugeisha, 1974.

Nihon-Esuperanto-Gakkai. *Nihon Esuperanto Undō-Shiryō, Vol. 1: 1906–1929*. Tokyo: Japana Esperanto-Instituto, 1956.

Nitobe Inazō. "Esperanto and the Language Question at the League of Nations." Geneva: League of Nations, 1921.

———. *The Use and Study of Foreign Languages in Japan*. Tokyo: Kyobunkwan, 1929.

Nojima Yasutarō. *Nakahara Shūichi to Sono Jidai*, vol. 7. Toyonaka: Riberoi-sha, Riberoi Sōsho, 2000.

Odagiri Hiroko. "Komaki Oumi and Henri Barbusse." *Journal of Comparative Culture*, no. 2 (2005): 1–18.

Oguma Eiji. *A Genealogy of "Japanese" Self-Images*. Melbourne: Trans Pacific Press, 2002.

Ohta Jotaro. *"Roshia Modanizumu" Wo Ikiru*. Yokohama: Seibunsha, 2014.

Oka Kazuta. *Okayama No Esuperanto*. Okayama Bunko 108. Okayama: Nihon Bunkyō Shuppan, 1983.

O'Keeffe, Brigid. *Esperanto and Languages of Internationalism in Revolutionary Russia*. London: Bloomsbury Academic, 2021.

Okrent, Arika. *In the Land of Invented Languages: Adventures in Linguistic Creativity, Madness, and Genius*. New York: Random House, 2010.

Osaka Kenji and Ujaku Akita. *Memlernanto De Esperanto*. Tokyo: Sōbunkaku, 1923.

Ōsugi Sakae. "Gokuchū Shōsoku." *Ōsugi Sakae Zenshū*, vol. 4. Tokyo: Sekai Bunko, 1964.

Ōwada Shigeru. "Komaki Ōmi 'Tane Maku Hito' He No Dōtei." *Shakai Bungaku* 35 (2012): 19–33.

———. "Tsuchizaki-Ban Sansatsu No Igi." In *"Tane Maku Hito" No Chōryū*, edited by Ōwada Shigeru, 60–82. Tokyo: Bunchido Shoten, 1999.

Ōzawa. *Fashizumu to Akita Ujaku*. Aomori: Bungei Shobō, 1970.

Pratt, Mary Louise. *Imperial Eyes: Travel Writing and Transculturation*. London: Routledge, 1992.

Puroretaria Kagaku Kenkyūjo. *Puroretaira Esuperanto Kōza*. Tokyo: Yōbunkaku, 1931. Reprinted 1968.

———. *Puroretaria Kagaku*, 1929–1932, reprinted by Hōsei Daikgaku, Ōhara Shakai Mondai Kenkyūjo, 1979.

Racine, Nicole. "The Clarté Movement in France, 1919–21." *Journal of Contemporary History* 2, no. 2 (1967): 195–208.

Ryan, Marleigh Grayer. *Japan's First Modern Novel: Ukigumo of Futabatei Shimei*. New York: Studies of the East Asian Institute, Columbia University Press, 1967.

Sasaki Kizen. *Sasaki Kizen Zenshū*. Tōno: Tōno City Museum, 1986.

Satō Jisuke. *Fubuku Nozura Ni: Esuperanchisuto Saitō Hidekasu no Shōgai*. Tsuruoka: Tsuruoka Shoten, 1997.

Satō Kentarō. "Taishō Jidai No Tōhoku Shinkō Undō." *Kokkai Gakkai Zasshi* 118, no. 3–4 (2005): 323–383.

Satō Ryūichi. *Sekai No Sakka: Miyazawa Kenji, Esuperanto to Ihatobu*. Tokyo: Sairyūsha, 2004.

Scalapino, Robert A., and George T. Yu. *The Chinese Anarchist Movement*, vol. 1. Berkeley: Center for Chinese Studies, Institute of International Studies, University of California, 1961.

Schor, Esther. *Bridge of Words: Esperanto and the Dream of a Universal Language*. New York: Metropolitan Books, 2016.

Shea, George Tyson. *Leftwing Literature in Japan: A Brief History of the Proletarian Literary Movement*. Tokyo: Hosei University Press, 1967.

Shibata Iwao. *Nakagaki Kojirō: Nichi-Chū Esuperanchisuto No Shi*, vol. 8. Toyonaka: Riberoi-sha, Riberoi Sōsho, 2010.

Shibata Iwao and Gotō Hitoshi. *Nihon Esuperanto Undō Jinmei Jiten*. Tokyo: Hitsuji Shobō, 2013.

Shimazu, Naoko. *Japan, Race, and Equality: The Racial Equality Proposal of 1919*. London: Routledge—Nissan Institute, 1998.

Shimoda, Hiraku. "Tongues-Tied: The Making of a 'National Language' and the Discovery of Dialects in Meiji Japan." *American Historical Review* 115, no. 3 (2010): 714–731.

Shockey, Nathan. *The Typographic Imagination: Reading and Writing in Japan's Age of Modern Print Media*. New York: Columbia University Press, 2020.

Silverberg, Miriam. *Erotic Grotesque Nonsense: The Mass Culture of Japanese Modern Times*. Berkeley: University of California Press, 2006.

Sims, Barbara R. *Unfurling the Divine Flag in Tokyo: An Early Bahá'í History*. Tokyo: Baha'i Publishing Trust of Japan, 1998.

Sluga, Glenda. *Internationalism in the Age of Nationalism*. Philadelphia: University of Pennsylvania Press, 2013.

Smith, Henry. *Japan's First Student Radicals*. Cambridge, MA: Harvard University Press, 1972.

Sōma Kokkō. *Mokui: Sōma Kokkō Jiden*. Tokyo: Heibonsha, 1999.

Stalker, Nancy K. *Prophet Motive: Deguchi Onisaburō, Oomoto, and the Rise of New Religions in Imperial Japan*. Honolulu: University of Hawai'i Press, 2008.

Stern, Ludmila. *Western Intellectuals and the Soviet Union, 1920–40: From Red Square to the Left Bank*. London: Routledge, 2007.

Tagore, Rabindranath. *The Spirit of Japan*. Tokyo: Indo-Japanese Association, 1916.

———. *A Visit to Japan*. New York: East West Institute, 1961.

Takaragi Minoru. *Rejisutansu No Seishun*. Osaka: Nihon Kikanshi Shuppan Sentā, 1984.

Takasugi Ichirō. *Yoake Mae No Uta*. Tokyo: Iwanami Shoten, 1982.

Takenami Kazuo. *Hyōden Narumi Kanzo*. Mutsu: Shimokita Bunka-Sha, 2010.

Takeuchi Jirō. *Puroretaria Esuperanto Undō Ni Tsuite*. N.p.: Justice Ministry Criminal Bureau, 1939; republished Kyoto: Tōyō Bunkasha, 1978.

Tao, De-min. "Negotiating Language in the Opening of Japan: Luo Sen's Journal of Perry's 1854 Expedition." *Nichibunken Japan Review* (2005): 91–119.

Thompson, Lee A. "The Invention of the Yokozuna and the Championship System, Or, Futahaguro's Revenge." In *Mirror of Modernity: Invented Traditions of Modern Japan*, edited by Stephen Vlastos, 174–190. Berkeley: University of California Press, 1998.

Tipton, Elise K., ed. *Society and the State in Interwar Japan*. London: Routledge, 2002.

Tipton, Elise K., and John Clark, eds. *Being Modern in Japan: Culture and Society from the 1910s to the 1930s*. Honolulu: University of Hawai'i Press, 2000.

Tone, Kōichi. *Teru No Shōgai*. Tokyo: Yōbunsha, 2006.

Tōno City Museum. *Nihon No Gurimu—Sasaki Kizen*. Tōno: Tōno City Museum, 2004.

Tryon, Darrell T., and Jean-Michel Charpentier. *Pacific Pidgins and Creoles: Origins, Growth, and Development*. Berlin: De Gruyter Mouton, 2004.

Tsu, Jing. *Sound and Script in Chinese Disaspora*. Cambridge, MA: Harvard University Press, 2010.

Usui, Hiroyuki. "Kokusaiha Kara Okkuruto Nashonarisuto He." *Japana Esperantologio* 4 (2010): 3–20.

Ward, Max. *Thought Crime: Ideology and State Power in Interwar Japan*. Durham, NC: Duke University Press, 2019.

Watabe Yoshiki. *Miyazawa Kenji Daijiten*. Tokyo: Bensei Shuppan, 2007.

Williams, S. Wells. *A Journal of the Perry Expedition to Japan (1853–1854)*. Edited by Frederick Wells Williams. Yokohama: Kelly & Walsh, 1910.

Wilson, Sandra. "Angry Young Men and the Japanese State." In *Society and the State in Interwar Japan*, edited by Elise K. Tipton, 100–125. London: Routledge, 1997.

Wright, Quincy. *Mandates under the League of Nations*. Chicago: University of Chicago Press, 1930.

Yanagita Kunio. "Jenēbu No Omoide." In *Teihon Yanagita Kunio Shū,* vol. 3. Tokyo: Chikuma Shobō, 1968.

———. "Suisu Nikki." In *Teihon Yanagita Kunio Shū,* vol. 3. Tokyo: Chikuma Shobō, 1968.

———. "Taishō 11 Nikki." In *Teihon Yanagita Kunio Shū,* appendix, vol. 4. Tokyo: Chikuma Shobō, 1964.

Yasuda Toshiaki. *Kokugo No Kindaishi: Teikoku Nihon to Kokugo Gakusha Tachi.* Chūkō Shinshō 1875. Tokyo: Chūō Kōron Shinsha, 2006.

Yi, Christina. *Colonizing Language: Cultural Production and Language Politics in Modern Japan and Korea.* New York: Columbia University Press, 2018.

Yi Sookyung. "Hansen Undo 'Kurarute Undo' Ga Nihon to Chosen Ni Utsutaeta Eikyo." In *Kurarute Undo to "Tane Maku Hito,"* edited by Yi Sookyung and Anzai Ikuro. Tokyo: Ochanomizu Shobō, 2000.

Yoshikawa Shōichi. *Naka San'nin Okareta Hito,* vol. 3. Toyonaka: Riberoi-sha, Riberoi Sōsho, 1996.

Yoshino Sakuzō, "Esuperanto to Watashi," originally published in *Kōgaku Yodan,* 1926; reprinted in *La Revuo Orienta,* June 1936, 21–22.

Zhong, Yurou. *Chinese Grammatology: Script Revolution and Literary Modernity, 1916–1958.* New York: Columbia University Press, 2019.

Index

About the Author

Ian Rapley is a senior lecturer of East Asian history in the history department of Cardiff University, UK. He completed his PhD at the Nissan Institute of Japanese Studies as a mature student, after a Daiwa Anglo-Japanese Scholarship in 1999–2001 and a brief undistinguished career in international finance.